# Illusions
# of Intimacy

# Illusions of Intimacy

*Unmasking Patterns
of Sexual Addiction and
Bringing Deep Healing to
Those Who Struggle*

## Signa Bodishbaugh

*with*

## Conlee Bodishbaugh

Sovereign World

Sovereign World Ltd
PO Box 777
Tonbridge
Kent TN11 0ZS
England

ISBN 1 85240 375 6

Cover design by CCD, www.ccdgroup.co.uk
Typeset by CRB Associates, Reepham, Norfolk
Printed in the United States of America

## Contact details

If you would like to contact Signa or Conlee Bodishbaugh, or would like to receive a quarterly newsletter from their ministry, *The Journey to Wholeness in Christ*, please write, fax or email:

The Journey to Wholeness in Christ
P.O. Box 50635
Mobile, AL 36605

*Fax*: 251-643-7626
*Email*: bodishba@aol.com
*Website*: www.christanglican.com

*To our three wonderful sons,*
*Rick, Matt, and Ben*

# Contents

# Introduction

Breaking newsflash! There has been a worldwide epidemic of terrorism unleashed, capable of wreaking devastation on every family unit. Begin to administer the antidote to yourself and your family immediately!

If you heard this on your local newscast or CNN today what would you do? Most certainly you would put aside all normal responsibilities, sacrificing whatever it takes to get the recommended vaccine that you and your family need to stay healthy.

This book is your newsflash! There is no need to panic but you *must* take its message very seriously to preserve your own health and that of your family.

The world has been inundated with a virus of sexual addiction and pornography. It is deadly! Millions of men and women have already been infected and are dying slowly because of its insidious effects. It is a silent killer, deceiving its victims until they find themselves nearly destroyed.

This book is an antidote to the present epidemic. It is a message of hope, not despair. It gives you valuable information: the history of the virus, explanations about how it started and what keeps it alive, and most importantly, practical and godly ways to come free from it. It also tells the stories of many men and women who have managed to find their ways back from

compulsive, sexual addictions to live exciting, healthy, productive lives.

If you are struggling with an unhealthy sexual fantasy life,
especially involving the use of pornography, you need this
antidote. Whether you are single or married, it will give you
the necessary tools for healing your emotions, your will, your
long-standing habits, and your distorted images of God's creation, including man and woman. The plan for restoration is one
that is so easily obtainable it is usually overlooked.

If you are in a close relationship with someone who is struggling with sexual addiction of any kind, you will have been
confused and deeply injured by his/her behavior. You will find in
this book helpful explanations as well as godly tools for you to
overcome the side effects of this deadly virus.

I have asked for prayer from many people over the months I
have worked on this book and I have been amazed at the urgency
in their voices as they have asked me repeatedly how the writing
was going and when it would be finished. Nearly all of my prayer
partners say they know someone who needs the ministry contained in this book; many of them say candidly that they need it
for themselves.

Many months of research have contributed to this book. I
have had to pray diligently as I discovered abominable facts
about what goes on in the sordid world of pornography. Much of
the material I uncovered is too graphic and too disgusting to
relate in a book in which I am asking God to cleanse the hearts
and minds of His people. He has been faithful to cleanse my
imagination and restore my innocence of such things as I have
submitted my will to His and stayed close to Him.

I have chosen to use theatrical terminology for the chapter
headings. Although I am not personally involved in professional
or even amateur theater, I can find no greater illustration of the
deception of pornography than that of the theatrical world.
Whether our emotions are moved to tears or laughter through
the drama presented on stage or whether we are astonished at
the magic and special effects we pay to see, theater itself
illustrates the mastery of illusion. It is a mastery so cleverly
executed that an audience can be moved to respond with
powerful emotions to what is being played out on the stage.
Theater may present a mastery of illusion so convincing that

often the actors themselves take on the characteristics of their cast of characters, sometimes resulting in identity confusion and depression. There is no better description of the diseased sexual fantasy life and the practice of pornography than that of *ultimate illusion*. When immersed in sexual fantasies, the participant soon forgets, and then eventually doesn't care, that it is all illusion. The play becomes more important than life. The illusory characters become more stimulating than close relationships.

*In Chapter 1 the cast of characters is identified.* Those who are captivated by sexual fantasy lives and the regular use of pornography for gratification, as well as those who are wounded by it, are everyday, ordinary people. They live next door to you, work with you, or go to your church. They may be in your own household.

*In Chapter 2 we listen to the overture*, the hints of a refrain that will re-occur throughout the illusion. Specific themes are introduced that will affect every person who becomes engrossed in the practice of a pornographic fantasy life. Hints are given about the eventual demise of those who get caught in its web.

*In Chapter 3 we are confronted with the plot.* It is the eternal plot that pits good against evil, blessing against curse, life against death, God against the enemy of our souls. It is not an equal battle; a large part of the illusion hides the fact that goodness, blessing, and life – all of which are synonymous with God – are always victorious in the end. We must choose the plan we will follow, that of the protagonist who represents life or the antagonist who represents death.

*In Chapter 4 we face the antagonist unmasked.* No longer is the enemy disguised but the stage makeup is removed and the illusion is uncovered so that we are allowed to see the backstage props that provide the framework for the illusion.

*In Chapter 5 we watch in horror as the three act play progresses.* We meet (Act 1) the "purveyor" whose illusion is that of entrepreneur, (Act 2) the "user" whose brokenness enables him to embrace the illusion, and (Act 3) the "addict" whose insatiable appetite for the illusion draws him deeper and deeper into the dark side of the plot.

*In Chapter 6 there is well-choreographed action.* The moves are predictable and deadly and the cast seems to be in mortal peril. There appears to be no way out, no resolution of the storyline.

*However, in Chapter 7 the house lights are turned up and every illusion is revealed.* All that appeared harmless in the beginning is revealed to be dark, confusing and sinister. The loving scrutiny and organization of the Master Director unmasks the plot for what it is.

*In Chapter 8 the finale is presented.* The illusion is destroyed and the steps to freedom from the bondage of pornography are illustrated and encouraged. The final curtain comes down and everyone goes home to reality and family.

*In Chapter 9 the play has been canceled.* "Dark theater" is the theatrical term used to announce that there is no performance today and that no illusion is showing. If you go to see a play on a "dark theater" night you will find the lights out, the building closed up, and the doors locked. No one is admitted. Personal ministry for maintaining purity is given so that no one will need to search for a place showing illusion again.

*In Chapter 10 the reviews are given.* These are the testimonies of fellow strugglers and overcomers. Each one gives two thumbs up to God!

While writing this book I had a dream about a person meticulously extracting small slivers of diamonds from the pages of a book. The accumulation of all the tiny slivers was enough to make something of great brilliance and worth. When I awoke I realized that the dream is my desire for this book, that you may find small glimmers of truth within these pages, so that when put together into a whole and applied to your life they may bring much spiritual wealth to you and your family.

Each personal story we have the privilege to tell about in this book is a priceless trophy of God's redeeming love. The people who have shared their lives, their struggles as well as their victories, have been courageous in their determination to get whole.

I am so grateful to Tim Pettingale of Sovereign World, Ltd. for believing in the necessity of getting this book in the hands of the Church and to Robert Brenner for making that connection possible. Throughout the long months of writing I have been encouraged by many men and women who struggle with pornography. The cries of their hearts have not gone unheard by the Father who wants them whole even more than they want it for themselves.

Without the prayers of my prayer partners this book could not have been written. I deeply thank Kellie, Alan, Becky, Kathy, Pris, Bert, Susan, F.G., Richard, Judy, Carolyn, Bernard, Sue, John, Marie, Jacque, Nancy, Bob, Claire, Frank, Diana, Micki Ann, Chuck, Kirk, Deby, Kay and Sterling.

May your interaction with *Illusions of Intimacy* bring you closer to our Father in heaven and His eternal desires for your wholeness.

*Signa Bodishbaugh*
Hamewith Cottage
September 2003

# Foreword

When you read *Illusions of Intimacy*, you will see a compelling picture of the depths to which a person addicted to pornography will sink when in the grips of this addiction. Also, you will find convincing information on the astoundingly widespread scope of the problem even among Christians as well as startling data on the huge profits made by the porn kings in this country. Most importantly, you are provided a clear way to appropriate the healing power of Christ in order to be set free from pornography and to deal with the underlying wounds of the soul which cause so many people to be susceptible to this, the "devil's candy."

However, as a pastor I am equally concerned about a less spectacular threat to men and their families which is much more pervasive than the habitual use of pornography. It is the threat presented by the infrequent, sometimes inadvertent exposure to sexually explicit material that comes through so many channels today.

While women are not immune to being affected by this, the difference in the nature of the way we men experience our sexuality makes us particularly vulnerable to the effects of casual, incidental exposure to pornography. By nature we are more easily aroused visually whether we see our wives in the privacy of our bedrooms or view scenes with which we have no emotional attachment. Whereas emotional attachment is an essential element of sexual arousal for most women, men can easily objectify the subject of their arousal and be titillated by sexual images almost before they realize what has happened. In fact many men can so objectify the source of the titillating feelings that they don't need to see a whole woman but can experience strong sexual feelings simply by viewing genitalia or other parts of a female body.

This difference in male/female sexuality is so pronounced that most wives have trouble believing that a faithful husband could be aroused by looking at another woman and yet believe that he has no desire to have sex with that woman. Sexually explicit scenes which a woman might view as being very impersonal and even disgusting can produce an involuntary sexual response in her husband, even as he is turning away from what he has no desire to see. This difference is often baffling to men and women alike.

Pornographic images, even when viewed very briefly and unintentionally, often remain imprinted upon our minds and imaginations. Pornography can leave this imprint even though we may not have been seeking it at all, and even feel genuine guilt about our reaction to what we know is not healthy.

Pornographic images, once imprinted, continue to whisper the lie that genital contact is what sex is all about. These images, when nurtured, offer the illusion of "ultimate sex" apart from intimacy of body, mind, and spirit experienced in a committed, monogamous Christian marriage.

This is a deep intimacy that is seldom achieved in the first year or even the first few years of marriage. Rather, it is an intimacy that evolves as a man and woman grow together in their faith in God and their commitment to one another. It grows as they build their lives together in ways that enable a solid foundation of trust to be the hallmark of their relationship. This happens as husband and wife openly share themselves with one another, whether dealing with crises or sharing moments of great joy.

Unfortunately, the *illusions* of true sexual fulfillment, apart from a tender, loving relationship, lead many – particularly men – to look for short cuts to the deep fulfillment of their God-given sexual desires. When these pornographic images surface in the marriage bed, a husband's thoughts and desires are not in sharing himself fully with his marriage partner but in getting his own needs met.

When the pornographic illusions dominate, a man's thoughts and actions become more and more self-directed. His wife is particularly sensitive to this and can tell in an instant when her husband has made the shift from her to the illusion, or worse yet, when his whole motivation to make love is geared toward living out some pornographic fantasy. This will be true even when she knows nothing about what he is envisioning. She simply senses that somehow she is being used to fill a role in her husband's fantasy rather than being an equal partner in a precious time of true intimacy.

The resulting unconscious, but very real emotional withdrawal by a wife in reaction to her husband's objectifying their love-making robs both of them of what God has made available in the covenant of marriage. Unfortunately, this emotional distancing can lead to distancing in other areas of their relationship thereby producing a chain reaction in the marriage.

It is ironic that I talk to so many men who tell the same story: his wife seems physically distant and unresponsive, yet he admits to going "occasionally" into adult sites on the Internet. Most men see no connection between the two. They are unaware that in perusing pornography they are sabotaging the very intimacy which they seek by refusing to do things God's way.

The truth is that pornography and perverse images leave long-lasting and potentially destructive impressions upon the imagination, whether viewed deliberately or accidentally. It is imperative that each of us be very intentional about avoiding exposure to pornographic material. When it happens for what-ever reason, we must immediately offer the images up to Jesus and ask Him to cleanse our imaginations. We ask Him to replace images of perversion and sin with images of His holiness, glory and beauty. We offer up to Him our own sexuality and ask Him to cleanse and purify our desires that they would be pursued in a manner He intends.

My prayer is that this book will be a call to greater holiness for all of us, reinforcing God's command that we put away all uncleanness from our midst, realizing that only in the obedient life do we find the fulfillment God has for us. May we as Christian men set an example that will restore a respect for purity and modesty in our communities and our nation.

*Conlee Bodishbaugh*
Hamewith Cottage
September 2003

# Chapter 1

## The Cast
*Who are the people involved?*

*"No temptation has seized you except what is common to man."*
(1 Corinthians 10:13a)

> I will never forget the look in my wife's eyes the day she found out about my involvement in pornography. That look cut me straight to the bone. I can close my eyes right now and see it. I can even feel it. I saw hurt in her I had never seen before and I knew it was because of me.
>
> I love her so much I can't believe how much I've hurt her. I watched her trust of me vanish like smoke. She looked like I had hit her with my fist.
>
> I still feel the sickening pain of having her find out. I felt like the slime from a slug.
>
> *Ken* (a youth pastor)

**Picture Jodi:** She's in her early thirties, full of life, feisty, loves the Lord with all her might, has an incredible amount of energy and has a heart for bringing healing to God's people. Her husband, Ken, an equally dynamic young man, is a full-time youth pastor. His wife is far more than his encourager and supporter; she is truly his co-pastor and she does all this with an active two-year-old.

Jodi grabbed me late one afternoon between sessions of a healing conference that Conlee and I were leading. "I've got to talk to you, **now**!"

She was beyond tears or even anger. She was deadly serious. "I've had it. I'm not going to live this way any longer. He can't stop looking at porn and masturbating and I can't ever trust him again. There is no intimacy between us and, at this point, I don't want any. What can I do?"

At this point Ken walked up and said quietly, "I don't blame her. She's absolutely right. When I tell her I'll quit I really mean it at the time. But then I'm drawn back into the old stuff so strongly it's like I'm doing it before I realize it. I don't think I can change. What can I do?"

## What can I do?

Both Ken and Jodi were asking the same question Conlee and I are asked repeatedly by individuals and couples. *What can we do about the hold pornography has in our relationship?* Some of them have tried everything they know to do – prayer, accusations, anger, threats, tears, denial, mind games, white-knuckles, gimmicks, cold showers, counselors, pastors, self-help books – then they give up.

Yet, somewhere deep within each one is a flicker of hope – *there must be a way out of this nightmare. There **has** to be an answer! If all things are possible with God why can't He deliver us from this particular distress?*

Without even realizing what they were doing, Jodi and Ken took a vital first step in their healing process and finding their way out. They brought their problem into the light! They took the huge risk of exposing their lives to another person they could trust. Painful as it was to talk about it, they chose to hide no longer the embarrassing things that had gone on behind closed doors.

Jodi put aside her pride that told her, "Only certain 'lower-class' people engage in such behavior." Ken threw away his arguments that, "It is just a 'guy thing' and all men do it from time to time." They both put their reputations as Christian leaders on the line and quit hiding behind a pious facade.

Unhealthy sexual fantasy lives and pornography have been taboo subjects for Christians to talk about for far too long. There is a desperate need for us to begin to talk honestly about the destructive effects of pornography on all of our society – not just people outside the Church but on those who *are* the Church.

A common belief is that men and women who are faithful church and synagogue-goers are not going to indulge in such things. Christian men and women who get caught up in the cycle of sustained sexual fantasy and pornographic practices feel isolated as though all the other pious-looking people in church would never entertain such thoughts and desires.

## Attempts to understand

In our feeble attempts to understand and justify what we feel about what is going on in our society, we often resort to sentimental explanations or even ignorant excuses for the increasingly serious involvements with pornography. These justifications are faulty and non-biblical. None of them promotes the deep healing that God promises.

First, there is the tendency to write off the beginnings of such behavior as part of an ongoing adolescent curiosity about sex that some people just haven't out-grown:

- Boys will be boys
- All kids are curious
- They're just sowing their wild oats
- I want my children to be popular so I can't be too restrictive in how they dress, what they do on the computer, what they read, where they go, etc.
- When they get married they'll change

## Conversations behind the dressing room door

This week I was trying on clothes in the dressing room of a local department store and overheard a conversation in a nearby stall. A mother and daughter were on a shopping trip for clothes for the daughter's spring break. The mother first told her daughter that a certain dress she was trying on could also be worn to church. (This told me that they were church-goers.)

Then the daughter tried on a two-piece swimsuit that she considered "way too boring" for spring break. The mother tried to talk her into it by suggesting she pull the waist down further to show off her belly-button ring. The daughter retorted that she was tired of her mother always telling her what to wear and what to do, even by insisting that she accompany her and her friends on their spring break trip. The mother *apologized* by saying that she only had to go as far as the lobby of the hotel to check them in because they were minors. She would then leave them alone for the rest of the week to do what they wanted to do. I had to bite my tongue to keep from knocking on their dressing room door and interjecting my opinion into their conversation.

This mother's need for her daughter to be "popular" had over-ridden the good of reason. She was giving permission to her daughter, and even encouraging her, to experience needless temptations and possibly uncontrollable behavior. No doubt this will be the mother who will scream someday at her daughter in trouble, "Why did you do this to me?" The trends in our society are moving more and more towards the bizarre and yet we rarely protest very loudly.

## Men are just Martians

Then there is the rationalization about the prolific use of pornography by men that says there are biological differences in sexual drives and desires. *Men just want sex more than women. They need an outlet for their greater sex drive.*

There is always the temptation for one involved in porno-graphy to justify his actions because he is not getting his needs met:

- My wife/husband just doesn't understand me
- I feel so lonely/isolated/anxious/etc.
- I need something to make me feel better

Eventually, everyone else is to blame except the addict because he/she begins to detach from the reality of what has happened to personal relationships and even what is happening to his own soul.

- I realize my family is upset with me, but I don't care
- They have no idea how important this is to me
- I can't give this up for anybody

No one wants to believe that the simplest beginnings of flirtation with pornography and sexual fantasy may eventually lead to uncontrollable behavior. *"I can quit anytime I want to"* can eventually become the cry of *"This is all I think about; I need help!"*

## God and sex

We are all aware of the trends towards more and more explicit sexual themes in movies and on television [1] but we don't want to appear Victorian in our attitudes by being too critical. After all, the subject is both alluring and appealing. We can't (and shouldn't) fool ourselves into thinking that sex is not fascinating to think about and desirable to enjoy.

Because of our innate fascination with it, it's important to have a biblical understanding of sex. Sexual relationship within marriage is really fun; it's exciting; it promotes intimacy between husband and wife like nothing else. It produces life, both physical life in the conception of children and emotional vibrancy between marriage partners. It is stimulating to all the senses and God uses sexual intimacy between husband and wife as the primary symbol to describe intimacy between Himself and His Bride, the Church.

In Genesis 4 we read of the intimate relationship that Adam had with his wife, Eve. We are told that out of their intimacy in which "they knew each other," they conceived life and birthed a child, Cain. The Hebrew word, *yada*, is used to describe Adam's *knowing* his wife. This beautiful word, *yada*, is used several times in the Hebrew text to describe other relationships that, like Adam's with Eve, come together in intimate, holy love to conceive life. These relationships are not always sexual, but the results of their intimacy are the same – love is conceived in their hearts for God and life comes forth. For instance, Moses "knew" God face to face and the life of a nation was conceived out of their intimate relationship.

God repeatedly encourages His people towards spiritual faithfulness and admonishes them to avoid spiritual adultery. The Song of Songs is inserted within the canon of the Hebrew Bible to denote very graphically the intimate relationship God has with His people.

In Matthew 7:22–23 where Jesus commented on this same

kind of intimacy, our New Testament texts use the Greek word, *ginosko*. The meaning is similar to *yada*:

> *"Many will say to me in that day, Lord, Lord, have we not prophesied in thy name and in thy name have cast out devils? and in thy name done many wonderful works? And then will I profess unto them, I never **knew** you . . . "*         (KJV, emphasis mine)

Of course Jesus knows the names of every person; this is not a question of being identified by Him. It is implied through the verb "to know" that Jesus is saying, "You never allowed Me to be in an intimate relationship with you where life could be conceived within you."

When Paul spoke about the intimacy between husband and wife, he commented, *"This is a profound mystery – but I am talking about* [the intimate relationship between] *Christ and the church"* (Ephesians 5:32).

Sexual intimacy within marriage is the earthly symbol of a spiritual union with God. This is why God hates adultery. When we pervert such a powerful symbol into a cheap imitation or illusion of reality, we not only lose the meaning of the symbol, we lose the meaning of the reality to which it points. Our present society has almost lost the pure meaning of this biblical symbol of sex and its reality.

## Intimacy within marriage

Notice how the symbol of sexual intimacy within marriage points us to the reality of an intimate relationship with God through Jesus Christ. When it is right there is nothing like it:

- It brings a fullness of joy to both bride and bridegroom
- It makes each one more real and alive to the other
- All creation appears to be more beautiful
- Our hearts sing, even while performing the most tedious tasks
- Our attitudes are softened and more forgiving
- Our compliments to others are increased

- We are much more generous because much has been given to us

However, when intimacy is contrived, it becomes something far less than that which God intended:

- It is manipulative, deceptive and destructive
- It is always found out, because we can only fake intimate relationship for so long
- Eventually it crumbles because pseudo-intimacy focuses only on self, rather than on the beloved

Unfortunately, if we practice the illusion of intimacy long enough we will fool ourselves into believing it is the real thing and settle for something far less than we were destined to have. We become content with the illusion and quit looking for something of real substance.

In godly, intimate relationships, no matter how long the relationship has lasted, each partner is always discovering new and wonderful things about the other. A shallow or self-serving relationship never allows for the delightful discoveries about the beloved that come with time.

In true intimacy, each one looks outside himself/herself and sees the beauty and reflection of God's glory in each other. It is in the mutual loving and respecting of one another that each person in the relationship is fulfilled.

Wholesome, appropriate sex is a gift from God and He wants His people to love and enjoy it within the secure, holy boundaries of marriage.

## The illusion unmasked

In contrast to this beautiful, exciting picture of the fulfillment of sex in marriage is the cheap, tawdry illusion of intimacy that is so pervasive in our society. Like the mother and daughter shopping for spring break, there are too many families who are imitating a distorted, perverted caricature of sexuality that is portrayed in the media.

Because God created men and women with the desire of

expressing their sexuality in deeply fulfilling ways and because the reality of godly sexuality is portrayed so rarely in a favorable light by the media, the elements are ripe for sinful substitutes.

The substitute that has taken on epidemic proportions to fill the aching emptiness of true, holy, sexual intimacy is pornography. An epidemic of unhealthy sexual fantasy and pornography has literally exploded behind closed doors, between secretive pages, and before silent computer screens. It is the epidemic of a deadly virus! It is terrorism at its worst because we condone and even invite it into our homes!

## How is the virus spread?

Picture a typically nice neighborhood in your hometown. Picture one that has the appearance of friendly homes, neat lawns, climbing roses, picket fences, beautiful people and few problems. This is the stereotypical image of "the perfect family" that most people strive for.

We are not Superman and Superwoman with X-ray vision, able to see inside the homes on a typical Maple Street, USA, but Conlee and I have prayed with enough people and heard their stories often enough to know that the following scenarios are no exaggeration. Behind perfect facades good people are struggling terribly. A lot of them are Christian men and women, attending church and in Christian leadership. A lot of them are respected in business and community volunteerism. Because they want to preserve a good public reputation, they are coping in their struggles by constructing respectable personae to avoid total self-destruction. Frequently they live very different lives behind the walls of their homes than those we see in public.

Let's look together, with God's eyes, into some of these "beautiful" homes. They are a composite of real life situations that are typical of the growing virus in our society. Perhaps one of them will seem familiar to you.

▶ *#217 South Maple Street:*
*Jack and Lynn Jones, two daughters and a son*
Jack and Lynn have been married 16 years. Jack works for an insurance company, Lynn teaches art classes part time. Both of them have been Sunday School teachers; last year he coached a

middle school soccer team, and they used to take a family vacation every summer before money became tight. Jack told Lynn that he would have to spend more time working late to make extra money. They have fewer family meals together. Several nights a week Jack comes home late, too tired to talk, but with work to do in his home office.

Jack's home office is the old storeroom in the basement which he has rearranged to hold his computer and some file cabinets. Six months ago he put a padlock on the door to "keep the kids from messing up his files." When Jack gets in at night he is too tired for conversation so he heads down to the basement to finish working. Sometimes he gets so lost in his work he may not get to bed until 2 or 3 am. When Lynn knocks on the door to bring him a sandwich or a cup of coffee he impatiently tells her he's busy and doesn't have time. Most nights she goes to sleep before he ever comes upstairs. The kids have quit asking about him.

Lynn finds her husband's aloofness and detachment both irritating and confusing. She misses the walks they used to take after supper. Jack had sometimes been moody before but never this preoccupied. They had always been able to talk about things. She also feels responsible for his working so hard. He says he is under tremendous financial pressure but he refuses to discuss it with her. Whenever she complains about her loneliness he tells her not to put any more pressure on him, that he's doing the best he can. Between guilt and suppressed anger she too, has learned to remain silent.

They haven't been out with friends in weeks. Jack has been too busy to even go to church the last few months. She can't remember the last time he initiated lovemaking and the nights she waited up for him to come to bed he brushed her off as being too exhausted. He is too tired to talk, too tired to socialize, too tired to be intimate. His only interest seems to be work and the computer.

Walking downstairs into his home office on a Saturday after-noon, Lynn found him playing some kind of online computer game with cartoon-like figures. He shut it down immediately. Hurt, because he was supposed to be working instead of spending the day with his family, she lost her temper. He reciprocated in anger and told her he had only taken a break for a few minutes from the work he was doing and to quit putting more pressure on him. She left the room in tears.

Days later, while cleaning out the garage – a job Jack used to do – Lynn found a hidden box of magazines and videos of men and women doing things she had never imagined. She felt dirty just looking at them. Intuitively knowing they were Jack's and yet wanting to deny the truth, she finally confronted him with the box. He was angry that she had snooped into his private stuff, but he assured her that the pictures of naked men and women had nothing to do with her and in no way interfered with the love he had for her. Lynn threw the box of pornographic stuff in the garbage but she doesn't know how to throw the images out of her mind. The pictures keep popping up at odd moments, prompting confusing, distorted feelings.

Lynn progressively feels more unattractive and more rejected every time she thinks about the pornography she found. She is both angry and hurt. One minute she reminds herself of what Jack told her, that men are different and they just like to look at things like that, but the next minute she is overcome with the few extra pounds she has put on and the stretch marks on her stomach and the little wrinkles forming around her eyes. Ambivalence reigns. She hates him for what he is doing but she hates herself too, feeling she must be to blame in a large part for his losing interest in her.

Lynn feels lonely and rejected, alienated from Jack. She doesn't want him to touch her. She feels alienated from her friends at church too. She is ashamed of what is going on in her family. She can't tell anyone about it, especially her pastor. She doesn't even want to pray. It's too embarrassing to think about it, even to talk to God about it.

Jack has suffered from a low-grade depression most of his life. He has been on medication, which helps somewhat, but he hates to talk to his doctor about it; it makes him feel weak. Since he has been married he has found outlets for his moodiness in activities like church work, coaching, and playing basketball with some friends. He used to pray for relief from the depression but without much success. He was disappointed that spending time with Lynn wasn't able to relieve the stress that builds up within him from time to time. But he loves her and realizes she has her hands full with the family and household. Sometimes the old feelings of loneliness and anxiety have been overwhelming even in the midst of all the activities of family and work.

Jack has always had pornographic magazines around since he was a boy. He had found his dad's stash in a closet and then started buying his own when he got older. The videos Lynn found in the box were hand-me-down's from his brother. Sometimes Jack used to get them out and look at them late at night but then he had fewer opportunities with an active family. He had almost forgotten about them.

Through some coffee break conversations at work Jack had heard about porn sites one of the guys had been exploring on the Internet. The talk became hushed and rather vulgar, but everyone else in the break room seemed interested so he didn't walk out. The next time he had privacy with his computer he accessed one of the sites. The leap from one glance to various links and chat rooms took about an hour. Jack was hooked!

It wasn't long before Jack found the computer offered something that seemed to work faster than the anti-depressants he was taking. In fact it was more like speed. Everything in him came alive when he was engaged in the online activities. He couldn't get enough of it, seeking more and more titillating sexual thrills while exploring the fantasy world of pornographic pictures and online conversations and interactive sexual games. He has found that the anxieties and emptiness he has battled all his life are forgotten when he enters the world of cybersex.

He has become consumed with finding opportunities to be alone with computer access and the never-ending search for the one more experience that will bring the ultimate satisfaction through fantasy and masturbation. Jack has begun to neglect and even abandon once important relationships and obligations with clients. His production at the office has fallen far beneath his capabilities. He is getting little sleep and is short-tempered with all his associates.

Now, the first thing he does when he comes home, the last thing he does before going to bed, and the first thing he does in the morning is check his e-mail. His relationships with his online friends have become more real than those of flesh and blood. Jack spends hours each day planning and playing out his role in the MUD[2] of his choice. He is finding very little distance between the reality of his life and the role of Hanspyth, the person he becomes online.

Intimacy with his real wife Lynn, has become distant and at times non-existent. Although he believes he loves her, he has little physical interest in her anymore since he depletes his sexual energy in the chronic masturbation that accompanies the pornography. He finds the excitement of secretive relationships with other women (or even other men) on the Internet to be more sexually thrilling than the one upstairs. He is quick to divert the blame to his fatigue and the lack of understanding he receives from Lynn. He can't turn away from the energy he feels when he is living in his fantasies. The rest of the time there is a deadness about him, physically, emotionally and mentally. His spiritual life has been reduced to meaningless ritual. There is no room in Jack's life for any real intimacy, not even with God.

Let's look across the street from Jack and Lynn inside another attractive home.

► *#220 South Maple Street:*
*John and Ann Smith, a son and a daughter*
Ann has been unhappy for a long time. She won't talk about it but she is quiet and withdrawn with John, impatient with her children and distant from her few friends who still call to check on her. Her whole day is organized around her favorite soap operas and reading her novels. John is never sure who she is going to be from one day to the next; her attitudes and personality seem to change with the calendar.

Although being a stay-at-home mom was important to both of them, Ann now has no desire to interact with her children, keep their home in order or prepare meals. As soon as the children are home from school she sends them out to play or puts them in front of the television for entertainment. There is little dialogue within the family. When John gets home in the evenings the breakfast dishes are still on the table and there is no thought of an evening meal. He is made to feel that he is an intruder in his own home.

He has been so concerned about Ann that he has asked her to make an appointment to talk to someone who can help her, perhaps their pastor or a psychologist. Ann has refused in no uncertain terms and John is at his wits' end.

For months Ann has brushed away all overtures for intimacy and she jealously guards her time alone. "Leave me alone," seems to be her favorite statement. She no longer fixes her hair, wears makeup or dresses attractively. Her femininity is withering and John doesn't know what to do with this woman he hardly knows anymore. Everything seems to be too much for her to handle and she constantly shifts all blame onto him. He doesn't know whether to push her to change or to get professional help or to give her the space she is asking for, hoping she'll snap out of it. He has even considered an intervention but doesn't know who to ask for assistance.

Ann felt lost when her children started to school. Her days seemed endless as though she had no life. The sadness she had felt as a child began to creep back into her thoughts. By turning on the television she began to find the companionship she craved. Without requiring any personal commitment she could enter into the worlds of Genoa City and Port Charles[3] and observe the activities and dialogues of the family she never had. By only lurking she would not be judged, rejected or abused. She could identify with any of the characters she chose and they gave her the life she had only imagined. She began to turn down invitations from friends in order to stay home and watch her soap operas. The lives of the on-screen characters consumed her thoughts during the day. She resented any intrusion of responsibilities and demands upon her time that interfered with her fantasy world.

Ann also discovered the lure of romance novels. When the soaps weren't on she would lose herself in the unreality of pulp novels, everything from syrupy sentimentality to dark erotica and horror. Her preference in romance novels, which began with simple, but tasteless, historical fiction, became more and more erotic after she found what a sexual turn-on there was in vicariously experiencing the bedroom antics of Skye O'Malley and Claire Randall.[4]

After the family purchased a computer with an Internet connection for the children to use for schoolwork, Ann discovered chat rooms during the day. Her new best friend is a woman she has never met but with whom she spends hours each day in such a room. She also flirts with men (or women) she will never meet, becoming a provocative, illusory woman who exudes sex appeal over the Internet. She has discovered that masturbation relieves her anxieties and stimulates her interests in the online relationships she makes.

Her children have become disrespectful and her husband is disappointing to her. The only times she feels alive is when she enters her electronic world. The rest of the time she battles depression.

Still on Maple Street, let's go back across the street and look inside the house next door to Jack and Lynn.

► *#215 South Maple Street:*
   *Bobby Morgan, his sister and his parents*
Bobby is eight years old. At home he still calls his mother "Mommie" and he sleeps with a stuffed rabbit whose right eye is missing and right ear is hanging loose. The only television shows he is allowed to watch are the Disney Channel one hour a day and selected Saturday morning cartoons. He likes to play soccer and enjoys second grade. He goes to church and Sunday School every week and sings in the children's choir. Sometimes he fights with his sister and he wishes his dad was home more often but he is a pretty happy kid.

All the neighborhood boys he plays with after school are older than Bobby is. To be included in their circle he tries to act more knowledgeable than he really is. The things they talk about it are mostly things they've seen on TV and Bobby usually feels a little left out.

The eleven-year-old boy next door at #217, found a pile of "dirty magazines" in the garbage can behind his house. The coveted invitation was issued to come take a look. Nothing prepared Bobby for what he saw. There were pictures of naked men and women, women together and men together, doing things to each other he had never thought about. In the very moment his eyes brought the contact of the images to his brain Bobby's innocence dissolved. No longer was he able to look at any girl or woman without the reference point of what these pictures conveyed to his memory bank. He has become shy and embarrassed around his sister and his mother. He has thoughts that are frightening to him.

No longer is he able to regard his own body without the images of what the men in the pictures were doing with the women. He has started to wonder if this is what it means to be a man. Is this what he is supposed to do someday? Is this what women do in their secret world?

Because his thoughts have become saturated with the images he is storing up, it doesn't take long for him to become obsessed with what else is out there that he hasn't yet heard about. Bobby's quest for "more" has begun. It is a quest that will go past curiosity toward the great unknown areas of conquest, sexual lust and domination. This child's life has been altered forever. Godly images of man and woman are now re-shaped by the pictures that have been imprinted into his soul.

At the end of the block on Maple Street is another attractive home with a very healthy, loving family inside.

▶ *#201 South Maple Street:*
   *Larry Bennett and his parents*
Larry is four years old. He has a new baby-sitter tonight because his parents are obligated to be at a company dinner. Larry's usual sitter who is busy tonight has recommended the 15-year-old baby-sitter, Lisa.

Larry is in bed and asleep by 8:30 so Lisa watches a show on HBO that depicts explicit sex. When it is over she makes a couple of phone calls to some older boys she met at the mall and the conversations get a little out of hand. Lisa feels inadequate talking with the boys and starts to recall the pictures of the man and woman she has just seen in the movie. She wants to see what real male anatomy looks like and realizes that she has a chance while Larry is asleep. As she undresses Larry and fondles him, he wakes up, confused, frightened and mute. He is left with the fear of revealing the events to his parents and also the fear of being left with Lisa again.

The events of this night are permanently imprinted into Larry's psyche. Way before his time this little boy is awakened to sexuality and its allure, both to a new connection with the feminine presence and the fear of what she wanted to do to him.

Larry will forever see women in a different light than the boys who have never experienced this kind of violation.[5] His mother's body now becomes foreign to him. He is at once afraid of her and intrigued with her. Ambivalence becomes the standard for all relations with women for the rest of his life. The images of man and woman that God and his parents gave him have now become distorted. He is afraid of what goes on in the secret world of grown-ups.

These are composites of what is going on behind closed doors in ordinary households. The damage being done is irrevocable unless deep healing is received. Most of these people will never talk about what is happening. Unless God intervenes, deep guilt, shame and destructive habit patterns will rule their lives.

The imprints of movie scenes, literature, Internet pictures, chat room conversations and phone sex are changing the course of our morality. When we see things enough we lose the shock factor of impropriety. And when we lose the shock factor we allow the content to descend to an even baser level.

## A normal day in my hometown

We were sitting at seminar desks in a hospital conference room, munching on our chicken salad sandwiches and potato chips. I had joined three of my friends and about a hundred other women at a luncheon to hear a local plastic surgeon talk about "reversing the aging process." The room was filled with chatter, enthusiasm and friendliness. It was a fun day's outing for a lot of us, a chance at the end of the summer to do something out-of-the-ordinary, like investigating a new kind of skin care that would, hopefully, take thirty years off your looks.

Chatting away at our little table, I was tapped on the shoulder from behind by a woman I hadn't seen in years. She had never been a very close acquaintance but was someone I used to see at our church before she and her husband joined another congregation that had less lively services than ours. Our paths had not crossed in several years but at least I remembered her first name and I was rather pleased with that.

"Signa, how have you been? Busy, I guess, since I read your article in *The Coastline* last month."

She was referring to a denominational church newsletter that several thousand people received each month. I had written an article called "The Christian's Battle With Pornography" which was the bare bones of this book.

"I'm glad you saw it. What did you think about it?"

"Well, I thought it was interesting, but I think it was lost on the audience you reached."

"Why is that?" I asked.

"Because you were writing to Christians and it's obvious they aren't the ones with the kind of problems you described. You weren't reaching the people who need it."

At that the lights dimmed, the speaker began to flash before and after pictures of women's faces on the screen, and I was sitting there stunned. *Christians don't have problems with pornography?!? Wow! Does she have her head in the sand!*

Sitting on one side of the room, I was able to glance around the darkened space, dimly seeing the faces of over a hundred women wanting to look younger and more beautiful. What were all their reasons? Were any of them there because they wanted to compete with the pictures of women that attracted their husbands? Were any of them married to good, church-going men who had affairs on the side with cyber-babes? How many of their homes had stashes of porn hidden away they hadn't yet found? My experiences in healing prayer told me that a lot of these women fit those categories!

## The people who need it

Later, at home as I reflected on the conversation with my acquaintance, I had to laugh. If this woman only knew who is addicted to pornography!

Almost all of the men who come to us for prayer are church-going, Bible-believing, born again, Spirit-filled, active laymen and ministers. We hear the confessions of pastors, lawyers, worship leaders, bankers, Sunday School teachers, insurance salesmen, youth leaders, construction workers, CEOs, and evangelists. They live respectable-looking and ordinary-looking lives. They are not bums, winos or what our society would call "perverts." They live in nice neighborhoods, protected by neighborhood watch groups and alarm systems. They pay money to guard the life-styles they have worked hard to obtain. They send their children to good schools and limit their friendships to other like-valued people. And yet they are failing to protect their families from one very invasive, insidious, destructive intruder.

This is not just a "Men's Club." The women who come for prayer are similar – above average in intelligence, some managing homes and caring for children, some with notable social reputations, others following successful careers.

Conlee and I have been praying actively with people for personal wholeness for over thirty years. What we lack in formal training we have gained through hours and hours of listening to the painful stories of hurting men and women and then even more hours of listening to God. After a while it becomes obvious that there are definite patterns in both the backgrounds and the behaviors of all these people. It also becomes obvious that there are definite patterns in God's requirements for wholeness. What is not so obvious is how blinded we have all become to the patterns of destruction in our society.

We seem to be ignoring and even condoning activities that are eroding the fabric of our families. We have gone even farther than re-making God in our own images (as if that's not bad enough!). Now we are re-making man and woman in an illusory image to satiate our baser instincts. We, not God, have become modern "creators" with more knowledge of evil than knowledge of good. It is very frightening!

## The way out

> "And God is faithful; he will not let you be tempted beyond what you can bear. But when you are tempted, he will also provide a way out so that you can stand up under it."
>
> (1 Corinthians 10:13)

In Christ, thankfully, *there is always a way out*, no matter what the situation. God's Word always provides the answer, no matter how complicated and/or distorted we make our lives. It may not always be the way we would choose for ourselves, the way of least resistance, or the least painful, but God's way is *always* the way that leads us to wholeness.

To find God's way for wholeness out of a downward spiral of pornographic addiction it is first necessary to define clearly the problem (bring it to the light as Jodi and Ken did). Then it is extremely helpful to name the spiritual pathology involved (this will include revelation from God as well as good biblical therapeutic diagnosis). Eventually one must realize there are some clear choices available in order to come free from the addiction (just knowing what the choices are is not enough; one has to exercise moral effort).

For the one obsessed with pornography, simply to name the problem for what it is: *"I have a problem with pornography. I am not able to quit using it even though I understand how it hurts my family"* – is to overcome a huge obstacle and cause a first change in one's heart. This first step is vital. It announces that "I am giving up and letting God in." Like Ken, the pornography addict has probably tried to quit many times, each time thinking this would be the last time. When Ken finally declared to himself, to Jodi, and to me that he couldn't quit, he was already on the right path to wholeness, even though his healing took time and hard work on his part.

This declaration and the same subsequent steps that bring wholeness to the addict will be immensely helpful to the other family members as well, especially for wives who desperately need to understand, "Why?" Just to hear Ken admit to someone that he had a problem and needed help gave Jodi permission to get back in the game and commit to pray for her husband and believe that there was something of value to salvage in their relationship. His confession of his struggle confirmed to Jodi that there was a legitimate problem in their family but one that they could tackle together now that Ken would be truthful.

Those who seek freedom need to walk out their godly choices through several practical and biblical steps in order to renounce and stay free from the practice of pornography. Besides acknowledging the problem, prayers of confession, forgiveness, deliverance, filling and empowerment are all vital to stay on the path of purity. Encouragement from others and accountability partners become like lifelines.

There is great power in the testimonies of those who have

already been down the same roads of destruction and yet found healing. Their stories speak to the deep heart of the one struggling with pornography. It can be very encouraging to hear about the struggles another person has had in coming free from the pain and chaos pornographic involvement places on the family, not because misery loves company, but because one comes free from the narcissistic lie that says, *"There's no pain like mine!"* It is necessary to hear the truth about other people's struggles as well as their victories. The "unspeakable," when brought to the Light of Christ, is transformed into healing power in many areas of a family's life together.

## The steps towards freedom

1. *Acknowledge that you have a problem you cannot conquer in your own strength.* Name the problem in straight talk without rationalizations. Tell it to someone you can trust to use discretion, prayer and spiritual encouragement, rather than someone who would respond with either sympathy or rage. This godly confessor might be a pastor, counselor, good friend, or perhaps your spouse. Then confess your sin to God and ask for and receive His forgiveness.

2. *Ask God (along with a trusted prayer partner or counselor) to help you find the root causes of your problem.* Be willing to allow Him to bring up pain from the past if necessary in order to make you whole. This step may involve forgiving others who have wounded you in various ways.

3. *Choose to exercise moral effort to stop the habitual practices.* It is a big mistake and a distortion of God's character to pray, "Lord, if You want me to quit this You will take away the desire." Of course He wants you to quit your sexual fantasies and sinful practices! Ask God to fill you with the power of His Holy Spirit to do what you will not be able to do in your own strength. Also, ask Him to strengthen your will to choose what is right.

4. *Maintain an accountability connection with someone for as long as it takes.*

The steps just outlined will be explored more intimately in further chapters. There will be the opportunity for you, the struggler, to make choices and participate in prayers that will greatly assist you in coming free.

There will be the opportunity for you, the one who lives with the struggler, to see the situation through other eyes, not just through your own sense of hurt, rejection or disgust. You will be able to see through God's eyes.

## There is hope

Acknowledging up front that Conlee and I are neither therapists nor counselors,[6] we have been overwhelmed in our ministry with the numbers of men and women who have come to us for healing prayer about their inability to give up pornography, usually either after they have gotten caught or after their involvement in pornography seems out of their control. Sadly, many of the people who have come to us have the mistaken idea that they are beyond help.

Some have already tried to stop by going cold turkey and have failed by eventually falling back into their old patterns of behavior. Some have tried to get help through group account-ability therapy programs without dependence upon Jesus Christ as their strength and healer. Unfortunately, many of those who were in groups without the power of the Holy Spirit to teach and heal them ended up with a lot of sympathy and understanding, increased guilt because they did not have the will power to stay clean and, unfortunately, some additional pornographic web sites from their fellow strugglers.

Some who come for prayer are dealing with broken marriages, fractured relationships with their children, and the shattered hopes of promising careers. Yet God gives new hope to all these!

> *"Everyone who has this hope* [of Jesus] *in him purifies himself, just as he is pure."* (1 John 3:3)

> *". . . I have put my hope in your word."* (Psalm 119:74b)

> *"Why are you downcast, O my soul?*
> *Why so disturbed within me?*
> *Put your hope in God,*
> *for I will yet praise him,*
> *my Savior and my God."* (Psalm 42:11)

Encountering beautiful families in disarray and very near destruction, we have simply done what we know how to do best. We have cried out to God for them and with them and we have listened to what He has said. God has spoken wisdom to us far beyond our understanding at times. He has shown us principles of healing for those struggling with pornography that are totally compatible with the biblical principles we all need to employ in our journeys to wholeness. Most of the spiritual principles contained in this book are either out of our own listening prayer journals, or received from God in prayer, or they are the direct results of applying God's biblical wisdom through healing prayer to those who seek help. The proof of the effectiveness of the principles is that through them, God has set many men and women free from years of bondage to a practice that once consumed their thoughts and actions.

The basic principles that are presented in this book were introduced to us first through Leanne Payne's ministry to the broken.[7] As God began to show her the most basic ways in which He wanted to heal His people, she began to pass them on in discipleship to those around her and, as we became more whole, we too passed them on to others. Her biblical understanding of ministering wholeness applies to any problem we have. As she so aptly says, "We are all healed the same way."

Healing from any addiction is a process. Once a person has declared his or her intentions to come free from the grips of pornography undoubtedly there will be setbacks. However, setbacks are not necessarily defeats. Today I spoke with Eric, a man who has struggled with his sexuality, and specifically pornography, all his life. There have been so many attempts to overcome his addiction he has lost count. He had finally come to the conclusion that he was destined to be broken, never to change. It was then, in the depth of his despair, that the victory came. His story will be told in detail later. Today however, he said he was so thankful that he didn't give up. Although the collaboration with God in his healing process was the hardest work he has ever done in his life, he said it was the best thing that ever happened to him. It was when he finally faced head-on the truth of his pathology and declared his helplessness and willingness to do whatever it took – no matter how painful – that the healing began to come.

Like overcoming addictions to alcohol, drugs, smoking, etc.,
there are serious temptations to turn back and give in to relieve
the anxiety of the moment. Often these temptations yield to
action and the work of self-denial is undone for a time. It is
important to start over with each fall, learning from the experience and seeking more and more of God's wisdom each time. It
is also important to understand, however, that one's marriage
partner feels increasingly betrayed with each fall, so that the
relationship suffers each time proportionately to the number of
times of betrayal. Your sense of helplessness and inability to
overcome the addiction by yourself must be conveyed to the one
you love. Otherwise you will continue to alienate the very
person God has given to you for true intimacy.

## Paint the dragon red

If we want to employ God's wisdom and healing effectively
when we confront the devastation that pornography leaves in its
wake, it is important that we thoroughly understand the
destructive nature of the practice. The picture is not pretty, but
the information is essential if we are going to confront the
deception with truth. As Jesus taught, truth always frees us;[8] we
should never be afraid of it. It is vital that we know exactly what
we are dealing with and how to approach the truth about
pornography in holy ways that do not dishonor God.

*Understanding* the deceptive nature of pornography is far
different than *experiencing* it. We should never immerse ourselves
in anything dark or become defiled by it in order to understand
the deadly dimension of its nature and how to combat its power
over us and others. Just as we don't have to (and should not)
dialogue with demons to send them on their way in the name of
Jesus, so we need not overly familiarize ourselves with the
darkness of pornography in order to help those who are seeking
deliverance.

Even the slightest flirtation with evil will leave stains upon us
that must be cleansed by the blood of Jesus. In reading many
books attempting to help strugglers from the deleterious effects
of pornography, I have felt "slimed" because too much explicit
information has been given by the authors in order to appear
credible or convince the reader that he can identify with their

problem. Some of the images that are constellated by well-meaning informers need to be submitted to Jesus, asking Him to do some holy washing of the mind and imagination. There will be the opportunity for you to experience this cleansing as you continue in further chapters of this book.

However, to bury one's head in the sand is not the stance to take when confronting such an insidious attack on the family. The deceptive, illusory aspect of pornography will only grow when the truth is not revealed.

We use the imagery of "painting the dragon red."[9] Our personal dragons are more like gigantic chameleons, having an amazing ability to adapt to our surroundings, camouflaging themselves against the circumstances of our lives. When we ask God to "paint them a brilliant red" so that they will stand out and be obvious, we are asking for truth to be revealed. I have encouraged many hurting wives, who know their husbands are involved in pornography and yet keep hearing avid denials from their lips, to pray a "paint-the-dragon-red" prayer. I cannot think of any such prayer that has not been answered over a period of time. God loves Truth!

Many times we do not know how to pray or we pray ineffectively for someone because we don't understand the severity of the problem. For instance, I will pray very differently for a person who has indigestion than I will for one with colon cancer, although the symptoms of abdominal pain may be similar. We need to be informed to be effective in our prayers and in our exhortations. When we begin to understand the underlying dynamics of an addiction to pornography we begin to pray for ourselves and others very differently than when we simply respond out of our hurt feelings, our sense of rejection, anger, or sympathy.

It is time for Christians to be not only informed but also equipped to enter this spiritual battle. And a battle it is! The war is being fought over the divine image in the human soul. If the enemy can destroy and pervert the divine image within humans he never minds leaving a battlefield strewn with the broken remnants of families, holy sexuality, and the innocence of children.

# Chapter 2

## The Overture
### The pervasion of pornography

*"For all have sinned and fall short of the glory of God."*
(Romans 3:23)

---

**por·nog·ra·phy** *n.* obscene literature, photographs, paintings, etc., intended to cause sexual excitement [fr. Greek *pornographos*, writing about prostitutes] [1]

---

### Something rotten in Denmark

While leading a *Journey to Wholeness in Christ* seminar in Florida, we were having lunch with a group of participants one day. One of the women at our table was Danish, recently married to an American who lived near the conference site. We were pleased to tell her that we had just returned from a ministry trip to Denmark and how exciting it was to see God's cleansing work among the participants. She wanted to know if we had been able to spend any time in Copenhagen since that was her home. We replied that we only had a couple of days there and, although it was a breathtakingly beautiful city, how difficult it had been for us. Of course we then had to explain why.

Walking through the Copenhagen airport, driving along the streets, even using the telephone, we had been bombarded with pornographic images in the most graphic ways. In 1969,

Denmark was the first nation in the world to rescind its obscenity laws. As a result, nearly anything goes. We saw large billboards, posters and other depictions of sexual nudity in nearly every public place, even on the cover of the phone book. Larger than life explicit sexual scenes from movies and novels (mostly American) were advertised in the airport and alongside the motorways. Interestingly, the same American movies and best-selling novels that were being highly advertised at the same time in the U.S. were the very ones that were being promoted in blatant sexual ways in this Scandinavian metropolis. The difference was that X-rated scenes that never appeared in the American versions were now plastered around Copenhagen. This kind of exaggerated content would never have been tolerated in such prominence in any American city.

The local television channels featured numerous offerings of sexual "enlightenment" documentaries. While searching for CNN in our hotel room we were literally "slimed" by just seconds of viewing several local channels. Their content was nothing short of erotic pornography in the guise of education.

One of the most heart-breaking scenes I remember was while we were window-shopping in beautiful downtown Copenhagen. Many of the shop windows were full of the bright primary-colored toys and clothes we always want to get for our grand-children while traveling in Europe. We stopped at the window of a book and toy store, admiring the intricate Lego village on display, when an adorable toddler, sitting in her pram at window level with the display, was wheeled right next to me. I followed her eyes to the Lego display and then watched her attention shift to something else – a large, brightly colored poster farther down the shelf. This adorable rosy-cheeked baby was cooing and gurgling happily, all the while gazing on the most explicit sexual coupling of two nude women on an advertisement poster for a book. I looked up at the parents who were seemingly oblivious of what their child was visually devouring. This child, along with many others, will grow up with an entirely different awareness of *man* and of *woman* than a child who has not been exposed to pornography.[2] How will these kinds of images affect the rest of her life?

Our Danish lady in Florida interrupted me before I listed off most of the reasons why Copenhagen had shocked me and said,

"Oh, my dear, no one really looks at that sort of thing. That's only what some lower level people get involved with. We just don't pay any attention to it. When you learn to ignore it it's really not that bad."

## Tell that to Pastor Nors!

Conlee and I had spent a lot of time in prayer with Pastor Nors in the healing seminar in Denmark. Mid-way through the ministry week we spent there he, in great despair, had asked for a prayer appointment. He was coming face-to-face with some realities of his life that he didn't know how to handle. Suddenly, God was shining His light on some areas of Nors' life that he had been keeping in the dark and he was asking us for help in sorting it all out.

He described his father as a "non-person." Although he had been around the home, Nors' father had left no impression upon his son at all, good or bad. It was as though he had never existed to Nors' memory.

His mother had been emotionally ill and fragile. He could not recall any times of his life when she was able to give him time, love or attention. Because he felt no connection with his mother at all, his heart and even his body were hungry for touches of feminine love.

Without an early attachment to mother – and to the feminine – Nors' images of woman had been formed as a child growing up in a society exposed to excessive amounts of pornography. He was obsessed on the one hand by an inordinate desire to give into the sexual lusts that began to consume him, the constant fantasy life of one sexual encounter after another, even to the point of violent fantasies. On the other hand he was plagued by feelings of insecurity and inadequacies. Because of a lack of connection with a father, his images of manhood were as perverted as his images of womanhood.

If, as pornography always projects, a man is supposed to be able to have sexual encounters with many women who beg for his attention, why did he feel so impotent? He no longer had sexual feelings for his wife. He had even had several nagging thoughts of homosexuality. *"What if I am really attracted to men?"* Only his frequent encounters with pornographic magazines and Internet sites kept him feeling alive. The rest of the time he felt dead inside. And through all his adult years of struggling with these problems, Nors was actively pastoring a church, ministering to the hurting and counseling the troubled. He was born again, genuinely loved the Lord, yet knew there was something terribly broken within him, something he felt powerless to handle.

Although he was willing to confess the obsessions of his thought life, he was quick to justify to himself and to us that he had never been unfaithful to his wife. What he meant was that he had never physically touched another woman in a sexual way. He discounted the numerous encounters with women in his fantasy life and through pornography, and the chronic masturbation that accompanied those illusory encounters. He also discounted the words of Jesus in Matthew 5:27–28, *"You have heard that it was said, 'Do not commit adultery.' But I tell you that anyone who looks at a woman lustfully has already committed adultery with her in his heart."*

I'll tell you how God helped him in a later chapter. But first let me tell you about Katye, his wife.

## What pornography does to a wife

Katye was one of those women it was easy to dislike instantly before you even got to know her. Upon our first brief introduction (before praying with her husband or knowing anything about their situation) I instinctively wanted to avoid her. She was rude, overbearing, had a superior attitude, and I was concerned that she would be a detriment to the ministry team for the seminar. Her countenance was stern and unpleasant.

After praying with Pastor Nors however, I knew I needed to make an appointment with his wife, but wasn't sure how to approach her. No problem! She bulldozed her way into a private conversation I was having with someone else and announced: "I need to talk to you!" And so later we met to talk and to pray.

We sat side by side, very properly in a small, private meeting room along a wall of banquettes. In this setting she was unexpectedly reserved and hesitant. At first I thought it might be because her English was not that fluent and she was reluctant to speak. But when I quietly asked, "Would you like to talk about your marriage?" she exploded. Even I (who keep saying I have seen it all, but haven't) was startled. She screamed, threw herself down upon the banquette, pounded the pillows, beat her head against the wall, cried, tore up a notebook, threw down her cell phone (several times), all the while shouting in Danish of which I understood not a word.

While this long tirade was going on I was silently and earnestly praying, asking God to show me what to do. Soon, I intuitively *knew* how to proceed to convey God's love and peace to her. I stood up and took her in my arms, holding her tightly as a mother would hold a child having a tantrum. I prayed that God's peace would flow into her and that He would love her through me. And like a child, her anger turned into hurt, then sobs, then shudders and finally peace. After a bit she began to talk to me about her life.

Katye had been affected by pornography since she was a child. Besides the proliferation of erotic material from her society, she had seen the pornographic magazines her father had kept at home. There had been no secrecy about them; they were out in plain sight. Sometimes she had observed her parents acting out some of the sexual fantasies she had looked at in the magazines. There had been provocative costumes and role-playing. Everything she saw in her family was also heavily reinforced in the world outside her home.

She soon learned to create her own fantasies, masturbating at an early age, dressing sexily one day and disguising her femininity the next. This ambivalence about her own femininity affected all her relationships. She was full of both rage and reticence. She was very confused and as a young woman, believed that marrying a quiet, gentle, loving man like Nors would give her a loving home and family. But instead, over the years, she had come to believe that he had deceived her. She now rationalized that, instead of loving her, he was incapable of loving any woman.

Because her needs were not being met, because he would withdraw from her and seldom affirm her femininity, because his actions caused her to feel unlovely and undesirable, and because of her own self-hatred, her hope for their future had deteriorated into anger and contempt. She had begun to despise his quiet, reserved manner. Even just looking at his demeanor often led her to feel disgust for him. When people in the church sometimes told her what a wonderful, compassionate man he was, her reaction was one of ridicule and disbelief. She began to store up a latent anger toward him that bordered on murder. I had just seen a lot of that anger released! Believe me, it was enough to kill!

Katye had lost interest in making love to her husband to the extent that the thought of sex disgusted her. She had even begun to put to death her own sexuality[3] and to withdraw from most normal social activities where she had to interact with people. She rationalized this detachment from others by claiming she didn't want to be a hypocrite.

## Giving away the ending

Later I'm going to tell you the details of what God did in the lives of Nors and Katye during a week in Denmark. But I want to give away the ending right now. At the end of the seminar, when it was time to leave, we were packed up, waiting to be driven to the train station from the conference center. The host team was at the door sending us off with their blessings. As I was about to step inside the taxi, Katye grabbed me. I had to look twice at this very different looking woman. How she had changed in six days!

She had curled her hair, her cheeks were blushed, and she had very femininely thrown a scarf around her plain sweater. But it was not hair spray, makeup or wardrobe that caused the real change; those were all external. She wore an inner glow of beauty that cannot be applied by hand. She looked better than one of the "after" pictures of the women who had gotten some of that expensive skin care stuff from the plastic surgeon.

"I have to tell you," she whispered excitedly. "Nors and I made love last night. It was so sweet. Not at all like the old fantasies. He was tender and loving, strong and vulnerable all at the same time. I realized there is a man there who really is wonderful and I can know him, really, intimately know him. I feel so free to be honest and respond to him without wondering about his motives. Thank you for praying for us."

As we drove away from the conference center my last view was of Nors and Katye holding onto each other, beaming from ear to ear, waving goodbye to us, hopeful for their future. That is a picture of wholeness!

## The proverbial frog in the pot

You know the story: The water in the pot is boiling and for some weird reason you want to put a live frog in it. You try and he jumps out. Frogs love water but not when it's boiling! However, when you take a pot of room temperature water and put a frog in, he likes it a lot. Then you *gradually* turn up the fire under the pot and he never realizes it until it's too late. You've cooked the frog![4]

When I reflected on my conversation with the Danish lady in Florida I realized that we in America are the frog. The water is heating up and we are not noticing. We're not boiling yet like they are in Denmark, but it's getting hot. You put me in Denmark and I jump out of the pot in a heartbeat. But you put me in Anytown, USA, with cable television, movies, bookstores and the Internet and I don't even flinch. Oh, I might think about it for a minute, but it's too much trouble to crawl out of the pot. Lord, have mercy!

According to Michelle Anderson, "We have become so accustomed to the presence of pornography that we have almost lost the ability to imagine an alternative – a market in which pornography does not monopolize sexual speech and quash dissent."[5]

So what are we going to do about this? It's bigger than Texas!

## Just how big is it?

If you don't like to read statistics you may be tempted to skip this next section, but if you persevere and wade through the following facts you will be amazed at just how hot America's pot of water is really getting while most people are just considering it a recreational hot tub. With each fact you read, be aware of the water's temperature rising.

- The number of major strip clubs in the United States roughly doubled between 1987 and 1992. In 1998 there were about 2,500 of these clubs nationwide.[6]
- There are more outlets for hard-core pornography in the U.S. (approx. 25,000) than McDonald's restaurants (approx. 9,000).[7]

- A survey of men who have attended Promise Keepers conferences shows more than 50 percent had been exposed to pornography within the week before the event. One in three reported that they struggle with pornography on a regular basis.[8]

- In 1996 pornography was a $13 billion a year industry, more than the combined annual revenues of the Coca-Cola and McDonnell Douglas corporations.[9]

- FBI interviews with 36 convicted sex killers, including serial murderers, show that all of them have entertained long-standing sexual fantasies of murder that are as real to them as the actual acts of murder, and 81% of the murderers regularly used pornography.[10]

- *Playboy's* electronic headquarters received 4.7 million hits (electronic visits) in a recent 7-day period.[11]

- Romance novels constitute 58.2% of all popular paperback fiction purchased in the U.S., resulting in $1.35 billion annual sales. 18% of all books sold are romance novels. 41 million people read them annually. 2,218 new romance novels were released in 1999. The main genres of romance novels are: traditional, paranormal, inspirational, suspense, regency, historical, contemporary, time travel, dark and erotic. The typical romance author publishes one new novel per year. The typical romance reader reads one novel per day. 57% of all romance readers are married. The average reader is: female, over 30, educated, middle income, white, non-working. 71% of romance readers read their first romance novel at age 16.[12]

- Porn video rentals soared to 665 million in 1996, accounting for 13.3% of all video rentals in America. Profits of sales and rentals of porn videos was $4.2 billion in 1996.[13] In 1996, "Americans spent more than $8 billion on hard-core videos, peep shows, live sex acts, adult cable programming, sexual devices, computer porn, and sex magazines. That represents an amount much larger than Hollywood's domestic box office receipts, and larger than all the revenues generated by rock and country music recordings."[14]

- A consultant hired to review the Clinton White House Internet logs in the summer of 2000, found that staffers, including those in the West Wing, had downloaded significant amounts of hard-core, XXX porn, including "teen sites," "gay and bestiality stuff, too." Although this practice is illegal in government offices, the White House, under the Clinton administration, admitted it had a "little porn-at-work problem."[15]

- Males who frequently read at least one of the following magazines – *Playboy, Penthouse, Chic, Club, Forum, Gallery, Genesis, Oui* and *Hustler* – are more likely to accept rape myths (such as women becoming sexually aroused by the assault) after exposure to pornography.[16] They are less sympathetic (both in personal attitudes and acting as jurors in rape trials) toward women who have been raped and they trivialize the trauma of rape.[17] These readers are also found to believe that women enjoy forced sex and being dominated in rough, physical ways. Furthermore, after seeing pornography that depicts female rape victims becoming sexually aroused by the assault, the men justify their aggressions and reduce their inhibitions against acting out their aggressions towards women.[18]

- Many sex offenders claim that viewing pornography affects their criminal behavior. Ted Bundy, convicted and executed serial killer, is one of the most well-known of these men.[19] Jeffrey Dahmer, convicted child molester and serial killer had massive quantities of hard-core pornography and videotapes in his apartment. Arthur Gary Bishop, executed in Utah, in 1983 for killing five boys, admitted to hard-core usage of pornography.[20]

- Of about 400 men who were surveyed:[21]
  - 77% believe they are addicted to pornography,
  - 72% are religious,
  - 15% have had their spouse tell them they are addicted to sex,
  - 50% view porn daily

- The average age a guy starts looking at porn is 11.

- 87% of all TV shows have sexual content.[22]
- 89% of all sex depicted on prime-time TV is outside of marriage.[23]

## The downward spiral

As this is written the most recent addition to the illusory world of pornography is DVD porn. With DVD one can experience virtual reality, entering the porn flick or game at any point in the action, interacting with the characters and choosing to view the action from any angle. It is said to be the nearest thing to having sex without really doing it. Who knows what will be available next year!

Once limited to dirty postcards, comic books, "girlie magazines," porn flicks, adult book stores, massage parlors, men's magazines, and XXX videos, the acquiring of pornography basically involved a person leaving the house and secretively buying or renting commodities. Where once a guy used to have to go to the sleazier parts of downtown to find porn, later he could go down the street to the local convenience or video store. Today he only needs to go downstairs. Downtown, down the street, downstairs – see how easy it has become? See which direction he is heading? Down!

Along with the huge variety of offerings available to satiate their customers with lust and addiction, the porn industry has found itself a real goldmine inside one of them – the Net.

## The Internet

We've looked at some general stats about the effects of pornography among us during the last few years. Now let's look specifically at the ways the porn pushers have capitalized on the PC in every home.

In the early 70s when Bill Gates said every home would have a personal computer in the near future he was laughed out of the boardroom. His original idea was of a world marketplace rather than an information superhighway.[24] In the world marketplace literally anything would be available to the consumer, with the interaction of consumers and sellers. Gates was right; not only can we now go anywhere on the Net, when we get there our options of things to buy, sell and browse are limitless.

The U.S. has an overwhelming lead in Internet users in the world with over 110 million people online. That is nearly 43% of the total 259 million worldwide Net users. It is estimated that by the end of 2005 there will be over 765 million people in the world connected to one another via the Internet. That is 118 people out of every thousand.[25]

The family home with Internet service is now linked to the most remote areas of the world and has at its fingertips information that exceeds any well-stocked library. I can sit at my computer and look at a live picture of my friends praying at the Western Wall in Jerusalem. Via a camera mounted on my computer, I can both see and talk to my little grandson in New Mexico. I can have online conversations with an expert in any field I choose. I can download more books than I can read in a lifetime. I can attend auctions and buy and sell. I can listen to music, keep financial records and send greeting cards. I can play any sport online, enter fantasy worlds of the future, chat with folks in Japan or Uganda, learn to cook, design a house and conduct business from nearly anywhere in the world.

All of that in itself can be exhilarating. Called "mindthrill, the Internet's constant stimulation of the senses of a cornucopia of electronic delights,"[26] can give some users such a rush that they will totally lose track of time. What seems like a twenty minute trip through cyberspace may in reality be three or four hours. When asked to leave the computer to join the family one may feel like he's being nagged every two minutes when in reality he's been asked twice in two hours. Some people report that they get on such a high when they get lost in the Net they resent anyone trying to break the spell.

When a friend recently announced via e-mail that she was online for the first time at age seventy, I sent her back this message, "Congratulations! You have just lost at least three hours of each day."

## First the remote control, now the mouse

In spite of its amazing capabilities, when we bring the Net, the ultimate communication system by the end of the 20th century, into our homes we also bring in one more intruder that can isolate us from our families and allow the values of the world to further infiltrate our environments. With the TV already firmly ensconced as most families' dinner companion and entertainment resource, we have become accustomed to having the interests of strangers, the fantasies of their imaginations through drama and comedy, and the excitement of sports events invade our space. The remote control takes us away from our present reality, sometimes into the merely mindless sounds and motion of TV Land.

However, we have no direct involvement with TV. We sit passively, pushing buttons that take us to a myriad of venues and people, but never given the privilege of entering into their worlds with them. The closest we seem to come to genuine interaction is through the immensely popular new genre of TV shows where we are given the opportunity to lurk at real life (*Survivor,*[27] *Big Brother,*[28] etc.) or to plan the wedding of a young couple[29] or the design and construction of a house[30] by voting for every decision that will be made.

On the Net however, we are given the opportunity to interact with people who appear to offer us what our real families cannot or will not.[31] Besides accessing reams of information, if we are lonely we can tell someone and they will respond. We can enter into "relationships" with people whose faces we don't see and whose voices we don't hear. We can become whoever we want to become without any responsibilities or judgments. What one tends to forget is that those who respond to us on the Net can be making up everything they tell us as well. There are no umpires, judges or referees. There are no rules, just endless opinions.

On television there are resolutions at the end of the show, the game, or the season. On the Net however, each site leads to another link, then another, then a dozen ... where does one stop? There are no endings, no time restraints, no monitors. And all of this time spent in cyberspace is time spent away from real relationships. Where once the wife's complaint was that her husband left work and went to the local bar to have a few drinks with the guys before coming home, now her complaint is that he comes home early only to huddle before the computer until he goes to bed.

Far more than the TV, the computer has isolated family

members from one another. Not only is the modern goal for every home to have a PC but the latest goal is for every family member to have his own PC. This further isolation from one another within the family now leads to the need to have "home networking," whereby all the PCs in a household can be electronically linked together so that the family members can communicate and share information.[32] Now we are trying to duplicate electronically what healthy families used to do – and are supposed to do – naturally.

According to Dr. Kimberly Young, the Top 10 list of neglected activities that suffer most due to excessive Internet use are:[33]

1. Time with spouse or family
2. Daily chores
3. Sleep
4. Reading
5. Watching TV
6. Time with friends
7. Exercise
8. Hobbies
9. Sex
10. Social events

Spending time online has become a sort of tranquilizer for many people, to the extent that some call it a new addiction. Often those (like Ann in Chapter 1) who find it very difficult to talk about their real feelings or anxieties to those closest to them will spill their guts to a voiceless, faceless persona in a chat room.

Last week in our very first experience of chat room "conversation" Conlee and I went into a room labeled "Romance" on AOL. It was an experimental investigation for us to see what the big attraction was for the millions of people who indulge in this activity every day. The inane conversation was reminiscent of a boring group of people seated at a bar. In fact most people were chatting online about what they were drinking at the time.

After "listening" for a while, finally we typed in, "Why is everybody here?" The consensus was that no one had anything else to do.

We eventually struck up a "conversation" with a woman who identified herself as Helen. Within mere minutes this is what we learned about her just by asking a few simple questions: Helen has an eight-year-old son, is divorced, is three months pregnant by a guy she "talked" to on the Net for six months, finally met and had sex with. As soon as he found out she was pregnant he split; she's lonely, has no money and her only companionship is in the chat rooms. She never once asked who we were, even if we were male or female. She just needed to talk to someone. She couldn't afford a psychiatrist's couch so she went online.

Can that be good? Perhaps, to the extent that Helen gets in touch with her feelings and names her problems, but extremely dangerous considering that she is receiving advice from unknown sources and that each pseudo "relationship" she makes online can be severed with the touch of a button, thus exacerbating her sense of loss. Her obvious vulnerability also makes her easy prey for another man like the father of her unborn child. In the online world there is no commitment to wholeness.

As our "conversation" ended we just said, "God bless you, Helen. I'm glad you didn't have an abortion. I hope you make it." Her response was, "Thanks for listening."

According to Sherry Tuttle, "computers offer the illusion of companionship without the demands of friendship."[34]

An interesting and surprising reaction to our one chat room experience was that I found myself thinking about Helen for a long time. In spite of my awareness that Helen may have been only a persona of a totally different person, I longed to help her. I felt I could minister to her. Perhaps I could pray with her. I was amazed at how strong the tie had become within about three minutes. I had to commit her to the Lord and *choose* to focus on other things. How could this have affected me so much when the whole experience had been carried out just as an experiment? What is the strong emotional pull of this activity?

## Addicted to the Net

*Is it possible to become addicted to an activity? I thought people were only addicted to substances that initiate chemical reactions in the body.*

There is a direct relationship between intense emotion (such as pleasure) and the subsequent release of chemicals in the brain (such as dopamine and serotonin). When certain foods (like chocolate) and/or experiences (like orgasm) are enjoyed, an imprinting occurs via the release of such chemical endorphins onto the cells of the brain. This "washing" of the brain cells releases the intense feelings of well-being.

Thus patterns or imprints of the pleasure experience and its source are embedded within the network of the brain. As the brain reacts to familiar stimuli (the foods, substances and/or activities) the behavior of a person can be permanently altered without the person being conscious of its happening. Tendencies become habits; habits become compulsions, compulsions become addictions.[35]

The "rush" experienced by many Net users can be just such a stimulus for the washing of brain cells to imprint the experience. Perhaps it is not fair to say one can be addicted to the computer or addicted to the Internet, but it is obvious that people can become addicted to certain emotional and mental responses they receive from their online practices.[36]

When we put these facts together with the "rush" many porn users expect as they enter into Web sites, chat rooms and sexually interactive games we see the potential for serious addictions. The additional sexual rush through masturbation and orgasm, which nearly always accompanies pornography usage, forms an even more thorough imprinting of each experience.

"Internet pornography has earned itself a reputation for being the crack cocaine of sexual addiction. 'It works so quickly and it's so instantly intense,' says Dr. Robert Weiss of the Sexual Recovery Institute in Los Angeles. 'We're seeing a whole population of clients who have never had a history with the problem, but for the first time, they're beginning one particular activity and getting hooked.'"[37]

## Back to your future

Caught in the net of pornography is not where you or your family is destined to be. This does not have to be your autobiography. There is more ahead for you than a life imprisoned by the greed of the porn czars and the lure of Satan. The cycles of your obsession with pornography can be broken! We're going to show you Who is going to do it and how it's going to be done. But first let's look at God's marvelous plan for His children's fulfillment and how the values of the world sabotage it.

# Chapter 3

## The Plot

*God's marvelous plan
and Satan's scheme to sabotage it*

---

**God's plan:**

*And I pray that you, being rooted and established in love, may have power, together with all the saints, to grasp how wide and long and high and deep is the love of Christ, and to know this love that surpasses knowledge – that you may be filled to the measure of all the fullness of God.* (Ephesians 3:17b–19)

**Satan's plan:**

*Your enemy the devil prowls around like a roaring lion looking for someone to devour. Resist him, standing firm in the faith, because you know that your brothers throughout the world are undergoing the same kind of sufferings.* (1 Peter 5:8–9)

---

Many of the men and women actively involved in pornography are in church every Sunday. They love God. They love their families. They often represent to the world the ideal family unit, sometimes teaching Sunday School, coaching Little League baseball, attending dance recitals and parent-teacher organizations. In fact, when not engaged in the compulsive habits of pornographic pursuits, they spend what little time remains in fairly wholesome activities. These may include church, work, and community activities with kids and friends.

In the midst of the increased activities of a family's life it is so easy for a husband and wife to avoid discussing a growing lack of intimacy between them. The first clue that there may be a problem with marital intimacy may be the simple fact that their lives have become filled with so many other obligations. This social activism may be the initial attempt to mask the pain of loneliness. The huge chasm formed between marriage partners may develop so gradually that, since neither one of them can recall a cataclysmic event that set it off, they tend to see it as a phase, ignoring it and hoping it will pass, instead of working on a solution.

Far more intimate than sexual intercourse, genuine dialogue from the heart binds a husband and wife together. In true dialogue every dream and desire is shared, every longing is explored; each one listens and respects, encourages and affirms. This kind of dialogue requires deep commitment to the relationship and the deliberate decision to give it a priority in the life of a family. It also requires vulnerability about one's needs and disappointments without projecting anger and frustration upon the other person.

When there are wounds that prevent this kind of vulnerability, or that promote the neglect of the kind of quality time that fosters trust between marriage partners, the typical result is a void or paralysis of this kind of deep intimate dialogue. When this dialogue is missing in an intimate relationship, each person tends to draw a curtain over his/her deep heart and close off the most tender part of oneself to others. And so each partner finds personal ways to fill the void of intimate relationship.

The attempts to fill these voids are highly motivated because each person created by God has authentic intimacy needs. God fashioned us that way so that our hearts would yearn to have intimate relationship and dialogue with Him. When God said, *"It is not good for the man to be alone,"*[1] it was the very first thing in the new creation that He did not bless as being good. It is normal for men and women to have deep inner needs to connect with other human beings on an intimate level. In fact, this is a healthy desire and it begins with life itself. It is when those innate intimacy needs are not met in godly, appropriate ways at God-appointed, appropriate times in our lives that things go askew.

## God's appropriate, appointed, perfectly-timed provision

God's perfect plan for the fulfillment of our intimacy needs is so simple we often miss it. It is so beautiful and so easily attainable we often take its brilliance for granted.

It begins with one man and one woman, united by God in the commitment of marriage, love and companionship, coming together to create life, thus fulfilling the commission given to Adam and Eve.[2]

For nine months the life that is created from their love is cradled and nourished by the body of the woman, protected and guarded by the strength of the man. The tiny life within the mother's womb is very secure and immediately absorbs the love expressed between the parents for God, for one another and for its own presence. For nine months this new creature is receiving constant blessing, welcome, acceptance, anticipation and love. This child-in-the-making knows nothing else but that there is a secure place wherein there is comfort.

Upon the signal of delivery, the baby begins the long passage of birth, withstanding the pain of the journey for the promise of what lies ahead. And at the end of the birthing journey are the welcoming arms of the one who has carried the precious life for so many weeks. The new-born baby feels her skin, hears her heartbeat, smells the nourishment she offers, and nuzzles into her embrace, totally absorbed in the continued awareness of the security of attachment and belonging. Every need is met. It is perfect! God has planned it so well.

David wrote about this amazing miracle of God in Psalm 139:13–16:

> *"For you created my inmost being;*
> *you knit me together in my mother's womb.*
> *I praise you because I am fearfully and wonderfully made;*
> *your works are wonderful,*
> *I know that full well.*
> *My frame was not hidden from you*
> *when I was made in the secret place.*
> *When I was woven together in the depths of the earth,*
> *your eyes saw my unformed body.*

*All the days ordained for me*
*were written in your book*
*before one of them came to be."*

For many weeks to come this newborn baby, yet unaware that there is a separation between self and mother, is totally dependent upon her touch, her look, her voice, her food, her protection and her care. Mother symbolizes life to the newborn. She is everything.

It cannot be emphasized strongly enough how important mother's love, care and affection is for the first few weeks – and even months – of the baby's existence. Initially, this new little life does not even know there is a difference between self and her presence. When the child becomes aware of mother's absence it is as though a part of himself[3] has fragmented. This sense of loss, even when experienced for only a few moments, will elicit intense emotions that are expressed in no uncertain terms until mother returns. He becomes aware of her absence and he cries until he feels the comfort of her presence again.

If her absence is prolonged the baby may experience an intensity of deep fear and anxiety that becomes imprinted upon his memory.

## God's divine order

After a few months (at just about the time when any new mother is longing to have a few hours all to herself), God establishes another level of divine order in the life of the baby. There is developed what is called "evocative memory." This is clearly demonstrated by watching a child interact with a little toy held in front of his face. For the first few weeks there will not be any noticeable interest. But there comes the day when the baby is extremely interested for a few seconds, then longer. Eventually, weeks later what happens when you hide the toy behind your back? Does the baby still lose interest as if the unseen toy ceases to exist? Or does the baby follow your hand and peer behind your back to find the out of sight toy? If so, the baby has developed a memory that can evoke an object no longer present – *evocative memory.*[4]

When the memory of the image of the unseen toy can be evoked to the baby's consciousness then we know that the child also has the capacity to evoke the memory of the image of mother when she is no longer present for very limited periods of time. However, the capacity to reasonably understand the absence of mother and anticipate her return may take up to three years. Therefore, the development of evocative memory does not mean that mother is excused to abandon her baby for long hours without consequences, but it shows that there is no longer the same sense of panic, fear of abandonment or rage within the child when mother cannot be present for every waking moment.[5]

With this kind of godly parenting whereby the mother sees herself as the primary caregiver, nurturer, and companion for the first few months, and the father sees himself as the primary protector of both the mother and the child, the child is given every possible chance to develop in healthy, contented, secure ways, knowing the worth and identity – the sense of well-being – that God has lovingly provided and bestowed. The child has become firmly *"rooted and established in love"*[6] and the image of God's character is being formed within his soul. It is so simple and yet our society has made it so difficult.

## The role of the father

The role of the father, although vital from conception, gains in importance as the weeks progress. From the first awareness of new life growing within his wife's womb, the wise husband will begin to talk to and bless his baby *in utero*. As he caresses his wife's belly the baby within absorbs his father's love. And at the moment of birth the newborn recognizes the familiar voice of his father among all the other voices around. Even in the delivery room, among many voices and noises, a newborn will turn his head towards the familiar voice of his father if he has become familiar with it while *in utero*. While deeply dependent upon mother, the infant is always aware of the masculine presence of father from day one.

But then there comes the day, after several months (up to two years), when the child realizes he has an identity, separate from mother's. No longer is there the sense that there is no identity apart from hers. There is now a real, separate little person who has desires apart from those of mother. This again is where the role of the father is so vital, to call this little life away from the total dependency upon mother and into the full identity of being male or female, of being loved and valued as a unique child of God.

Both little boy babies and little girl babies need to know they are separate from mother. It is especially important for the father's voice to call his sons into their masculine identity, which is so vitally different from mother's. This masculine calling forth, for both sons and daughters, according to God's plan, is the voice of love, of protection, of acceptance, of affirmation, of joy and of safe boundaries. It is invitational and at the same time it totally affirms the unique love the mother still offers.

This masculine voice, calling us out of a totally dependent relationship with mother and into a vertical relationship towards God, is equally as important as the mother's presence during the first few weeks. The father's voice mimics the voice of God, the heavenly Father, calling us all into our own person-hoods and affirming us in our true selves.[7] It also resembles the voice of our heavenly Father who calls us all out of our dependency upon the world and our bondage to sin, to come walk in the Light with Him, living out our true identity as a child of the Light, accepting Jesus as Lord.[8] It is through our positive responses to these callings-forth that we become the persons God created us to be.

What a vivid picture of this we see in the family picture album of the baby's first attempts to take a step! Here the baby is turned away from mother, yet the little hands are still firmly grasping hers, daddy's arms outstretched a few inches away, his masculine voice encouraging baby to turn loose from all that is familiar and comfortable and walk into the protection of his safe arms. The toddler wants to take those first steps of freedom but hesitates, turning back to make sure mother is there. Then finally, with a burst of courage, the little adventurer is off and running, stumbling at first, but gaining more stability with practice, always knowing there is a secure place, still within reach and firmly imprinted in his heart, that keeps him well-grounded. He has been well-rooted and established in love.

## The world's ways of parenting

*"... now the prince of this world* [Satan] *will be driven out."*
(John 12:31b)

Let's take a look at what happens when, instead of following God's plan, we follow the model that the world and its prince (whose destiny is determined) are condoning as parenthood.

The world's systems of parenting are totally different from God's plan of security for our children. The propaganda about the kind of parenting the world endorses is so convincing and so appealing to our selfish natures that we tend to rationalize its tenets and even defend its existence. When we hear something touted enough without resistance, we tend to acknowledge it even though we know it contradicts God's Word.

When we don't stand firm for a truth that never changes, soon we too can hear our thoughts and voices joining those of the world who say that God's plan is lovely, but too idealistic, too simplistic, naive, impractical, too primitive for our progressive society, too old-fashioned, etc., etc., etc.

Well, let's examine the alternatives that the world encourages. In contrast to God's divine plan, what is popular today in child raising and what are the results?

Newborns are often secondary to the selfish ambitions or lifestyle of the modern parent. Many are born without the protective love of a father who provides a secure place for the mother while she is caring for the baby and whose masculine voice calls the baby into his/her own identity.

Where are the modern fathers during this critical initial period of their children's lives? Statistics tell us that 38% of all American homes have no father present.[9] If he's present at all, he often plays a minor role:

- I provide for my family. I go to work everyday and bring home a paycheck to pay the bills. That's how I show them I love them. I want to make sure my kids have the best.
- I'll get involved when my boy can throw a ball! I'll root from the bleachers!
- I'll even go to her recitals someday when she gets older.

- I'm just not a "touchy-feely" kind of guy with my kids. I'm a busy man. I tend to be more like my dad and I turned out OK.
- Right now, while my kids are little, this is woman's work.
- I'm too worn out at the end of the day to spend time with my kids. They'd rather be doing something else anyway.

Where are the modern mothers when the infant barely knows there is a separation between her presence and him/herself? Today 90% of American homes have working moms.[10] Many women barely interrupt their careers to become mothers.

- I really need to get back to work so we can make our house and second car payments. My daughter is so little she doesn't know the difference whether I'm here or at work.
- The day care facility is exceptional.
- I give quality time when I'm with my baby, even though I must be gone most of the day.
- I'm sacrificing this time by working for extra money so my child can have all the advantages possible when he is older.
- God has given me a good mind and it would be a sin not to use it to its capacity in the workplace.
- If I don't keep this job while my baby is little I'll be forfeiting all I've worked for and lose my place in the job market.
- Being a stay-at-home mom is just not my gift. I'm going stir-crazy sitting around this house all day with an infant![11] I really need to stay in touch with the outside world.

The modern world's idols have become self and mammon, and as you can tell from the above popular responses to God's plan for parenting, these idols are gradually replacing God Himself. Making more money, pursuing careers at the expense of family, doing what seems right in our own eyes, and accumulating more stuff has taken precedence over the desire to give 100% of ourselves to parenting our children.

Those who are unparented thus become parents and pass along the legacy of non-attachment, leaving generations of men and women to grow up with huge deficits of motherlove in their hearts. One would reason that, after thousands of years of many generations, men and women would learn to live without the internal bonding of a mother's love and attention. They should be able to be self-sufficient without prolonged periods of experiencing her face and voice and touch. They shouldn't need the constant protective presence of a father and his strength and encouragement.

But no, the passage of time, even of many generations who have experienced this loss, never erases the God-ordained need that humans have for parental bonding. In fact, its prolonged absence, along with its accumulation of devastating affects, makes the need more apparent.

## But what about *me*?

Dr. Laura Schlessinger says she is inundated on her call-in radio show with parents complaining about their children. "Though callers may mouth concern for the welfare of their children, they inevitably whine, 'But what about *me*? What about *my* happiness? When am I entitled to what makes *me* happy? When am I going to get what *I* want?' "[12]

She quotes a great, back-to-reality answer to these whiny voices from Lloyd Olivia Davis,

> "You don't get to resign from parenthood. You don't get to tend to your 'inner child' at the expense of your real ones. You don't get to have the childhood you wish you had or wish you still had, while your children are having theirs. As long as you have dependent children you are responsible for being a parent, whether you want to be responsible or not. And you don't get to opt out of your responsibility because your lover needs a place to stay or you need the school clothes money to make the payment on your Corvette. And you don't get to snort cocaine on your posh leather sofa or smoke crack on your tattered vinyl recliner because you've had a hard day. Sorry. So grow up."[13]

Hard words? You bet! But I would add even more. Today's parents need to be healed, not coddled with sympathy which is what they're getting from most of the world's systems. They need to be healed because they're wounded!

## The walking wounded

Although they are mostly invisible and often ignored, huge gaping wounds of loneliness and emptiness are afflicting many men and women who attempt to lead meaningful lives. They have been deprived of basic infantile needs for attention, bonding and security. They have had these wounds so long, they have gotten used to their existence. They bleed; they are infected; they ooze pus and they don't heal. Many have gangrene and have had amputations on their emotions because of the severity of their infections. Some are so severely infected they are dying. But before they die, they are infecting those closest to them. So who are the world's "healers" these wounded ones are visiting? What are the "treatments" that are being prescribed?

The treatments these wounded ones find in the world are only temporary tonics passed off as cures. They are self-medicating themselves with illusory relationships, pornographic titillation, idealized fantasies of men and women, misogyny (the hatred of woman), misandry (the hatred of man), fornication, adultery, pedophilia, masturbation, rape and violence.

The treatments are self-prescribed and self-administered. They are, for the most part, endorsed by the world and the mastermind behind them is the destroyer of our souls. They are not God's solutions and because they are not, they are ineffective and destructive. People are not getting whole; they are getting a fix. Those who rely on them are only temporarily relieved and yet, find they are becoming addicted. The next hit has to be more potent than the last to give the same amount of relief. If we think illegal drug trafficking is causing a increasingly serious problem in society we ain't seen nothin' yet!

## A baby's need

We have already noted that when mothers separate themselves from their infants so that the baby must cry and cry for her to come, the child may be wanting far more than milk or a clean diaper. The baby needs *her*! She is his link to comfort and security. In her loving presence, the infant is at home, at peace, and growing quickly into a sense of belonging and well-being. Admittedly, for the parent, God's plan is time-consuming and self-sacrificing. It requires putting one's own plans aside for a short time for the sake of another, and offers few immediate rewards. But then God's plans are often that way – look at the life of Jesus!

However, without the constant, intentional presence of mother, the child's world quickly becomes a foreign place, full of insecurities, dangers and fears. Because in her absence there is no longer any sense of attachment, the child may experience a sense of abandonment or rejection and will let everyone around know of this predicament by loudly expressing anger and even rage.

All newborn babies will readily protest the absence of mother. When they become aware that she is not present they cry! However, when their needs for her presence are left unanswered for prolonged periods of time, these protests may progress from whimpering to crying to anger to wailing.[14]

If her absence is prolonged repeatedly to the point that the child begins to experience a familiarity of abandonment or rejection the whimpering may turn into a despair of her ever returning. And if her absence persists for days or even longer, the child may detach from her entirely so that when and if she does return, the child will not accept her embrace.[15]

For an infant, fifteen minutes may seem like a week. There is no understanding of time for a baby. His thought processes do not reason, "If I only wait a little longer she will come." When mother is absent from the newborn it is as though she does not exist. And without her existence there is no sense of being for the child.

## Other reasons for separation from mother

There are many reasons why parents separate themselves from their babies for considerable amounts of time during the first few days or weeks of the baby's life. Yes, sometimes there are deliberate intentions on the part of parents that are based on faulty or self-centered reasoning, such as previously mentioned. But many separations occur because of ignorance or are even beyond the control of a loving parent. Unfortunately, for the child, the results are often the same.

The ignorance of the parents may be due to a lack of education, the bad advice of health care professionals, including the insensitive birthing techniques required by some hospitals that require hours of separation after birth, or perhaps because of extreme family poverty which robs parents of the ability to provide emotional security for their children.

Sometimes severe damage can be done to an infant, not due to physical separation, but emotional separation for various reasons. Infants have the capacity to internalize the sinful reactions of their parents without words being spoken. Parents who are disappointed with the sex of their child, or detached because they never wanted the child at all, who attempted abortion or even had strong considerations of abortion, can unknowingly project their emotions onto their unborn children. These emotions can be internalized intuitively within the unborn child as fears of rejection or death.

There may be the stigma of illegitimacy or the violence of rape, which can allow unexplained shame to reside in a child's heart. It is possible for true evil to reside within a family in which curses are placed upon children while they are still in the womb.[16] A sense of guilt may be imposed upon a child because of the mother's sickness, weakness or mental and emotional instability.

In addition, the child may be given up for adoption, lose the mother due to prolonged illness or death or suffer a deep deficit of love and affirmation because of severe emotional woundedness in either or both parents.

A substantial deficit of attachment can also occur when the child has to be isolated at a very young age for treatment because of his own illness.[17]

The violent disruption of innocence at any age through sexual abuse can certainly short-circuit any security a child may have acquired.

During adolescence or young adulthood a child who has acquired a healthy sense of being from conception may even abdicate it himself if he gives himself over to drugs, drunkenness, violence or the occult. Even a mental breakdown and electric shock treatments have been known to diminish or disrupt a healthy sense of attachment and belonging a person has once had.

For whatever reason if, *especially* before the evocative memory is established in the child, a sense of abandonment and rejection is formed, it will be extremely difficult for the child to escape from the effects of these losses. The deficits very likely may become imprinted within the heart of the child who often retains them into adulthood.

These losses lead to a kind of progressive anxiety, thus forming a basic part of the child's developing personality. The inner sense of the baby's own existence and acceptance into his world is threatened and these anxieties may lead to such basic insecurities as being unsure that there is really a place for him to belong. He can develop such a lack of a sense of permanence that the patterns of restlessness and insecurity, including an anxiety about exploring the world in normal ways and through normal relationships, may haunt the child permanently, unless healing occurs. The older child may either express these separation anxieties in a very clingy, overly dependent manner or may remain extremely detached from others, or vacillate between the two.

## Separation anxiety

According to Dr. Frank Lake,[18] an infant, deprived of his only identification with being (his mother), may begin to live out of an identification of non-being. He calls this "a dangerous waning of hope and expectancy, a certainty that one will not be able to last out long enough, a feeling that time passed in solitariness is equivalent to an imminent death of the spirit."[19] This feeling is in the nature of *separation anxiety*. It is "a painful state of non-acceptance and rejection; of being shut out from life as a person, cut off from 'being' itself."[20]

One of the characteristics of deep separation anxiety in the infant is the clutching of the genitals. Anxiety can produce severe tension and even pain in a child's body. This pain is often centralized in the child's most sensitive physical area, the genitalia. The child, like an athlete rubbing a sore muscle, will clutch the genitals to relieve the pain. This action, while providing a short-term comfort, is not a sexual response in an infant or small child. Rather, it is a typical reaction to anxiety.

When the deprivations of childhood, that are the primary source of this kind of anxiety are not healed, the adolescent or adult may continue to experience similar genital reactions. Now eroticized, the symptoms of tension and anxiety can be activated by loneliness, rejection, criticism, emptiness, frustration or anger. To attempt to relieve these anxieties he/she may find short-term comfort in "anxiety-driven" masturbation or even frequent sexual encounters.

These patterns of release for the build-up of inner tensions and anxieties may become habitual, not based on lust nearly as much as on relieving the anxiety. When this means of comfort has become imprinted within the child's memory bank, the action of genital rubbing can be repeated habitually throughout a lifetime to soothe the tension that emanates from distress and anxiety.

Trying to fill and relieve an inner emptiness may become the driving force in one's life. Finding ways to alleviate anxiety becomes very important in the life of a person suffering from the deprivation of healthy attachments and relationships. Frequent masturbation is not at all uncommon, but it is not a healthy response. In spite of what modern educators tell us, the chronic habit of masturbation will continue to focus all of one's attention on self and divert one's desire from finding the true roots of the anxieties and thus healing from them. The practice of masturbation and its accompanying fantasy life will eventually replace the healthy desire for loving relationships with others and the need for godly attachments.

## The gift of imagination

When God saw the prevailing evil in the time of Noah He spoke of *"every imagination of the thoughts of* [men's] *hearts* [were] *only evil continually."*[21] Their thoughts or imaginations projected what was already in their hearts. When our imaginations are polluted with unholy images they need to be cleansed, but our hearts need to be cleansed even more.

The imagination reveals the thoughts of the heart:

> *"As water reflects a face,*
> *so a man's heart reflects the man."*          (Proverbs 27:19)

From the time the imagination (a wonderful gift from God) becomes established, there is the temptation for the wounded child to use it to create a fantasy world to cover up the loneliness of his heart and his failure to come into an appropriate sense of being. For the child with attachment deficits this can very easily go way beyond the normal imaginative activities of make-believe and play-like. It becomes rather a place of escape, where unreality becomes more real than the actual people and situations surrounding the child. It probably accounts for the increasingly growing interest in fantasy and role-playing games such as *Dungeons and Dragons* and MUDs. These games are opportunities for the in-depth assumption of other identities in a world of unreality whose paths explore darkness, where there are no boundaries or godly justice, and where the events and characters of an unreal world can begin to control one's thoughts and actions.

What this unreal world of fantasy is offering the player is another identity and a purpose for life of one's own making. This can seem to be a tremendous comfort, like a salve for the one who has no sense of being and identity in his/her own family. But the salve is not a healing balm. Rather it is a temporary, gooey ointment that attracts all sorts of unhealthy vermin to cling to its aroma.

Although disgusting, this graphic description of what the diseased fantasy life is like is perhaps too mild. Because the aim of the enemy is to destroy the true self in each human made to be the image of God, when a person gives him/herself over to what is far less than a true self, the minions of the enemy (demons) flock to the site like the vermin to the sticky ointment. Any home that is used for unholy purposes will just naturally attract spiritual forces that are unholy as well. One might as well invite them in. Conversely, when holy thoughts and activities are freely enjoyed in a home, the Holy Spirit dwells in the midst of them.

When the imagination is used in ways contrary to the development of a healthy soul, the images imprinted upon it will begin to put to death the true self – the one God created – and the illusory self becomes dominant.

## The illusion of existence

Joyce is an intelligent, attractive, witty woman we met about ten years ago. She was married to a pastor, had a gifted ministry of prayer and also a full-time job. We had lost touch with her for several years until she came to a "Journey to Wholeness in Christ" seminar. We couldn't believe the change in her appearance. My first thought was that she was dying of some disease. She truly looked as though she didn't have long to live.

When we had a chance to talk she began to disclose the events of the past few years that led to her present condition. She spoke of her husband's adultery, the secrecy, her depression, the loss of her job, and her gradual involvement in fantasy games on the Internet. Joyce had internalized her husband's sinful behavior and applied it to her own heart.

It is natural for a woman to experience deep pain and a sense of rejection when her husband has been unfaithful repeatedly and is unwilling to repent. Joyce's pain however, began to wrongly re-interpret her true self. To compensate for her deep loneliness and sense of rejection Joyce had constructed a whole new persona that came to life in an interactive online fantasy world. She named the illusory woman Rachel, and soon Joyce was spending up to sixteen hours a day on the Internet becoming Rachel. She told me that eventually Rachel became more real than Joyce. Indeed, as I looked at her, Joyce appeared to be dying.

Through many weeks of prayer and courageous effort Joyce faced reality. Facing it was painful because, she had to speak the truth about her husband and also to make decisions about what to do about her marriage and the rest of her life. She began to listen to God, to obey Him, one step at a time, to confess her sins, and receive God's forgiveness. She learned to set holy boundaries around the evil in her life and she literally had to put Rachel to death.

Joyce's imagination had to be cleansed and renewed by the breath of God. Today, after much hard but rewarding work, Joyce is free, productive and exploring the God-given ministry gifts she once exercised.

## Imprinted patterns

Each pattern of healthy attachment and each pattern of a lack of attachment in our lives, once developed, tend to persist into adulthood. The person who has been loved, affirmed and protected from conception will take for granted the confidence of life and the peace of living with a healthy sense of being. It is as natural as breathing. It is vital but one is seldom aware of its presence unless, as with Joyce, it is thwarted.

The person who has grown up with a lack of sense of being, as has been described previously, accompanied with insecurities and anxieties, also will not have known life in any other way. His world consists of far different emotions, reactions in situations, thought patterns, and responses to relationships than those God intended. This person frequently doesn't realize that there are *diseased* attitudes controlling his behavior. He too is seldom aware of a lack of sense of being until his own pain or the pain he causes others becomes overwhelming.

## Neurotic dependency and the feminized man

In contrast to the parents who put their own needs for fulfillment before their children's, by paying others to care for them or by neglecting them, there is also the sad situation of the parents who tend to find their sole worth in the lives of their children, living vicariously through their offspring.

Here you find the mother who never came to a sense of being herself, has poor relationships with her family and sees in her child, rather than in a career or social reputation, the opportunity to have an identity. This is the situation where the child is never given the opportunity to come free from the maternal embrace in a healthy way, for to do so would jeopardize the mother's misplaced sense of well-being, and impose immense false guilt upon the child.

This child lives under the manipulative control of a clingy, overly protective mother who sees the father's role in her child's life as a threat to her own fulfillment. The child, plagued by false guilt and the internalized fears of the mother, is thus reluctant to leave her suffocating embrace at the appropriate time (or ever) because of the implied hardships the mother would suffer. Many of these children grow up believing that their sole purpose in life is to make mother happy.

For the rest of his life (without God's help), the boy who grows up with this kind of mother becomes "feminized."[22] He is not necessarily "effeminate" (looking or acting like a girl), but his thought patterns, reactions, lack of ability to call forth in himself and in others the strength to press through difficulties or to initiate action are more like the false feminine than the true masculine. He tends to be dependent upon women to make decisions for him and would prefer the company of women over men. His behavior is characterized by passivity rather than initiative.

In his world women are supposed to take care of him. They are supposed to provide for all his needs, emotionally and physically. They are supposed to cater to all his sexual fantasies and his only responsibility is to receive. He may develop a strong ambivalence towards women even though he is deeply dependent upon them, stemming back to his frustration about not being able to detach from his mother in appropriate ways.

He may have been his "mother's little husband," hearing inappropriate emotional outbursts and opinions from her, even about his own father. He may continue to be her confidante, made to believe that he is the only one who truly understands her.

He too, looks to the world of fantasy to live out his life, always expecting grandiose things to come his way, never content with the ordinary pleasures of life. His failure to find a genuine comfort in the arms of a woman (his wife) may lead him to many sexual exploits, perhaps even to explore homosexual relationships.

The feminized man forever will act like a little boy, always expecting someone to rescue him and take responsibility for his actions. He has never been called properly into his manhood by the voice of his father.

To receive the healing he needs from God he will have to kill the whiny little boy within. One man who worked through this difficult healing process described "putting that internal, self-pitying, obnoxious, little boy on the altar to become an Isaac, bound and ready to be slaughtered. The only difference was that I was also Abraham, and I had to use the knife and actually kill the sacrifice. I put that old, sick part of myself to death once and for all so that the real man could live."

It may be more difficult for the feminized man to come into his healing because he may have a deep love and respect for his mother and what she did for him. He will be able to thank her for what was good and bless her for this, but, releasing all sentimentality, it will be necessary for him to name his inordinate dependency on her and other women. His healing will depend, even in adulthood, upon making a healthy separation from her and receiving his true identity from God the Father, the Eternal Masculine voice. This kind of godly separation always results in the opportunity for the wounded mother to receive God's healing as well.

## The fruit of the plan of the world

In an effort to see how vital God's plan is to our proper sense of being, it is unfortunately necessary to look at more of the disastrous results that happen to men and women as they grow up trying to fill their inner emptiness with the offerings of the world and broken parents.

So what is happening to young people who are growing up into adulthood without the abiding, internal, secure attachments to the parents God gave them? Well, for one thing they are starving for true intimacy; they have the need for intimacy that God put within them, but it was not fulfilled as it should have been at the appropriate time. This need for genuine intimacy thus begins to be mis-translated into the language of the world.

Starting at an early age, perhaps even at four or five when social interaction with others begins to develop, children may shut down their emotions and become withdrawn as "loners" or they may attempt to find the fulfillment for their emptiness in the inordinate attachment of a "best friend" or a gang or the obsessive preoccupation of being teacher's favorite. This kind of attachment continues to go far beyond the normal relationships children should be developing. It is in the insecure, neurotic attachment to another person in order to find one's own identity that the ingredients are combined to form a toxic mixture.

The child (and later adult) who continues to look for that "one idealized person" to be the sun and moon for his existence quickly will learn to manipulate, lie and use emotional bribery to keep the object of his attention close by. Such a person frequently will develop a classic ambivalence toward the object of his neediness. He will want to be with his "best friend" constantly and yet is critical and paranoid about the relationship. The slightest word of disagreement or criticism may elicit deep feelings of anger or rejection. In spite of constant companionship the needy one may feel intensely lonely, incompetent and negative. It is as though nothing one does is enough to satisfy the relationship.

These characteristics make it very difficult to be close or intimate with such a person. To protect oneself, a friend will have to set good, healthy boundaries in their relationship, but to the needy one, those boundaries only accentuate the pain and his sense of incompleteness deepens.

Other wounded ones may cut themselves off entirely from healthy relationships, finding a safety net through detachment to avoid the pain and rejection they have experienced in the past.

While these traits may begin in early childhood it is easy to see the way they become ingrained in a person's personality as he gets older.

The adolescent may find himself depressed with powerful negative feelings that disintegrate the good of reason. He may feel incompetent, experiencing personal rejection from relationships and situations where no actual rejection is occurring. He may become a loner or he may develop addictions that provide short-term pleasure to assuage the pain, insecurity and anxiety he feels inside. The inordinate attachments he has made to people may be transferred onto objects, fetishes[23] or substances. He is looking for intimacy and is willing to settle for its illusion if it provides temporary relief and requires no responsible investment of commitment.

## Emotional dependency

A person becoming so much less than that which God intended is the bleak picture of the development of one deprived of healthy attachments. The extent to which one reacts to his environment varies. One might think that little children are too young and immature to have the kind of emotionally dependent relationships described above, but the needs are intense at any age. Lori Rentzel says that "emotional dependency occurs when the ongoing presence and nurturing of another is believed to be necessary for personal security."[24]

Does that statement sound familiar? Isn't it the very kind of relationship we have been describing for an infant to have with his mother? If that proper relationship has been achieved at the proper time, in the appropriate way, and then weaned at the appropriate age to a more mature identity in one's true self – all as God ordained – then the neurotic needs for connection in childhood, adolescence and adulthood become unnecessary.

Mrs. Rentzel also warns that no matter how wonderful the feelings might be at first for those who find their identity in another person, the end result is always a bondage more horrible than one can imagine.[25]

As adolescence progresses many of these intimacy needs are eroticized. The arms of another person may become a ready substitute for the real affection of the parent and of God.

## Fathers and daughters

The masculine voice of a father that lovingly calls his daughter into her true identity of the woman God created her to be is her lifeline to fulfillment. She is (perhaps unconsciously) aware of his protection, his strong boundaries, his encouragement, and his reassurance to her at each stage of her journey. Ideally, her father is listening to his heavenly Father, praying for his little girl and asking for God's guidance as her life is shaped by his attitudes and actions. A father may have no prior experience with little girls, may have no clue as to how they think, what their interests are, or what to do with them. However, as he learns to hear God's voice and bless her in the same ways God blesses him, he collaborates with the Lord to bring life to her ever-expanding world.

As Conlee and I have watched our sons, Matt and Ben, raise their little girls we have marveled at the expertise they appear to have in being fathers to daughters. Matt and Ben were raised with brothers and no sisters, and now Matt has three daughters and Ben has twin daughters in addition to a son. In spite of their lack of experience of observing daughters in the family where they grew up, the strong maternal bond of feminine love they achieved from the moment of birth was lovingly and sensitively nurtured by Conlee as they were each called away from their attachment to me and into Conlee's masculine identity. Matt and Ben are no more expert in fathering little girls than any other dad; they have just applied what was positively modeled for them and they have learned to collaborate with their heavenly Father on a day-to-day basis.

At every age a daughter needs to dialogue with her daddy. She needs his blessings, his compliments, his good-natured teasing, his exhortations, his praises, his discipline, and on a regular basis, his undivided attention to something of interest to her. She needs to feel his appropriate touch and sit on his lap. Without this, males can become foreign creatures to a girl, at times even threatening.

Many an adolescent daughter has turned to a young boy's hormone-energized body to provide the loving affection she has been denied from her emotionally absent father. Her father may be unable to affectionately affirm his daughter emotionally because he has had no healthy attachment to the feminine in his own life, apart from sexual encounters. Fearful that he might even overstep the bounds of intimacy with a daughter whom he loves, this is the kind of father who establishes rigid, artificial boundaries in their relationship. The daughter, needing her father's affectionate, loving affirmation, calling her forth and blessing her as she matures into budding womanhood, interprets his distance as critical and uncaring, even believing that she is unlovable. Inevitably, she will seek other masculine arms to prove that she is desirable.

Sexual involvement is only a by-product of such relationships between teenage boys and such unaffirmed girls. It is not sex that the emotionally deprived young woman is wanting, it is affection and affirmation. How often we have heard these words from women who describe the years of their wasted lives: "I just wanted someone to hold me, someone to tell me I was pretty, someone who would make me feel feminine. If I had to have sex with guys to get that I would, but I never enjoyed the sex."

These women end up feeling used, cheap and abused. They either learn to put up hard shields around their emotions or they become blobs of self-pity.

Occasionally, although rarely, a daughter will be so rejected by her father, or abused by him, that she will reject and fear all male companionship. She may retreat from any healthy connections with others or experiment with female sexual relationships to find an identification with the feminine that was denied her in appropriate ways. These relationships are seldom long-lasting and do not produce the desired affirmation she craves. If she continues to search with a genuine desire to become whole she will find the eternal Father who will call her by name and bless her as a woman, thus initiating the healing process.

## Mothers and sons

From the moment of birth any child, boy or girl, has a God-given need to be immersed in mother's continuing love and embrace. This has been described previously in detail. For the son who does not experience this in a healthy way with his mother, there is going to be a continuing ambivalence toward women. He knows that he has a strong need to connect with feminine presence in his life, however he keeps himself at arm's distance from her because he has intuited rejection at the time of his most critical need, those first few months. This ambivalent tension can accompany him into adulthood: needing a woman, yet rejecting her; attracted to a woman, yet ridiculing her. This describes not only the way many boys relate to girls (or all women), but also the way many husbands relate to their wives.

First, look at the way some little boys relate to their mothers: needing her, yet pushing her away; dependent upon her, yet angry with her. This behavior further translates into adolescence and dating relationships. Many a young man, missing from infancy the warmth of true feminine presence in the form of a loving, unselfish mother, sexually pursues girls way before he is ready for emotional involvement with them and then abandons them.

His need for a connection with the feminine is so strong that he is drawn towards inappropriate, unhealthy relationships with girls at an early age. He often prefers to "go steady" with one girl at a time so that he can feel a temporary sense of connectedness to the feminine presence. His one girl "belongs to him." He may feel a proprietary interest in her, attempting to quash her identity to conform to his interests. Although he professes to care about her and feels a need to be with her, at the same time he ridicules her (and girls in general) as "silly," "illogical," even "inferior."

He may begin to fantasize about touching girls in intimate ways to the extent that he ceases to see them as real, whole persons, but only as fragments of persons (such as breasts). His ability to relate to girls in normal, healthy ways will be greatly hampered by his need to "get what he wants."

The bravado and bragging about imaginary sexual conquests that often marks the conversation of a group of teenage boys can be extremely threatening to the young man who so desperately needs an attachment to the feminine. His feelings of inadequacy about what it means to be a man begin to shape his life. He tends to size up other men and compare himself to others to find his worth.

Now look at how these same symptoms of a mother-love deficit can translate into the relationship between a husband and wife. He truly loves his wife and wants to be with her, perhaps even would lay down his life for her, but he is frustrated that she cannot fill the emptiness within him. Because the need for feminine love was not fulfilled at birth (or was disrupted or abdicated for some reason later) he has extremely unreasonable expectations for his wife. She is expected to fill every longing he has ever had and when of course she can't, he becomes very frustrated. He both desires her and pushes her away. His actions reinforce the deep life-long sense that he will be rejected by the feminine presence. Therefore, he protects himself emotionally from his wife so he will not be rejected by her as well.

This can be extremely confusing for a wife married to such a man. She will know she is loved and yet find his behavior towards her baffling. His only way of connection to her in intimate ways will be sexual, and yet no matter how much she gives of herself to her husband, it is never enough. Because of this unfulfilled need for intimacy a husband can easily fall into the practice of pornography and/or a sexual fantasy life, rationalizing that his wife just doesn't meet his needs.

Apart from the appropriation of God's love into the deficit in this man's life, he will strive in vain to find what he craves, only to face one disappointment after another. The eternal Word of the Father will fill the void, however. His Word often comes in surprising ways and just one Word can fill a lifetime of emptiness – an emptiness that perhaps defined a man's personhood for as long as he can remember.

## Mothers and daughters

Every little girl and every little boy has a mother as the first model of womanhood. This of course can be either a positive or a negative influence that can shape the child's future. The little girl's perception of mother however, will be entirely different than the little boy's. The daughter will be watching and interacting with her mother to learn what it is to *be* a woman, not just how to relate to women. She will either want to be like mother, or vow never to be like her mother. Both responses will affect her life tremendously. Same-sex attachments are vital in childhood. When healthy, parental same-sex connections are denied or lost, the need for them becomes intense in the child as he or she moves into adolescence and young adulthood.

If a mother has unselfishly bonded with her daughter in ways that affirm and bless the truly feminine in her, there will be a much easier road to womanhood for her daughter. This little girl will still have the usual struggles through adolescence to maturity, the usual sense of competition with her mother in her awkward struggles for independence and the normal feelings of inadequacy. But in spite of these difficult passages the daughter who has had a genuine, godly, feminine model of unselfish love and affirmation from her mother, will look forward to womanhood with a security in who she is and a relative ease in each transition.

Female friends will have an appropriate place in this young girl's life because she will not be using them to find her feminine identity, rather she will be enjoying the company of those with same-sex interests. Even her interaction with male friends will be somewhat easier since she already has established a healthy sense of who she is and will be able to resist being formed into any teenage male expectation of what girls should do to please them.

Compared to the daughter whose mother was too busy or unable to bond with her and provide a viable symbol of motherhood and womanhood, the former little girl's passage to adulthood is a cakewalk. Without a healthy mother's attachment and then appropriate disengagement to allow self-discovery, this passage to womanhood can be painful and prolonged if a daughter is forced to walk it alone, blazing her own trail through unknown territory. She often gets lost and wounded along the way.

A young girl who has little or no healthy connection with her mother may question her own femininity to the extent that she is obsessed with thoughts of "What's wrong with me?" as she moves from one stage to another.

Seldom feeling at home in her own skin, she may develop artificial ways of relating to herself and others. She may analyze herself constantly, seeking to find out what's wrong. She may "walk alongside herself,"[26] always watching how she looks, listening to her own voice, hating what she sees and hears. She will watch others to see how they react to her, attempting to alter her personality to become what she perceives they expect of her.

The false feminine persona may replace her own sense of feminine inadequacy. Syrupy, insincere sweetness, an inordinate need to please, exaggerated responses, constant touching and pawing at others in pseudo-intimate ways, manipulation to get what she wants, and lack of healthy emotional and physical boundaries are ways she might adopt to compensate for her lack of connectedness to her true femininity. She tends to relate to other women by secret confidences, invading their physical space in conversations by getting too close or "in your face," exaggerating or manufacturing details of information to secure another woman's attention, or wanting to talk about subjects too intimate for casual conversations.

An alternate response to an insecurity with the feminine is to over-exaggerate feminine characteristics in a seductive manner. This is the behavior that screams, "I'm not secure in who I am so I am proving I am a woman by how I dress, walk and look at you!" Clothes that are too tight, hair that is too big, make-up that is too artificial, attitudes that are too calculated – all these point to a woman who is trying desperately to be feminine but has misinterpreted womanhood.

If she is particularly cut off from a healthy connection to the feminine or wounded by her earliest interactions with the feminine model in her life she might discard any semblance of what it means to be female. Her appearance and attitude may reflect her abhorrence of anything "girlie." She can assume an androgynous look, putting to death within herself that which would reflect the woman God created her to be. Or, in extreme cases, her own hatred of herself as a woman (perhaps projected through her mother's self-hatred) can lead her to distort her appearance and withdraw from social interactions with others.

In other cases of disconnection from the feminine at an early age, deep emotional dependency may develop towards other women, to the extent that normal relationships find no place in this woman's life. She may even reach out for a same-sex connection that becomes eroticized, believing that she can be completed only by her intimate connection to another woman. Of course this cannot be accomplished and when one relationship after another disintegrates she stores up further layers of rejection and hurt.

God the Father is the sole affirmer of those who did not connect with the source of love and security He provided at appropriate times. Any other attempts to find this divine connection of *being* through another person or through artificial means will be frustrating and eventually end in failure.

## Fathers and sons

A father's call of love for his little son to come out from his utter dependency upon mother and into the paternal embrace is vital! Although the father's blessing towards his daughters is essential for them to move out gracefully and assuredly into their womanhood, it is even more important for the calling out of his sons. His voice will disengage his son from a dependency upon mother and into his own identity which is so *other* than hers. This seemingly huge chasm of separation between femaleness and maleness can be so easily and effortlessly navigated by the son if only the father's voice is one of love, invitation and blessing.

In his invitation to manhood the father not only welcomes his son to join him, but in doing so, he blesses and respects womanhood in his wife, the boy's mother. The son should never be put in a position of seeing manhood and womanhood in opposition and competition with one another. Neither is superior or inferior; they are different, yet complementary.

It has been said that the most important thing a father can do for his children is to love their mother. By doing so, he sets a healthy model for his children to see the masculine presence respecting and honoring the feminine presence in the family. This will bind truth to the hearts of both sons and daughters. The healthy bond to mother is not thrown aside when the son is called into his own male identity; rather the son is encouraged to expand his capacities to love and become the person he was created to be.

When a little boy perceives a non-threatening sameness in himself and his father, he is drawn to him like a magnet. He will imitate what he sees if he perceives he will be safe in his father's presence. This begins at a very young age.

We have a photograph of our little grandson Caleb, taken when he was just beginning to walk. The picture shows him standing, only wearing a diaper, in the open door of his parents' closet. He is looking at a row of shoes neatly lined up, his daddy's on one side, his mother's on the other. You can see easy access to some Birkenstocks that belong to our daughter-in-law. For a little guy who is still unsteady on his feet, it would not have been difficult for him to negotiate sliding his feet into her shoes if all he wanted to do was to dress-up like an adult. But in this picture, little Caleb has put his foot into his daddy's big work boot. That took some effort for a toddler, but he was motivated to do it so he could be just like daddy. This is the picture of a son, barely a year old, loved and affirmed by both parents, moving out into his own identity of maleness at the invitation of his same-sex role model.

A son needs to see his father in a genuine way, not as perfectly in control all the time. Healthy dads are still men who have emotions and feelings; they exhibit joy, sorrow, grief, sadness, fatigue, laughter, anger, passion, etc. A man's children watch closely to see how he expresses these emotions, where he takes them, how they are shared in a family, how he affirms and yet directs genuine emotional outbursts from his children.

So many adults relate to us that the only emotion they ever saw their fathers demonstrate was anger. This seems to be the one emotion that an unhealed person cannot keep contained. A child needs to learn at an early age that it is not a sin to be angry; it is a sin to project one's anger onto others or turn it onto one's self. Rather, anger is to be taken to the Cross. Otherwise, it destroys all in its wake.

A good old-fashioned saying about a son is, "You are never a man until your father tells you that you are." The exact word of a father saying to his son, "Today you are a man!" may not be absolutely necessary, but the implication of those words is essential to any man. We have prayed with dozens of adult men who begin to weep when they recall how desperately they have always wanted to hear those words from their dad's mouth. "I love you, son!" has the same result when spoken from the heart of a father.

If a son doesn't hear those words from his father (in whatever way they may be communicated) he may spend his life trying to prove his manhood to himself and others in foolish, risky ways. Recklessly walking the high steel beams of a construction site, sky-diving and other risky activities, dressing in a "macho" way, driving "manly" vehicles, driving too fast, drinking heavily, coarse talk – all point towards a man's attempts to assert his manhood to himself and the world. A man may try to prove his manhood to himself and others by engaging in numerous, perhaps even meaningless, sexual conquests. Apart from actually participating in sexual activities, he may develop a sexual fantasy life that keeps a sense of his mistaken idea of manhood alive in his imagination.

There was a time when fathers and sons worked alongside each other from the time the sons were old enough to be responsible. A dad would begin to take his little boy into the fields with him as he worked the land, or in the shop with him as he plied a trade. There the two rubbed shoulders, shared common experiences and the little boy learned of life from his daddy's knee.

Today, fathers and sons go in different directions for most of the day. It is seldom possible for them to spend long hours together on a regular basis, and thus it becomes so important that fathers and sons engage in some kind of physical activity with one another. Wrestling on the floor together provides healthy skin-to-skin contact that nourishes the boy. Just throwing a ball to one another provides an activity that binds a father's undivided attention to his son's soul.

Taking on a project together will provide hours of interaction, instruction and modeling of patience and perseverance. The goal is not to produce a perfectly executed project – the goal is the experience of spending quality time together with a common theme of partnership.

Even with the best dad, a boy may still be tempted to look to the male role models of the world as much as, if not more than, he looks at his father to discover what it is to be a man. The world is holding up some pretty unsavory role models and it is easy for any young man to feel inadequate when pitted against the macho personae that are projected to the public.

If a healthy relationship has not been made between father and son, the intense yearning for a same-sex attachment can become eroticized during adolescence. The adolescent, confused feelings of whether one might be homosexual are not uncommon if this is the case. Unfortunately, we are living in a society that is encouraging our young people to experiment with their sexuality (both heterosexually and homosexually) and to disdain the practice of self-denial. Young lives are being irreparably damaged by the false encouragement of amoral heroes.

Yet, for the son who has heard his father's voice call him forth into manhood, that voice does not go unheard. Its words will ring in his soul throughout a lifetime. For the son who has never heard his father's invitation, there is the eternal invitation of his heavenly Father who will woo him and call him to look upon His character and follow Him. This heavenly voice fills every void when welcomed and appropriated into a man's heart.

# Chapter 4

## The Antagonist
### How pornography is attacking the family

*"He* [the devil] *was a murderer from the beginning, not holding to the truth, for there is no truth in him. When he lies, he speaks his native language, for he is a liar and the father of lies."*
(John 8:44b)

---

**Pornography**: The graphic, sexually explicit subordination of women [primarily] through pictures or words, including the presentation of women [or men] in a dehumanized way as sexual objects or commodities; as enjoying pain, rape, or humiliation; as body parts (such as [breasts or genitalia]); or in any other way that sexualizes degradation, pain, or subordination.[1]

---

### A new kind of candy story

Life holds a variety of alternatives for those who lack a secure connectedness with God's love. Most of these second-rate options have been with us for a long, long time. But in this present age we are confronted with quite another set of substitutes for true intimacy.

In my lifetime I have experienced the progressive pull of the media, including contemporary literature, movies, television and now the Internet as enticements to fill the voids left in modern families. It seems that each time a vacuum occurs within the family, the world's system (and the prince of this world, our enemy Satan), provides another way to fill it.

As a child growing up in a troubled family with little demonstrative affection, I could easily become lost in television shows such as *Ozzie and Harriet, Father Knows Best, The Donna Reed Show, Lassie*, and *Leave it to Beaver*. These were shows with a family structure: a father, a mother, children, rules, order, right behavior being rewarded, wrong behavior being punished, the family engaged in conversation at table, and a happy ending every thirty minutes. These shows provided positive role models of what it meant to be in a healthy family. My hungry heart absorbed the content of these dramas to the extent that I would put myself into the story, becoming a member of the families and pretending that my own family was different from reality. The shows I watched as a child provided wholesome, temporary measures of fulfillment for my neediness.

The loneliness of my heart still ached however, and so I attempted to fill it with literature. I read incessantly, much to the chagrin of my parents who considered it to be a waste of time. And so at a very young age, reading became a furtive, secretive past-time, whereby I would hide away and comfort myself (with a small degree of guilt because I knew I was displeasing my parents).

The novels I read as a very young girl, innocent as they were (like *Rebecca of Sunnybrook Farm, Little Women, The Bobbsey Twins, Five Little Peppers and How They Grew, Nancy Drew*, etc.), became like drugs to me. I knew when the oppression became too heavy in my family I could retreat secretively to a corner with my fantasies.[2] Knowing I might be interrupted and scolded only enhanced the pleasure. It became a way of life and I would plot and plan how I could find the opportunities for my special time with my heroes and heroines.

## How times have changed!

Today a child raised like I was several decades ago is faced with options to alleviate loneliness and neediness I never dreamed of. Instead of *Rebecca of Sunnybrook Farm* or *Father Knows Best*, children are bombarded with eroticism and sentimentality about sin years before they even reach puberty. These two genres of eroticism and sentimentality of sin have taken the place of wholesome literature and family role models on television.

Fewer children find solace in reading now that television is so accessible. Much of the children's literature found in school and public libraries is nothing more than sentimental fluff or excursions into the occult. Children reading it are affirmed in their confusion and loneliness and are encouraged to esteem themselves even in their sinful states. Seldom are discipline and order lifted up as virtues in a child's life through contemporary literature. More and more children are drawn to books romanticizing darkness and their fantasies without moral value.

The effects of television on our children's souls are extremely detrimental. Where once a child was able to look at wholesome family situation dramas and be drawn into them to see healthy role models, now they watch situation comedies where fornication is exemplified, sex is seen as the goal of every young person, and even homosexuality is lifted up as amusing and acceptable. The people portraying these immoral values are cute, stylish, attractive, "hotties," "hunks," and wanna-be's to our young people. Immodest ways of dressing are in style and grade school kids have moves that rival those of strippers. They are copying what they see on television! We have allowed this medium to become the role model of the present generation.

Both sentimentality towards sin and eroticism are greatly lacking in their ability to fill our souls in healthy ways, but in addition, there is a danger in today's offerings of an erotic, pornographic illusion of intimacy that is detrimental in ways we are only beginning to understand.

What are modern children reading? What are they playing with? What television shows are they watching? What video and photographic images are they storing in their memory banks? What are they hearing adults talking about?

Fantasy romance, erotic literature and books about witchcraft, visual images of men and women in sexual positions that can be seen in movies and television, and the subject matter that is discussed on daytime television or even on the nightly news are filling our modern children. And they are demanding more!

Their hearts are susceptible to this because we as a culture, have forgotten how to parent them according to God's divine plan. They are hungry for intimacy! They are viewing ungodly material

– illusions of intimacy – and absorbing it, not rejecting it, because it is temporarily filling a void. That void is parent-induced!

We can blame our society all we want; we can rail at the media and the pornographers, and we can denounce the politicians who give us ambiguous laws about obscenity. But in reality we, the parents who have been too busy to follow God's plans, are responsible for the fertile ground these despicable substitutes for intimacy have found.

## The big lie

There is a destructive nature to the world's temptations that is eroding the godly image of man and woman that was intended by our Creator. The enemy of our souls, Satan himself, has as his chief goal the desire to rob creation of its divine imprint. If he can pervert our minds and our imaginations with ungodly thoughts and fantasies, he's got us, because whatever occupies the thoughts of our hearts will reveal what we treasure.[3]

If I am occupied with thoughts of my own pain, loneliness and ways to alleviate it, I am treasuring (or worshiping) self. However, if my thoughts are centered on whatever represents the bounty of the Kingdom of God (truth, nobility, righteousness, purity, loveliness, etc.)[4] my treasure is in heaven and in Him.

What occupies the time and thoughts of our children today? Thanks to the media, and what the public supports, the average twelve-year-old has witnessed 8,000 murders and over 100,000 other assorted acts of violence, not to mention the proliferation of profanity. In the average American family every adult watches 4 hours and 41 minutes of television per day, every teenager watches 3 hours and 6 minutes and every child watches 3 hours and 30 minutes.[5]

What images of man and woman and the values they live by are being implanted into the minds and hearts of these families every day? What is filling their souls so thoroughly that godly, wholesome images of loving relationships have become to them "nerdy," "dorky," and "totally uncool"?

The message being broadcast loud and clear to American families today is that **sex** is what they really need to make them feel secure and good about themselves. If they can get sex, more sex and better sex they will find happiness. Sex is now selling the most wholesome products America has known. Only last night I saw an Uncle Ben's rice commercial on television and it was being touted by – you guessed it – sex!

*If you serve her Uncle Ben's she'll tear off her clothes and do what you want. If you serve him Uncle Ben's you'll look like a sexy babe in his eyes,* was the message being projected via the thirty-second drama.

The frightening thing about this is its success. Mainstream manufacturers are succumbing to these ad techniques because the bottom line is: it sells products. People must believe the lie enough to go out and buy the stuff. If we see the lie often enough we always end up believing it must have some truth to it.

## How do kids go from a TV commercial to porn?

The following is taken from a legal testimony given in 1985. Did you catch that? This stuff is not new!

- 100% of all high school age males surveyed reported having read or looked at *Playboy* or similar "men's entertainment" magazines.

- 16.1 issues of pornographic magazines is the average number seen by male high-schoolers.

- 92% of males in junior high report exposure to *Playboy* or similar magazines.

- The average age when viewing the first issue is 11 years old.

- 12.8 years is the average age of exposure to first R-rated film.

- A larger portion of high school students had viewed X-rated films than any other age group.[6]

## Simple math: 2 + 2 = 4

Put together the facts that more and more fathers are absent from the home, more and more mothers are working in the marketplace, more and more infants are being separated from their mothers at a very early age and even so-called Christian experts are telling parents that it is OK to let your babies cry for prolonged periods of time if they are clean and full of milk. What is the result? We have several generations of children, adolescents and adults who have internalized an emptiness and longing for attachment that they did not receive at the God-ordained, appointed times. They are desperate for something to fill the voids.

## Where do they look?

If they are not avoiding them altogether, they look first to relationships, but, in their neediness, they are like bottomless pits. They will exhaust friends, spouses, counselors and pastors. For instance:

- Being Sally's friend is not enough; she insists on being your *exclusive* friend and is jealous when you do anything without her. Her pettiness and jealousy becomes too much and you find yourself avoiding her phone calls and making excuses to keep from being with her.
- Being married to Fred is exhausting; he refuses to engage in intimate conversation but insists on making love more frequently than his wife is comfortable with. His lack of vulnerability makes him seem uncaring and cold.
- Jason always has a crisis to report to his counselor; he never seems to make progress in his therapy, although he is extremely cooperative. He only seems to find energy when he is angry with someone or seeking revenge.
- Richard's pastor is confused by Richard's inability to find fulfillment in his family and work; he always seems to be seeking more than he is experiencing. Although a committed Christian and willing prayer partner, he never seems to believe he is truly loved by God.

Finding only eventual disappointment in each relationship, these needy ones like Sally, Fred, Jason and Richard will descend into either further isolation and separation or rely on manipulation or deception. Not one of us will ever find our identity in another person, not even in a loving spouse. Adam and Eve couldn't find their identity in each other, and we are no different. When we try to find ourselves in another person we will only wear out the relationship and still have little more substance than when we started. The reason is that when the initial, primary attachments are not made according to God's plan, then *only God can fill the void that is left.*

After looking for people to meet their needs and becoming disappointed, discouraged and desperate, the Sally's, Fred's, Jason's, and Richard's of the world then look to *things*. Here a temporary satisfaction may be discovered. Short-term pleasure can be found for many in food, alcohol, cigarettes, drugs, pornography or sex. However, just like with the first cigarette, or the first hit of dope, or the first dirty magazine, they don't realize the power of the addictive nature of all these activities.

The double whammy that often hits the victim is that, on one hand he may know how empty, desperate, wounded and help-less he is, but on the other hand he is so angry with God for "allowing" his situation that he won't turn to the One who alone, can provide the help needed. We have met such men and women many times. They have been exposed to God but not His love. They have heard God-talk, but not His voice. They have prayed but only for selfish desires. They have been terribly disappointed and, of course, blamed God. He becomes the last one they want to go to for help.

The more typical Christian who has such an internal deficit may acknowledge that God is the answer but has no idea how to access His healing. This is the kind of Christian who becomes so susceptible to the hard-hitting lures of sex and pornography. He has prayed for God's strength and deliverance but the problems persist. To him, either God cannot or will not answer his prayers for deliverance and so he goes further and further into the deception.

To understand the degree to which the invasion has pene-trated the Christian family we must face the enemy squarely and learn the tactics of our antagonist.

## The calculated invasion on the family by the porn pushers

"The president of a company that produces a popular Internet game site for teenagers was horrified last May when, trying to call up his site, he got instead a screenful of lurid sex scenes. Worse yet he could not escape. Every time he tried to move on, he got more pornographic scenes."[7]

In searching for the most innocent web sites, such as information on "gourmet recipes," or "weather facts" (or in doing research for this book), instead of the information requested, up pops a succession of sex scenes, many animated, urging you to "click here for more!" The more you close them out, the more they keep coming. The only way to end the succession is to log off the Internet or shut down the computer.

The first time this happens you might think there is something wrong with your carrier or your computer. The second time it happens you begin to realize there is a conspiracy.

In reality it is the result of an Internet fraud devised by a Portuguese hacker and an Australian pornography company. The fraud has affected as many as 25 million Web pages, more than 2% of the World Wide Web. Commonly referred to as "pagejacking" or "mousetrapping," it involves the cloning of legitimate, respectable sites so that when you, the computer user, inadvertently reach the cloned site you receive a porn site in its place. Every time you use your mouse to click your browser's "back" or "home" buttons, you receive another porn site. In effect, you are "mousetrapped."

The perpetrators of this scam make money in three ways: by selling advertising on the Web sites (almost exclusively to porn companies) based on the amount of traffic, by inflating the value of domain names (URLs or Web addresses) at auction for hundreds of times their original cost, and by offering the viewers the opportunity to see more Web sites by paying for them. It has become extremely lucrative.[8]

## No such thing as a free look

According to VisaUSA one of the top three complaints they have from their credit card users is that they are being charged for browsing free pornographic Web pages or taking "online tours" that are advertised as free.[9] To browse many porn sites listed as "free" the consumers are asked to provide credit card information to prove their legal age of 18. They are told they will not be charged for the free tours. Once the porn site receives their credit card numbers the browsers may become their victims. The porn merchants know most people will be too embarrassed to fight back.

One man claimed, "he'd signed up for a 1-week free preview, supplying his credit card number. 'They sent me an access code for the site. But the code required seven numbers; they only gave me five. I e-mailed my cancellation request numerous times, but they didn't respond. They charged me for membership three months in a row. It's going to be embarrassing to call my credit card company, but I've go to do it.' Many victims of these scams simply pay up rather than 'fess up."[10]

Forgotten in the heat of the moment is the advice everyone has heard, "Do not give your password or credit card number to **anyone** on the Internet (with the exception of using your credit card for making a legitimate online purchase)." In their curiosity and desire to go a little further into the porn world these users throw all caution to the wind. It is common for sizable charges to show up on the credit card holder's bill the next month. The Web sites usually offer no phone number where the charges can be questioned and if a number is given no one ever answers. The only solution for most upset cardholders is to cancel their credit cards. Recently there was a lawsuit filed by the Federal Trade Commission against dozens of porn Web sites for this kind of fraud. It is estimated that porn merchants collected $188 million from 1997 to 1999 via credit cards. There have been tens of thousands of complaints.[11]

## Phone scam

Focus on the Family reports:

> "Adult web sites have also expanded beyond credit card fraud, into more legitimate means of taking your money. Recently AT&T issued a consumer alert because some customers had unwittingly triggered international long-distance charges when they accessed some sites. *The Washington Post* reported, 'The [customers] said they were unaware that while surfing X-rated Web sites for a "free" preview, or by clicking hot links in steamy e-mail spams, they had stepped into a new and apparently legal billing

ploy.'[12] By failing to read the small print the unwary surfer granted permission to terminate the modem connection to his local ISP and connect a long-distance call to another country. The article ends with the following sober advice, 'AT&T advises that other than never visiting adult entertainment Web sites, there is no fail-proof measure to take.'"[13]

## Phone sex

One man reports that over the last several years he has accumulated over $12,000 indebtedness for phone sex. It's no wonder then that a New York market research and consulting firm found that late-night sex lines are a $6 billion per year industry.[14] Sadly, U.S. phone companies estimate that 70% of the 500,000 daily calls to dial-a-porn are made by minors.[15]

## Porn spam

Unsolicited pornographic e-mail messages can be a huge nuisance as well as an uninvited lure into temptation territory. Commonly called "porn spam," these commercial e-mails will occur in cycles. They will always give you the option to "unsubscribe" even though you have not subscribed in the first place. Once you "unsubscribe" however, you have just informed the sender that your e-mail address is working and your name can be sold to other porn companies. These sites are manned by paid stay-at-home clerks who send out thousands of e-mail lures to lists of people.

We have tried several forms of defense to combat this nuisance; we have forwarded the messages to our Internet Service Provider (never receiving a response), checked the ID of the sender (when available, they are usually identified as single, older people), and sent firm messages to the sender (i.e.: "Tell whoever you work for to take my name off their mailing list immediately."). Many of the messages we sent came back as "mailer demons," – no such address. No matter what route we took to get rid of the garbage, it always seemed to be just a matter of time before they would take us off their lists since we never logged on to the sites they were touting.[16] For us it was merely a disgusting, invasive nuisance to find unsolicited e-mail with pornographic words in the subject line pop up on our down-loaded mail. For those with children using the computer to send and receive e-mail, it is much more than a nuisance.

## Wrong address

I recently had a phone call from a young man who has been struggling with pornography for several years and has made huge strides in overcoming his temptations through healing prayer. His wife has been his prayer partner in this effort and her level of trust in him has increased as she has seen his progress. But his phone call revealed a desperation and plea for help. "Would you please talk to my wife? She checked our e-mail this morning and found this obscene invitation to enter a porn site and it said that if I wanted to unsubscribe to click the button. She can't believe that it isn't something I subscribed to and we've regressed months in our healing just by opening up one e-mail."

I did indeed talk to his wife, assuring her that we too get numerous invitations exactly like the one they had received. She admitted that her heart had nearly stopped when she feared that her husband had regressed into the old patterns.

So, how in the world do they get your e-mail address in the first place? According to a *Newsweek* reporter:

> "A typical strategy is to write a program that harvests valid e-mail addresses from public forums like newsgroups and member directories of ISPs, such as America Online's massive one. These directories are open because, like the telephone white pages, they're intended to let you find e-mail addresses of long-lost friends and family.
>
> Another common tactic is what's known as a dictionary attack, in which a spammer creates possible addresses using every name in the book, in myriad permutations: JoeA@hotmail.com (JoeB@hotmail.com, JoeC@hotmail.com), etc.
>
> Spammers then mail out e-mail pitches in huge batches; it costs no more to send thousands of messages than to send one."[17]

The messages all have one intent: to get you to spend your money.

## The bottom line

The pattern one can see clearly in all these scams is that big bucks are involved. Knowing the heavy pull that lust has on men and women, the porn merchants are looking for a quick, fat pay-off and getting it! They know all the steps that lead to addiction and they play their game very well. They are becoming very, very wealthy at the expense of needy, and often unsuspecting men and women.

These are the means by which porn is diminishing the family pocketbook – money that could otherwise pay for household expenses, family vacations, college tuition, church tithes, charitable contributions, etc. What is it doing to individuals?

## Get 'em hooked while they're young

When kids start exploring the World Wide Web they are exposed to more things than the average adult has seen in a lifetime. On the Web there are no police, no bouncers, no chaperones, no one to check IDs. A lot of graphic porn sites carry the warning: "No one under 18 permitted to enter." They may then ask the user to click on the button, "Yes, I am at least 18." Realistically, how many kids are going to decide, "I can't go there; I'm underage." Once that click of the mouse is accomplished the seamy world of pornographic sex opens up.

Craig, age 16, from Massachusetts, said:

> "Porn is everywhere on the Internet. If you don't seek it out, it comes to you. Most often you'll see advertisements for it on 'warez' pages, where you can illegally download software that you haven't purchased. Apparently the people that run those 'warez' Web sites think that software pirates are also very interested in porn. If you're seeking it out, it's definitely one of the easiest things to find on the Internet."[18]

Gio, 15, from Florida, said:

> "It seems to be very easy for kids to find porn on the Internet. Most of the time I stumble upon the porn sites. For instance, I was looking for pictures of elephants for my

aunt and I stumbled upon pictures of women having sex with animals, not a pretty picture.

My school has put in filters so that kids won't be able to access porn material. Online porn is changing the minds of young kids, kind of putting the message in their minds 'porn is OK' and perverting their minds. Online porn is not OK and it is ruining young children."[19]

There is also a risk for our children when we restrict them to kid's chat rooms. Some of these have age limitations such as "only kids 11 and under allowed." This is often fertile lurking ground for pedophiles who pose as kids to "meet" victims. This can become the first step in getting acquainted, exchanging phone numbers, and meeting in the park. They can spot in a minute the kids who feel isolated, lonely and rejected, in other words, those who are easy prey.

Many porn sites preview the "behind-the-doors" content up front. Lurid sexual scenes appear just by accidentally opening sound-alike domains for innocent purposes. Some of the most publicized are the hard-core porn sites like "whitehouse.com" which can easily be opened instead of the legitimate governmental information site "whitehouse.gov." The lure is the copy-cat name and the main purpose of the lure is to get subscribers to pay at least $9.99 a month to look at more of their pictures. Many porn sites use domain names (URLs) that are set up to intentionally confuse and lure the innocent Web traveler, especially those underage. They know that once the kids get hooked they have them for a long time and with them comes big bucks.

Many URLs are intentionally set up with misspelling so that by changing one letter in the spelling you can end up with hard-core porn. Most letters that are different from popular, respectable domain names are next to each other on the keyboard so that they are common slips typists make. (For instance "m" and "n" might be interchanged.) These sites appear and disappear quite regularly so as to keep from being obviously discovered. There are thousands of such sites at any one time on the Net.

Porn merchants also deliberately set up explicit sites that will be found when someone uses Internet search engines to look up innocent information such as toys, dolls, pets, etc.

We also must take into consideration that kids are curious. They have heard enough about sex at school and from TV to want to know more. Natural curiosity is to be expected but if the Internet is where they go to get their information they will be bombarded with the baser instincts of men and women and the worst of the smut that the porn merchants are touting. It takes only seconds to type into a key word search the word "sex" and any person, adults included, will be slimed with pictures and descriptions that severely degrade the beauty of sexual love between husbands and wives and the godly images of man and woman.

Once these pictures and descriptions are imprinted into one's mind and imagination they are impossible to get out without God's help. (We will offer helpful steps in allowing God to do such a cleansing in another chapter.) Once any of us is exposed to graphic sexual content, our innocence cannot be regained, barring a miracle.[20]

Concentrated supervision by parents and information about using caution and setting healthy boundaries are vital when we allow our children to have access to the Net. A lot of kids know more about the Internet than their parents, so it is often hard to successfully monitor what they're viewing. I can't imagine any family with children living at home with Internet access not having some kind of filter service or clean ISP such as "Mayberry.com," "Net Nanny," or "SmutStopper.com." These kinds of filters are not 100% effective but offer a much greater protection for our children's innocence.

## Guidelines for your kids about internet usage[21]

It could be very helpful to go over in detail the following guidelines with your children, making sure they know the importance of each imperative. Although most parents are reluctant to confront their children about such unpleasant subject matter until there is a warranted reason, this is an area, much like staying out of the street, that must be addressed before irreparable harm is done.

- Never fill out questionnaires or any forms online or give out any personal information, including your real name.

- Never agree to meet in person with anyone you have met online.

- Never enter a chat room without Mom and/or Dad's presence or supervision.

- Never tell anyone online where you will be or what you will be doing without Mom and/or Dad's permission.

- Never respond to or send e-mail to new people you meet online.

- Never send a picture over the Internet or via regular mail to anyone you've met on the Internet.

- Never respond to any belligerent or suggestive contact or anything that makes you feel uncomfortable.

- Always tell Mom and/or Dad about something you saw that is upsetting.

## The zoning board

The job of zoning boards in responsible communities is to prevent and shut down businesses that are considered inappropriate for a certain area. This may include the "seedy" pornographic bookstore that could possibly be opened next to the neighborhood dry cleaners or across the street from the school. However, today the porn merchants open and close up shop at will in an electronic territory that no zoning board can regulate.[22]

Once upon a time we felt the responsibility to pressure the entertainment industry to clean up what was in the movies and on TV. Once upon a time we worked hard to keep sleazy products and magazines out of the local convenience and drug store. But today the job is overwhelming. Who in the world has the time and resources to tackle such a monumental giant?

There appears to be no zoning board regulating home e-commerce. Porn merchants are the creative pioneers of the world-wide marketplace. They were the first to use shopping-cart technology and credit cards for online payment. They bring in more profit than any other online business. Stock trading is a contender for the profit title but its profit margins of about 0.2% profits are paltry next to porn-site profits, which are often as high as 30%. The estimated revenues of pornographic Web sites in 1999 totaled $1.1 – $1.2 billion.[23]

We have no idea what innovations are just on the horizon for the technologies that make illusions seem real. Not all of the senses have been satiated electronically yet. I'm sure someone out there is working right now on digital touch, taste and smell. As each "impossibility" comes to life it only seems to open the window for hundreds of other never-thought-of-before technologies. And with every subsequent digital innovation, porn is being reshaped and transformed into other forms of temptress sirens who continue to seductively lure their victims only to dash them upon the rocks of destruction.

This is the plot of the enemy of your soul. When he gets his way you are lured into experiencing one more hit of pleasure to compensate for the lack of meaning in your life. And then just one more … *But wait, here's something even better … Look, here! This is even more exciting!*

I hope these facts have made you angry, especially if you have been victimized, either through someone you love or by your own gullibility. I hope you realize that you have gotten caught up in a scheme to extort money from you at your weakest level. I hope you understand the futility of ever finding fulfillment through pornography. I hope you are seeing the illusory side of the attraction.

Even if you respond, *yes! yes! yes!* to all these hopes of mine, there most probably is still a place within you that says, "Intellectually, I agree, but I still don't want to give it up. I need that rush to feel alive and I don't think I'm strong enough to walk away."

You may not be strong enough to quit cold turkey. That's why the success rate for those who try to abruptly stop any addictive behavior is so low. We all need help. The important thing is to get the right kind of help, the kind that brings deep, thorough results. You may be highly motivated right now but tomorrow morning at 3 am when you wake up feeling desperately lonely and anxious and you know that one or two hits on the computer will bring you some temporary relief, you may not have the same motivation. You need something more than a pep talk. You need something that works from the inside out.

## Five smooth stones and a sling

The porn industry and its lure is a huge Goliath for little Davids like us to tackle. Like Goliath the Philistine, this enemy of the family looks formidable. It has grown so large there doesn't seem to be anyone who can overcome its immensity – not even the government's regulations. Its influence upon individuals and the addictive quality of the practice seems even harder to overcome.

According to 1 Samuel 17, Goliath was over nine feet tall. He wore a bronze helmet on his head and a bronze coat of scales of armor that weighed about 125 pounds. He had bronze leggings and a bronze javelin with a 15-pound point as well as a sword in a scabbard. He also had a shield bearer who went before him to take the first blows and ward off any attacks. He believed he was invincible – and he looked it! He had wealth, strength and clout.

Goliath's verbal threats were no less intimidating. He taunted the Israelites to come down into the valley from their mountain-top to take him on. He defied their ranks. The goal of battle was that the loser would give total submission and servitude to the overcomer. The outcome of the battle affected not just Goliath and his immediate opponent, but all the people they both represented.

A nation's allegiance to the god they served was at stake – either Yahweh or Baal. Baal, the god of sexual orgy was the god the Philistines served and worshiped, along with Ashteroth and Molech. The practices of those devoted to these gods were called abominable by Yahweh. They indulged in lewd acts and used pornographic symbols, such as the Asherah poles (ancient phallic symbols), to enhance their worship. They sacrificed children as offerings to their god. Their temples were ornate and wealthy. They were the predominant religion in much of the history of Israel.

The troops of Baal looked immense, wealthy and powerful to the Israelites, and they seemed to have the advantage. But Yahweh, the one true God, put all His eggs in one basket – a young shepherd boy from Bethlehem, a most unlikely one to defeat such a formidable enemy. He was the least of a small tribe. No one in his family paid much attention to him. He was young, inexperienced and had done only menial jobs.

When David, the shepherd, saw the fear in the men from

Israel, as they ran away from the giant and his threats, he began to ask questions: "Why? What is to be gained? Who is this giant really?" Everyone from the king to David's own family members told him he wouldn't have a chance in the world to defeat the enemy. But David had a weapon that the Philistines knew nothing about. He had seen this weapon used to great advantage in the most ordinary circumstances and he had come to trust in its efficacy. *He understood the power of Yahweh.*

Even after the gauntlet had been thrown down and David was chosen to stand against Goliath, the men of Israel attempted to prepare David for battle by equipping him with the weapons of the world. He was outfitted with the best the world had to offer, even the armor of the king himself. But David found that the armor the world proposed was too rigid and would prove to be ineffective, hampering his ability to do what he knew best – rely upon the strength and power of Yahweh. He would either trust in God alone and do what He said or he and his family and even his nation would be defeated by the enemy.

For David to face Goliath was a no-brainer – no one else was going to do it. If he didn't make an attempt the whole nation would fall to Baal. There would be no one left to stand for holiness and righteousness and the joy of wholeness. The leadership, the religion, the family – all would be given over to the lusts of the flesh and the baser instincts of men and women as they worshiped idol gods.

David felt pretty insignificant and inadequate in the flesh. His personal arsenal consisted only of five smooth stones he picked up from the stream and a shepherd's sling. But the weapon David knew he would use, and the one which prompted him to volunteer for the mission that would bring the victory, was the presence of a mighty God. God Himself was the shield-bearer who went before David into battle. David was approached by the giant Philistine who was threatening and cursing and using the power of his god, the wiles of Baal. But in his weakness, something rose up within David and he shouted back at Goliath, *"You come against me with sword and spear and javelin, but I come against you in the name of the* LORD *Almighty, the God of the armies of Israel, who you have defied."*[24]

That day, using only one of the five stones he had gathered, David struck Goliath in the head and using the Philistine's own sword, cut him down to the death. The armies of Baal retreated and David took the weapons of Goliath out of circulation.

The fatal "blow to the head" that has always been promised to the enemy of God since Genesis 3:15, was once again powerfully illustrated. The weaponry used for victory is what is always so surprising, not only to the enemy, but often to us as well. A little stone can pack a big punch when used in the right way.

Like David, you have to throw aside the lies from the enemy:

- Who do you think you are to make a difference?
- Who would listen to anything you say? You're weak! You're a hypocrite.
- You're addicted to this stuff. You won't ever be able to live without it.
- Who cares anyway? You have rights. You need to feel happy.

You, too, have to discard the defensive weapons the world would give you to use to fight the battle:

- Be energized by your anger.
- Use the power of your influence.
- File a lawsuit.
- Let everybody do his own thing. Don't be judgmental or mean-spirited.
- If you want to quit, just do it cold turkey. If you really want to you can.

Like David, we have to pick up the extraordinarily simple weapon that God gives us and have faith in its power to overcome. *The truth of the Word of God will set us free.* Only then will we see victory. This will prove effective regardless of which venue we are called to fight the battle: the pulpit, prayer groups, counseling offices, our homes, our neighborhoods, the courts, or our own hearts.

## Taking stock of the situation

Are you ready to face the truth? A lot of God's people are in trouble, but not defeated yet. Their cause is not hopeless.

Perhaps you or someone close to you is feeling defeated by living so long with the destructive patterns of behavior that seem to be a part of who you are. You may feel it is too late to change. Perhaps you have already defined yourself as a failure or a pervert. You may see no hope of recovering broken relationships and being restored to genuine intimacy that brings fulfillment. All the other forces, even your own pain (or numbness, emptiness, anxiety, obsessions, etc.) may seem too large, in fact, overwhelming.

Write all that out before God right now. State in absolute truth the condition in which you find yourself, without blaming anyone else or excusing your own behavior.

Now, look at the confession you have made to a holy God in your own handwriting. Be brutally honest. Do this prayerfully, asking God to reveal anything else hidden to you that displeases Him.

To help you get real before God concerning your problems with pornography, answer the following questions and let God speak to your heart. If you answer yes to any of the questions, write that out in your confession.

## Search my heart, O God!

1. Do you routinely spend significant amounts of time viewing pornography (magazines, videos, or Internet) or visiting chat rooms with the intent of finding sexual stimulation?

2. Do you feel preoccupied with using the Internet to find online sexual partners?

3. Do you frequently use anonymous communication (phone or Internet) to engage in sexual fantasies not typically carried out in real-life?

4. Do you hide your online interactions and/or pornographic materials from your family members?

5. Do you anticipate your next encounter with pornography with the expectation that you will find sexual arousal or gratification?

6. Do you experience significant physiological changes when you look at sexually oriented material (magazines, video or Internet) (e.g. increase in heart rate, sweaty palms, etc.)?

7. Have you paid to enter pornographic web sites?
8. Do you need sexual images that are increasingly more graphic than those viewed before to attain the same level of sexual excitement?
9. Do you masturbate while viewing pornography?
10. Are you less involved with your spouse because of your experience with pornography?
11. Have you ever told yourself that you would stop your sexual behavior with pornography, then broken that resolution?
12. Do you look at pornographic web sites or magazines while at work?
13. Do you have sex sites that you check frequently to see if they have been updated?
14. Are you worried about how much money you spend on pornography?
15. Do you have a sense of guilt or shame about your involvement with pornography?

## A clean slate

*Part 1:*
Now that you are facing honestly some difficult truths about yourself it is time to start a brand-new prayer journal. In it you will observe an honesty code with God. This journal will contain your heart's cry to the only One who can effectively change your life for good. See your life through His eyes and describe it. Is He pleased? Is He grieving? Allow Him to release any grief that has been stored up within your heart. Take it to the Cross. It is the only place to put it.

Have you stifled grief by turning it into anger and projecting it out on those around you? Who have you wounded by your words or your silence? Have you been embarrassed to admit that you have childlike needs to be held and cuddled and protected? All these answers and revelations should go into your journal.

*Part 2:*
Now, for the other important part of your journal: Listen to what God is saying to you. This is vital for your wholeness. Let me

start by sharing one important thing He always says to His children:

> *"If you say you have no sin you are deceiving yourself and the truth is not in you. If you confess your sin, God is faithful and just to forgive you your sins and to cleanse you from all unrighteousness."*                                 (1 John 1:9 personalized)

Write this out in your journal as well. You have just confessed your sins and God has forgiven you. Without this vital first step you will not be able to stay the course. After writing the scripture, write in your own words:

> I receive Your forgiveness. I embrace it and make it part of who I am. I am a forgiven child of the Living God.

This is your identity and you need to celebrate it. Now the cleansing can begin!

# Chapter 5

## Act 1, Act 2, Act 3
### Purveyor, user, and addict

*" ... do not let sin reign in your mortal body so that you obey its evil desires. Do not offer the parts of your body to sin, as instruments of wickedness, but rather offer yourselves to God, as those who have been brought from death to life; and offer the parts of your body to him as instruments of righteousness. For sin shall not be your master, because you are not under law, but under grace."*
(Romans 6:12–14)

### Act 1: The purveyor

For those of you born after 1960 it's as though God added some "techno-genes" into your DNA. You are the ones who feel as much at home at a computer keyboard as you do with a spoon in your hand.

The rest of us could better be classified as "techno-peasants." We're always trying to eat with chopsticks. We may master the technique enough to make do but it still feels awkward and with the slightest glitch we feel totally helpless. Conlee and I frequently have to call our adult son in Seattle to talk us through a computer problem. We're always amazed at the ease and familiarity he has with the internal workings of our PC and software.

Those who have found it like second nature to construct their own computers, design their software and modify the internal structures of their PCs to do what they want them to do have become the young entrepreneurs of the twentieth and twenty-first centuries. They travel the world with their electronic laptops and notebooks; they dream of an impossibility and make it happen; they rely on e-communication and technology to accomplish instantly what used to take days.

Their ingenuity and talents have developed areas such as Silicon Valley and established amazingly lucrative, albeit off-the-wall, companies. These young computer wizards have become unbelievably wealthy at a very tender age and are contributing to the fast-paced progression of computerized devices and gadgets that are filling our homes.

## Technical overload

You realize all this is quite overwhelming to me, sometimes resulting in techno-overload. I can still remember my grand-mother telling me stories of her family's move from the country to the city before 1900, a 75-mile trip in a covered wagon, taking three weeks. She could hardly believe that we would hop on a plane and be in another part of the world in a matter of hours.

Conlee began his engineering studies with his trusty slide rule, never dreaming that he might ever need computers in his offices to make his successful contracting company more modern. But today our sons, also engineers, are electronically connected to a network of offices around the world.

This deluge of innovative electronic design has certainly changed all our lives. We live in a fast-paced state of overload most of the time. We are bombarded with devices to enhance our lifestyles and as a result, some of the most menial chores have now become technical challenges for many of us. The last time I bought a new microwave was a frustrating experience. Remembering the first one I ever had (a huge, no-nonsense Amana that was the top-of-the-line in 1969), I asked for a model with just a very simple on/off switch, a timer-dial, and a defrost cycle. I found there is no such creature anymore. Instead I have to study a manual and learn to program a microwave just to heat water, melt butter and warm up left-overs!

In spite of my inadequacies, I delight in my cell phone, my answering machine, my laptop computer, my palm pilot, the remote control, the VCR and the DVD. They are all fun to have and have brought worlds of knowledge and convenience into my life. For this I am grateful to the computer wizards who have had the dreams and visions to make such things realities for all of us.

## The modern El Dorado

Some of the same kinds of young techno-wizards out there who were more fascinated with making lots of money than developing new technology found a get-rich-quick path that obliterates the California Gold Rush. The kind of money they have tapped into is nearly obscene. The product they are pushing is definitely obscene.

The popularity of the camcorders in the 1980s launched an ever-increasing appetite for putting pornography into homes. Camcorders were advertised to record weddings, graduations, a baby's first steps and birthday parties, but it became obvious that many people were using them to record sex. Because of the home movies with explicit sexual content that were being exchanged, an underground market was developed for the amateur videos, later to be capitalized upon by more professional entrepreneurs. Those watching realized the potential gold mine for such a product if you could just perfect the distribution.

Pornography, already proven in popularity, was thus the pioneer product used to get e-commerce established as the big business it is today. Due to the incredible response the tech-heads got to their initial advertising of online porn, some of their success resulted in developing shopping-cart technology and the use of credit cards for online payment. It was the porn merchants who were the early adapters of streaming video and banner advertising. They were also the ones who devised ways to disable your browser's "Back" button and to gratuitously open window after window to prevent you from leaving their sites.[1]

The innovative electronic techniques that have sent pornography so easily into the home have resulted in a bonanza for the porn merchants. In early 2000, there was a 10% increase in porn-site traffic each month.[2] Such a booming business brought in over a billion dollars in 1999 to those peddling the erotic websites.[3]

One particular company, the fastest growing distributor of pornographic "entertainment," New Frontier Media, Inc., has nearly 40,000 interconnected adult porn sites and is owned by public stock holders, traded on the Nasdaq. Its CEO since its beginning in September of 1995, Mark Kreloff, reported the company's payment of $5.2 million in taxes on $48 million in revenue for the fiscal year ending March 31, 2000. He says he expects the company to nearly triple its pretax earnings the next year.[4] The company, based in Boulder, Colorado, reports that its networks reach 31 million addressable subscribers and that from June 2000 to June 2001 they had an increase of 130% in its subscribers to its pay television subsidiary, The Erotic Networks.[5]

Another Internet subsidiary of New Frontier Media, IGallery, claims over 1,300 Internet domain names and 30 thematically organized consumer sites. Together these sites generate over 30 million visitors a month. In addition, New Frontier operates 27 web sites and 6 pay-per-view erotic channels, available on many cable and satellite providers.[6] Twenty-five million homes currently receive New Frontier's pay-per-view channels, with the average home purchasing 2.5 to 3 adult movies per month at $7.95 to $10.95 per 90 minutes.[7]

With the vast amounts of money that the porn czars such as Mark Kreloff are making, comes an incredible amount of power. Not only do these CEOs influence the money market because of the huge profits they are able to generate, they also are receiving the power to shape the future generation into an image of humanity far baser than anything God ever intended. This power can be intimidating and the czars like it that way. Their lives reflect an arrogance about their misuse of power that gives them control over many lives and pocketbooks. Listen to some of the arrogant statements that come from the big leagues of pornography:

> "I have all the money I need now, and I'm not really motivated by it anymore. The most important contribution I could make would be an end to the obscenity laws."
> (Larry Flynt, founder of *Hustler* magazine)[8]

> "You have to try really hard to lose money in this business."
> (Steve Orienstein, president of Canoga Park-based Wicked Pictures)[9]

> "If you look around at a lot of the other dot.com businesses out there, they're not profitable. We are. We are very, very

profitable. We've learned what it takes to make a dollar. Not just make a dollar, but make a dollar and make a dollar and make a dollar."

　　　　　(Jonathan Silverstein, president of Cybererotica) [10]

"For a while it was a manna where everyone could graze, but now there will be a rapid evolution so there's a survival of the fittest in the next few years ... Rich people go where the money is, so it was only a matter of time until morality got thrown out the window."

　　　　(Scott Maslow, age 26, one of four partners in Pornication,
　　　　　　　the leading provider of interactive video,
　　　　　　　　now sold out to NuWeb Solutions) [11]

When asked if he would consider selling any of the roughly 3,000 domains his company owns that direct traffic to its 14 paying porn sites, Joe Elkind replied, "That's small-time thinking; unless you have to, would you sell Broadway in Monopoly?" (Joe Elkind, chief executive of The Cyber Entertainment Network). [12]

Because of this profusion of innovative technology and the enormous profit associated with it, sociologist Charles Winick notes that the sexual content of American culture has changed more in two decades than it had in the previous two centuries. [13]

With every digital innovation that comes along, the scent of more money is detectable to the pornographers, and pornography is being reshaped constantly, transformed into the latest tempting venues to those who are susceptible to its wiles. The pornographers and those who peddle it do not care about the souls of the users. They have one mission only: to accumulate wealth at the expense of the public. They will argue in courts about the legitimacy of their profession, distort and then defend the laws of this nation, and then go to new depths to persuade the user to continually go a little further into their dark world.

## Act 2: The user

Not every person who dabbles in pornography is caught in its web. Curiosity is a powerful emotion that leads a person to areas of life that are unknown. Without a natural curiosity many progressive and wonderful inventions would never have been inspired; without a normal curiosity great territories would never have been explored. But, like many other helpful emotions, curiosity needs healthy boundaries. Limits must be set so that there are definitions as to how far we will go when we seek what is unfamiliar. It can take only a small step to move from a soft, mushy area to quicksand where one is swallowed up and seen no more.

There are increasingly more "soft areas" in our society where we assume, arrogantly, that we can tread without danger. However, we must be very careful to watch each step. As Christians we often presume upon the grace of our God in some dangerous areas, even though He has told us expressly not to walk down those paths. Thinking we will be exempt from the downfalls of many others, we often stride out with a false confidence on the road to destruction.

## Just say No!

The proliferation of pornography in our society leaves very few people, if any, totally untouched by its reach into our lives. One almost has to live in a cave to be unaware of the influence of pornography in our daily routines.

The morning paper, the TV news, advertisements on billboards, magazine covers in the grocery store, art, etc. – it swirls around us in varying degrees of sensuality. What was considered risqué a generation before is now considered normal. It is happening so fast it is frightening.

A small, family-oriented shop I used to frequent catered mostly for women who often had their children with them. One day, while doing business there, I noticed a new, fairly large, colored poster on the wall depicting close-up nude body parts of a man only barely covered by a woman's foot – an extremely provocative position. Twenty years ago everyone would have definitely labeled it "pornography." Today, I guess most people would say it bordered on being pornographic.

Not seeing any possible reason for the poster to be there, I decided to speak out. When I asked the manager why such a picture would be placed in her shop, she merely shrugged and said, "It's just an advertisement we received from the manufacturer of the toe rings we sell." It took a moment to discern that the woman's foot was actually wearing a toe ring.

Not letting it drop, I pressed the point. "Do you put every advertisement you receive from manufacturers on your walls? Why this one?" Her answer was a shrug. She didn't know and evidently didn't care.

I then decided to act like the person I profess to be. "I really believe that poster is totally unsuitable for your customers, especially children. Would you consider removing it, because it is sending a message that is not wholesome? In fact, it's nearly pornographic."

The manager said she didn't agree with me and refused to remove the picture and I, very nicely, told her I would not be coming in anymore.

That was a very small thing in the huge scope of pornography. But that is why we have become desensitized to the problem. We have allowed the little foxes to spoil the vineyard.

## Compromising Christians

Most casual users of pornography think of it as harmless and recreational. Before we were committed Christians, in the early '70s we, like the other young couples we knew, had a subscription to *Playboy*. Hugh Hefner had done his job well, because it seemed to us that his publication was something every sophisticated family should receive in the mail each month. I can't remember our ever discussing the effects this magazine might have on our young sons in the home. We didn't hide it – it was out in plain sight.

Granted, *Playboy* magazine in 1970 was hardly what it is today. However, the message was the same. To young children this was what adults were interested in and what they should grow up to be interested in. In spite of its being relatively benign material as compared to what is available today, we sinned against our children by polluting their home.

One of the first things we did after we committed our lives to the Lord in 1972 was cancel that subscription! We knew it was not what we wanted in our home in the Lord's presence.

In case we give you the impression that we have been pure and spotless since 1972, we must confess that there have been many times we have compromised God's holiness to fit in with the world. We have sat through several movies that we should have walked out of thirty minutes after they started. When you think about it logically, there is just something wrong with paying to see images that you then have to ask Jesus to cleanse from your imagination!

Frequently as I pray for people at our church during the Sunday morning service, they want to confess watching something in a movie that displeased God. When they come into His presence on Sunday morning to worship Him, He begins to show them areas that need cleansing so that they can enter His holiness. In trying to live holy lives, they are aware of the pollution of such things on their soul.

We found the answer to this particular dilemma – we quit going to movies. We just rent those that friends assure us are worth watching. We had to get over the idea that we had to be the first to see every movie that was being touted in the press. It turns out that the good ones are just as good three months later, and the objectionable ones don't get our money to keep them going.

It's a bit easier at home to just change the channel when something objectionable comes on the television. The subject most situation comedies focus on is sex. This is the primary objective of the traditional, modern thirty-minute slice-of-life. And most of the sex they show and talk about is outside of marriage. If you don't think this is a problem, ask some six-year-olds what sit-coms they watch and then ask them to explain the storyline. Fornication sounds very different coming out of the mouth of a child. These shows are greatly influencing the morality of our society.

Busy productive lives have little time for mindless television watching. If vegging out before the TV is a long-standing habit in your family, ask God to give your family a project. It won't take long at all before the interaction of the family members will become far more meaningful than the vegetative state of tube watching.

Another habit I had to put to death was wanting to read every best-selling novel that came along. I had this need to be "in the know" about the latest books people were discussing. Within the last couple of decades, however, the term "best-seller" has almost become synonymous with "pornographic." The subject matter of many highly touted books is obscene and is further-more, a waste of time.

Much more discriminating in my choice of reading material, I now find my mind actually has expanded to take in far more than I used to be able to read and absorb. I am reading far more difficult, challenging and informative books that I would have thought possible ten or twenty years ago. I have put aside books that do not lift me to a higher place.

The music we listen to in our home is calming and it glorifies God. Occasionally however, I have the radio on in the car. Curious to hear what is popularly being listened to, I have tuned in to the lyrics. Most of them glorify fornication and adultery, drinking and drugs.

## What harm does it do?

*So, what's the big deal?* You thought this was about hard core porn, right? Well, that's the end result of a society who begins with the simple things I just mentioned: public advertisements, movies, television, books and music. We are the consumers of all these things and what we support and patronize speaks to the people at the top. If we *allow* a greater use of immoral and pornographic material to be used in everything that surrounds us, we might as well be *requesting* it. That is the trend right now and it will only increase as long as it pays off financially to the purveyors.

## What the casual use of porn is doing to marriages

Before the Fall, described in Genesis 3, man and woman only had a knowledge of goodness. Their source of all information came from God Himself. They were filled with things that were true, noble, just, pure, lovely, things of good testimony, of excellence, and worthy of praise.[14] There was a purity of intimacy with God that was modeled in the purity of the love relationship Adam and Eve had with each other.

When the knowledge of evil was introduced into the human race by Adam and Eve's sin, everything was changed, except who God is. Sin distorts the beauty of creation. What began as perfect love in a Garden, sin perverted. Adam and Eve eventually grieved over the loss of one son, and the actions of another. A life that was intended to be so beautiful became horrible. Their marriage was never the same, although God promised a way of deliverance for them.

In our modern society, infused with a knowledge of evil and even professing that it is not harmful, marriages are still affected in horrible ways and husbands and wives are experiencing heartbreaking circumstances. This will continue until the husband and the wife look to God's boundaries of protection.

## A luncheon encounter with sin

Sitting across the luncheon table from a handsome, energetic, young European pastor and his wife, I was asked what sort of book I was presently working on. I explained to them the inspiration for this book and how great the need is for healing and deliverance from this epidemic of pornography.

"Oh, yes!" he exclaimed, enthusiastically. "I engage in this activity from time to time. All men do. But it is outside of me, not part of the real me."

I hastened to explain to him how even occasional excursions into the pornographic world contribute to the distortions of the images of woman and of man – the image of God – and of our sexuality. We will never see ourselves or others aright when we fill our imaginations with such distorted images.

This young pastor looked at me as though I were telling him he no longer needed air to breathe. Such is the picture of many Christian men worldwide. They have been addicted to pollution to the extent that the purity of the imagination no longer holds the promise of reality to them.

I glanced at the young pastor's wife, seated next to him. She had just heard his bold declaration of occasionally using pornography. Her reaction was that of lowering her eyes and blankly staring at the white tablecloth. I could sense her feelings of rejection and helplessness. I could even see the chasm in their relationship by her reaction.

How could this couple truly become one when there were many other women's images in intimate proximity to the husband's needs?

## Pornography and women

When pornography begins to influence a society women lose their relational value. Because they are the objects of most pornographic venues, they become compartmentalized, seldom seen as whole women, but merely as the sexual parts that comprise the whole woman.

When a husband begins even to casually use pornography, he takes this compartmentalized view of woman into his heart. "When a man, after weeks of [Internet pornography], actually sleeps with his wife, he's in for a letdown," says Greg Gutfeld.[15]

The wife of a man who dabbles in pornography will never live up to his fantasies – because they are not real, and she is! He will be tempted to ask her to do things he saw in magazines, videos or online. He will be disappointed in her responses to him. In reality, he has taken other women into his bed as he makes love to his wife, constantly comparing her to them and wishing she were more like his imaginary lovers.

*The New York Times* wrote an article about a thirty-four-year-old woman who had found out that her minister-husband had an online porn habit. "How can I compete with hundreds of anonymous others who are now in our bed, in his head? Our bed is crowded with countless faceless strangers, where once we were intimate."[16]

## God's holy boundaries

Far from being a God who doesn't want His people to have any fun, God delights in His people's joy. He just knows that often what *we* call fun is leading to death. We often find ourselves crying out, "O, Lord, why did You let this happen?" when we find ourselves at the bottom of a pile of rubble, composed of broken relationships. We are quick to blame God for disasters of our own making, yet so reluctant to heed His loving boundaries that promote the ultimate joy for our lives.

The Judeo-Christian understanding of sex espouses a higher view of it than any other religion. "That's why it has the strictest rules about it. Anything so important has to be handled carefully. If you pursue pleasure for its own sake, two things happen. First, it disappears. Philosophers call this the 'hedonistic paradox.'

Second, it steers you wrong, because pleasure can result from doing wrong as well as doing right."[17]

If we choose to pursue sexual pleasure for its own sake, instead of restricting our enjoyment of it to a benefit of God's love in marriage, we will never have enough and never feel fulfilled. We will move from one relationship to another, or one distorted stimulus to another. We will have mis-translated God's intention for sexual pleasure into the language of a hedonistic society. The meaning is never conveyed accurately in this venue. It always *appears* to be narrow, boring, unexciting, uninteresting, and merely dutiful.

Sexual pleasure within marriage is like the spark plug for a car.[18] In the whole of a marriage, the amount of time a couple spends actually experiencing the throes of sexual pleasure is relatively small, compared to the rest of their shared experiences. However, small though it may be, it is as essential as the spark plug of a car to set the whole mechanism in motion.

Sexual pleasure in marriage brings husband and wife together in such a way that the Bible speaks of them as becoming "one flesh," while at the same time, no other human activity so "accentuates one's own identity and self-awareness, at such an elemental level."[19] When joined with one's beloved so intimately, one becomes more fully alive in his/her own identity. As the husband and wife each give of themselves more completely to the other, they each receive a greater sense of self-pleasure in the sexual embrace.

God created us with the capacity to enjoy sexual pleasure. He meant for us to enjoy it within marriage, for this provides the safe boundaries in which our deep emotions and vulnerabilities will be protected. We cannot and must not dilute God's intentions for sexual pleasure because of a broken world or because we have a distorted compassion for those who are not married.

A godly, holy view of sex depends upon healthy marriages for its continued existence. We cannot view it separately. There is no potential for the depth of joy that God intended sex to give His children, apart from the loving boundaries of commitment in marriage. Those who attempt to find it in other places will soon become fragmented and dissatisfied. Casual, uncommitted sex, outside of marriage, "endlessly joins and severs. Imagine what it would be like to repeatedly tear off and reattach your arm. There would come a day when no earthly surgery would suffice; the reparative power of your body would be lost. It is the same when you repeatedly tear off and reattach your various sexual partners. Eventually they will all seem like strangers; you just won't feel anything. You will have destroyed your capacity for intimacy."[20]

## Fragmenting a good relationship

Whether one goes from one sexual partner to another or seeks to find sexual thrills from the occasional use of pornography, a fragmentation of the soul occurs. Even the infrequent user of pornography will begin to have a much different view of sexuality than he once did. The images he has seen, and the feelings associated with those images, will draw him back to a lesser symbol of man and woman coming together. Even the most wholesome relationships between man and woman will become tainted by the residue of what pornography leaves in its wake.

I think every woman can relate to the discomfort that is felt when, in a normal conversation with a man, he repeatedly glances at her breasts. She feels that he is not really interested in who she is or what she is saying, but in a particular part of her anatomy. Or, just as disconcerting, when in his efforts not to look at her breasts, he begins to dart his eyes around and avoids looking at her altogether. Both actions diminish the real woman.

The wife who is married to the casual porn user is aware that something is not right even before she has proof. Men find this hard to understand, but wives have special antennae for things like this. A husband may lie about his involvement with pornography up until his last breath, but a wife has a built-in sensitivity to notice if there are other women in her marriage bed. She can sense when he is focusing his desire on something or someone other than herself. She may rationalize it, try to deny it, and make excuses for it, but when she finds out the truth, invariably, she will look back and think, *I saw all the signs and ignored them.*

## Polly and Sam's story

Polly and Sam had been married for about twelve years when she came to us for prayer. She told us that Sam had just confessed to her that he had been watching pornographic videos and found them exciting. He wanted her to watch them with him so that they could share the "thrill" and make their lovemaking more exciting. Her question for us was, "As a Christian wife, am I obligated to do this because he wants to?"

We asked her if their sexual relationship had been pleasing to both of them before he started watching the videos. She said it had been up until a few weeks before, when she became aware of herself pulling away from him emotionally. She said she had had little interest in sex since that time and had begun to make excuses to avoid his invitations. She, at his suggestion, had even been to see her gynecologist to see if there was a physical problem. As she began to think about it she realized that her emotional detachment occurred about the same time Sam had discovered a backroom in a video store that rented pornography.

Polly began to realize that she was really angry with Sam for bringing into their home the images of what other men and women did together in bed. She didn't want to become one of the porn queens in his videos; she wanted him to desire her for herself. At our suggestion, she asked Sam to come with her at her next visit to us.

Sam attempted to relate in detail about a guy at work who loaned him the first video, telling him how it really "spiced up" his marriage. Then, he moved on to his discovery of the store where they rented them and the hours he had spent looking at the things various couples did, all the while maintaining he was doing it for Polly and their marriage. When we finally confronted him with, "What was wrong with your marriage that made you want to use porn to jazz it up?" his answer was very revealing. "Well, I didn't think anything was wrong with it until I started looking at what was possible. After that, it seemed pretty boring."

Sam started flirting with illusion and it became more enticing than the loving reality he had at home. He nearly jeopardized the wonderful family he had for the sensate illusory world, which says, "Enough is never enough."

Sam and Polly did some confession, renunciation and reconciliation work in their marriage and learned, painfully, the value of what God had already given them. They came very near to disaster, but because they loved God and, above all, wanted what He wanted, their marriage was restored to an exciting, trusting relationship. They had not gone too far down the path of destruction before they realized the bridge was out. They turned around and went back on the right path.

Unfortunately, when a person has abused his emotions to the extent that he only seems alive when pursuing the "rush," his profile changes. He moves from being a "user" to becoming an "addict."

## Act 3: The addict

Once a person has moved beyond sexual curiosity and experimentation into the realm of "I can't live without it," he begins the slide down the slippery slope. Relationships are in jeopardy and so is anyone or anything else that gets in his way.

Dr. Victor Cline, of the University of Utah, has studied the adrenalized escalation of sexual arousal through pornography and has made the following conclusions: "Soft-core pictures of women in lingerie will soon become boring and you will seek full nudity, and as that loses novelty you will look for something more enticing."[21]

Dr. Cline then lists the four typical steps[22] of such a de-escalation:

### 1. Addiction

In addiction, pornography has become a regular part of your life. Your thoughts are obsessive about it. Every woman (or man) is measured against the images you have stored up in your imagination. You plan for times to be alone to look at magazines or get online. You limit conversations and reduce relationships to the barest necessities so that nothing will interfere with your porn time. You bargain with yourself to get the rewards of looking at a new magazine or going to a favorite porn site if you get a certain amount of work done. You're still in awe of the vast amounts of porn that are out there that you haven't yet explored. The supply seems endless. You feel alive and excited in ways you haven't experienced before. You're hooked and you can't quit.

### 2. Escalation

The initial thrill has worn off. When you look back at the first magazines you had they look tame. It was hard to believe you got so excited about them. Where is that titillating feeling of expectation you used to be able to have by just turning the page or booting up the computer? Like coming down from a drug high, you feel worse than you ever imagined. There was so much out there when you first started looking. You need to find a little more advanced level since you have obviously "graduated" from the elementary levels of pornography. You start to look for more graphic pornography that has some shock value but also awakens the responses you once had when you first started. The areas you begin to look at were once repulsive to you, but you now find them enticing. The rush of endorphins that bring the old sensations back over-ride the disgust you once had for this new subject matter.

### 3. Desensitization

After a time of getting into more and more disgusting material, your emotions are finally, permanently severed. No matter what depths of degradation you go to, the images no longer arouse you. There is nothing else you can find that will bring back the arousal you once felt. You become desperate in your search for the old thrill and the temporary sense of comfort it once gave you, but it is no longer there. No other relationship matters to you as much as regaining the feeling you once had. But, you can't find it. You begin to feel numb towards the images you see. Even the most graphic porn is no longer arousing.

### 4. Acting out

In a last measure of desperation you recall the images of sexual illusion you have stored in your memory bank. These scenarios have been rehearsed over and over in your mind. Now you plan how you can begin to physically act out the images. This becomes the over-riding obsession of your life, planning your participation in what was once only mental fantasy. The acting out may eventually include using prostitutes, children, rape, animals, torture, or even, in extreme cases, murder. Reason is thrown away and dangerous liaisons only heighten the excitement; even the fear of getting caught, arrested, infected, or killed becomes a turn-on. The human soul, once created to contain the image of God, has plummeted to its basest level, total depravity.

## God restores and heals

In spite of the dismal description just given of the de-escalation of sexual arousal through pornography, and its end result when one gives himself over to it, God is still God. God is the God who sees into our hearts, hears our cries, and brings true life to those who are repentant.

"A pornographic culture is not one in which pornographic materials are published and distributed, but is one which accepts the ideas about sex on which pornography is based."[23] Our culture's philosophy has become, "Sex is the answer to loneliness." The fixation so many people have with sexual fantasy, while looking for something to alleviate the loneliness they experience from a lack of intimacy, is therefore not surprising. Sexual intimacy is the deepest symbol to the adult heart of what it means to join with another person completely, to be one with that person and enjoy a closeness that compares with none other.

God's answer to our cultures's philosophy comes from Psalm 68:6:

> *"God sets the lonely in families,*
> *he leads forth the prisoners with singing;*
> *but the rebellious live in a sun-scorched land."*

God intended sexual pleasure to bring a special closeness to bind the hearts of husband and wife together in order to establish and protect the unity of the family. Therefore, it is not surprising that within the deep heart of one who has suffered a tremendous loss of intimate connection from childhood there is triggered a strong need for connection at moments of great stress, fear, fatigue or anxiety. The desire to be soothed and comforted comes to the surface, along with the need to alleviate the pain of being disconnected.

The old warning signs of genital tension may accompany the restlessness and anxiety. At this point a person has several choices concerning what to do with the rising temptations. If he[24] chooses the ways God prescribes, he will be as one who has been bound (a prisoner), now set free to follow the Lord with a throng of joyful, singing kindred. For the one who chooses to follow his own, downward spiraling desires however, the end is devastating. He will live in a scorched, arid place without the intimacy his heart needs.

# Chapter 6

# The Action
*The cycle of addiction*

*"Religion that God our Father accepts is this: ...*
*to keep oneself from being polluted by the world."*
(James 1:27)

## Identification of patterns of addiction

If you want to find the healing place of comfort and security in God, rather than follow the world's path, begin by looking for patterns of experiences that trigger the stressful responses that then lead you to seek a pornographic fix. Seeing these patterns from your past can help you begin to understand the cycles you continue to fall into today.

Perhaps Jon's story, which follows, is a familiar scenario. Watch the order of successive responses that Jon has, once an old familiar emotion is triggered within him. As long as he rides the wave of his emotions he is headed down his usual, destructive pathway. As you read his account, notice where, at any time, he could have interrupted the cycle he was in to disrupt the familiar resolution.

## Jon's story

Jon's field supervisor has been asking Jon to do more tasks than normal for the past few weeks. The workload in the whole company has increased and everyone is putting in overtime. Jon already has a desk piled high with backed-up job reports to tackle when his supervisor comes into his office on a Friday morning with a stack of folders for Jon to analyze a.s.a.p.

This new assignment triggers a helplessness within Jon and a sense of inadequacy that overrides the reasonable response of dialoguing with the supervisor. He says nothing, but spends the whole weekend at his desk. However, instead of feeling he has made a significant dent in the paperwork, he feels bogged down with the amount of work still left undone. Although attempting to get through his work, he feels he is slogging through mud.

By Monday morning Jon has become so obsessed with a sense of failure that his work efficiency diminishes. Mistakes are found in what he did over the weekend, giving place for the supervisor to criticize his competency.

A paralysis of clear thinking takes over and Jon begins to spiral out of control. He considers quitting, but knows that would be foolishly throwing away his benefits and pension plan. The thought comes to Jon's mind of one thing he knows would bring a temporary relief to his anxiety – the latest hard-core porn magazine he can pick up at the newsstand on the corner. He hasn't bought one in a while and he can soothe himself with it after he leaves the office. Soon nothing else matters except finding that moment of comfort to his wounded soul. He believes if he can just get a quick fix to calm his anxiety he can then think more clearly and be more organized. For the rest of the afternoon, all Jon thinks about is how he is going to reward himself for simply staying on the job.

Jon's "comfort fix" might be anything from a drink of whiskey, a cigarette, a glazed doughnut, a buying spree, a visit to an Internet porn site, a sexual encounter, to masturbation. And it might actually relieve his tension and give him the temporary respite he needs to regroup and apply himself more efficiently. But Jon is flirting with disaster by going in the direction of self-medication.

## An objective look at Jon's situation

Let's look at Jon's situation with an eye of reason. This was a relatively simple and normal beginning towards a slippery slope – a supervisor was unaware of Jon's already full work schedule.

Jon could have chosen to respond immediately to his supervisor's request by saying something like, "Let me show you what else is on my plate today. Perhaps you would like to help me prioritize all these jobs so that I can be of greatest assistance to the company." Then Jon would have shared the burden with someone else in a responsible position and also, would have identified and brought to the light, the stress-causing problem.

Of course the supervisor could have responded unreasonably and the process would have begun again, but continuing to identify the problem is a huge step towards finding healing for anxiety-driven responses.

Jon's instant sense of helplessness and inadequacy under pressure did not originate with his supervisor's requests. The situation just enabled Jon to tap into an internal reaction to anxiety that had probably been with him since conscious memory or before. He was reluctant to dialogue with his supervisor because dialogue was not his natural response to conflict. Why? Was there little dialogue in his family as a child? Was he afraid of being criticized by an authority figure? Was he afraid of being ridiculed in public? Of exposing his facade of competency? What other fears were lurking within Jon's heart as he began to hide away within himself?

There is no way Jon will be able to know how his emotions originated within his soul unless he asks God and then listens to what God reveals.

### Call a trusted accountability and prayer partner

Another option Jon could have chosen was to make a quick phone call to explain the situation to a friend or pastor with whom he has already shared his problem of pornography, masturbation, drinking, or whatever. This would, of course, be contingent upon the fact that Jon has recognized that he indeed has a problem, and has been willing to admit it to someone else. This "911" call for help would enable Jon to admit that there are some things he can't do without the assistance of others, a trait he has always considered "weak."

The ability to begin to dialogue with a trusted person who will be prayerfully objective, without having to make excuses for why he is feeling so anxious, would be helpful for Jon to then begin a meaningful dialogue with his supervisor.

It is comforting just to know that someone is lifting you up in prayer when your life seems out of control, besides the fact that there is real power in the prayers of the faithful. Through them the power of God is released to disengage the immediacy of the pressure until you give Him the opportunity to do some deep healing in your soul.

### Leave the scene for a moment to disengage the tension

Just leaving the scene of the turmoil for a few moments can disengage the anxiety if you have not allowed it to control you. Jon could have gone to the men's room to have a moment of privacy to pray. He could have washed his face and hands as a reminder that God, when asked, washes him with the Blood of Jesus and cleanses him with holiness. Jon could have walked outside for a few moments to breathe deeply of fresh air, reminding himself that God's breath brings life to his soul, whereas self-pitying, destructive thought patterns bring death.

### Exercise moral effort

Jon could also have made a conscious decision: "No matter how much this hurts I will press through this difficulty and not give in to the temptations that I am having."

Many people ask us if such pain can kill them. The answer is an unqualified, "**No!**" It is the behavior that results from the pain that kills. We have far more reserves of moral effort within us than we realize. Just beginning to act on what we know is right will often give us the momentum and energy to then continue the journey away from self-pity, anxiety and tension. We always have choices and when we are trying to think in a fog of emotional pain we make terrible choices. At such times we cannot rely on our own responses but must rely on the authority of God's Word and the choices He lays out for us when we ask Him.

Here are the steps of moral effort one man shared with us. He kept this list with him in his wallet at all times for several months and relied on this procedure to get whole.

1.  I realize I am not alone.
2.  I have changed my prayer from "take this from me," to "I give it to You, Lord."

3. I have become accountable to a close male Christian friend.

4. I view this struggle as a matter of winning or losing. I am tired of losing.

5. I have asked my wife to forgive me and to pray for me.

6. I have stopped masturbating and am using a calendar to mark the days I abstain.

We did not describe Jon's having a fall. We described a serious moment of temptation. Many men and women are tempted to relieve their anxieties in sexual fantasies, visits to porn sites and accompanying masturbation. This is an unhealthy response to anxiety, but it is not necessarily addictive to everyone who goes there.

## Temptation is always lurking

Pornography is always available, in a variety of ways, to fill the chasms in hearts that never got mended in holy ways. It is always there, ready to bring a titillation and temporary comfort to the outer layer of the problems of the soul. The need for a quick fix can be so great that one may forget the option of searching or waiting for the deep total healing that God wants to bring to the roots of the neediness. Even Christians, knowing that the character of God is to heal His people, can be distracted from the deep, thorough healing that He promises. The fast-food, drive-through mentality of our age has affected the ways in which God's people, as well as unbelievers, are looking for relief, and are reluctant to wait for God's timing.

The person who is looking for pornography to ease his/her anxiety and emptiness is always dealing with surface symptoms, wanting to quickly alleviate a raw, primitive hunger with a quick, topical salve rather than face into the painful wounds of the past and seek godly help. It is not unlike the person who has chronic stomach pains and chooses to only take more antacids and over-the-counter relief rather than go to a doctor for a proper diagnosis and effective treatment. The relief of the symptoms seems to be more urgent than the permanent correction of the problem. *I just don't want it to hurt!*

To continue the physiological analogy, perhaps the person

with stomach pain is fearful of discovering a very serious disease, having to come out of denial, having to bring it to the light, take responsibility for it and discuss it with health care professionals. What if it is *very* serious, perhaps cancer? Maybe it runs in the family and there is the fear of death. "Besides," one incorrectly rationalizes, "the antacids seem to be working – most of the time." It just seems that you have to take a lot more medication than you previously took to achieve the desired numbing effect.

But meanwhile, the cancer is still there, growing and multiplying. It is always beneath the surface, screaming, with its painful warning signs, for surgery and healing. And meanwhile the person is slowly dying, with an addiction to the ever-growing medications and the harm they are causing.

## Taking the bait

"Okay," you say, "I admit it. I do use pornography once in a while, sometimes just out of curiosity, sometimes when I need a break. But I really don't think my problem is nearly as bad as the pictures you've painted. What I do doesn't hurt anybody. Nearly every guy I know has done the same thing. I don't let it control my life."

There are probably many men, and women too, who have investigated pornography without being pulled into a dependent relationship with it. This frequently happens with teenagers who are coming into an awareness of their sexuality and are exploring some of the temptations of the world. The very *least* consequence that will occur in their lives is that they will retain an unhealthy residue of distorted images of man and woman in their imaginations. They will forever see themselves and others in ways far inferior – less human – than that which God intended. Their images of sexuality will be soiled with the pollution of sinful fantasies and illusion. Their need to confess this practice and to be cleansed by God is vital, even if it was only restricted to earlier years, only done out of curiosity, and/or only done occasionally.

According to Bob Gordon, a member of our *Journey to Wholeness in Christ* prayer team, these occasional voyeurs are like a fish that has been cleanly hooked. The bait has been thrown in the water and the fish has nibbled on it and even, perhaps, made a clean bite. The fish definitely has a hook in its mouth but it can either spit it out or the hook can be cleanly removed and the fish can be tossed back into the water and still survive.

## Gut-hooked and pan-fried

It is a far different fishing story that depicts the many men and women we have previously described who have a "hole in their soul" for real intimacy. These are the ones who have suffered a deficit of proper, healthy emotional bonding and attachment with mother and/or father in early childhood and who lack a sense of being, a true identity. If this deficit was never filled in appropriate ways as they grew older perhaps they have attempted to find their identities in their gifts, jobs, religion or talents, rather than just securely *being* the persons God created them to be.

Some men and women with such deficits have no idea who they are supposed to be apart from the personae they wear. These personae may be so well developed that the person may appear to be very confident and secure. But beneath the carefully constructed facade may lie the agitation of a mass of insecurities and emptiness.

As Bob Gordon describes them, these are like the fish that is starving for something of substance, grasping here and there, ignoring the hook, only seeking the appealing lure. This fish literally gulps the bait and swallows it, hook, line and sinker. It becomes "gut-hooked." To try to remove the hook from this fish is to literally tear out its guts. Although it has been temporarily satiated by the bait, barring a miracle, it will surely die.

Those who have been "gut-hooked" by pornography thought they were finding an instant, responsibility-free, secretive, exciting balm to alleviate hidden pain and insecurities. In fact sometimes the hidden pain of deep emptiness is relatively unapparent until after the drug-like rush of titillation that accompanies pornography floods through the mind and body. When the rush abates and the soul tries to accommodate once again the wounded heart, a hidden sense of non-attachment, pain and emptiness may be uncovered that can, at times, become unbearable. All one can think about is the next hit. It initiates a dreadful cycle.

## Who is susceptible?

Generally, pornography is going to be more appealing to men than to women. However, often-wounded women too, can become hooked by the practice because of their deep inner needs to connect relationally that were never met in proper ways. Because men, by both nature and conditioning, are less relational and more easily stimulated sexually by visual images, they find the salve of pornography an instant camouflage for an empty heart.

Women (and some men) may gravitate to erotic literature and romance novels as a primary source for spawning such an active sexual fantasy life. However, some visual sexual images can come from the fantasies constructed within one's own imagination. Those with really active imaginations and highly developed picture-making faculties have no trouble manufacturing their own little worlds to which they can retreat.

Many times we minister to men or women who are ready to renounce the practices of adultery or homosexuality or pornography in their lives, and yet they still have a dreadful time giving up their fantasy lives. They may be ready to quit acting out in sexual ways, but it is much harder for them to deny access to the fantasy life within. In fact it often seems virtually impossible to them to do so. Everyone will benefit from the regular spiritual exercise of cleansing the imagination (see Chapter 8).

Men and women who have found it very difficult to form healthy attachments to others may find temporary solace through the *simulation* of sexual attachments and erotic relationships without ever having to become emotionally or intimately involved with another person. Their desire to fill the aching need for authentic emotional attachment is thus deviated into an imaginary sexual attachment with every aspect of the "relationship" under their control. They find an alternative to disclosing the nature of their emptiness and anxieties and being vulnerable to another person. To the one who carries a lingering sense of rejection and abandonment, the thought of being vulnerable is wrought with fear and anxiety. And yet the need for attachment persists.

## The cycle of addiction

Once begun, the habitual practice of pornography takes on a life of its own. The addict always thinks he is in control, able to quit whenever he wants to, but like the drunk who insists he can stop drinking anytime, he never wants to stop.

The reason why it becomes so difficult to come out of the cycle is that patterns of behavior and response are imprinted into the brain. Once acknowledged, emotions such as fear, loneliness, emptiness and anxiety keep popping up in their heads, begging to be healed. The repeated reminders of our weaknesses are God's way of making us aware of our need for His order in our lives. Unfortunately, too many people wait until their pain gets bigger than their pride and their suffering gets bigger than their shame before they cry out for His help.

Instead of responding immediately to the pain and suffering in godly ways, so many people tend to "self-medicate" the problems, thus forming a cycle that requires more and more "medication" for them to continue to function. These cycles are repeated with growing intensity and regularity. As they are repeated they move in a constant downward spiral (as illustrated below), becoming more imprinted in the brain.

*The downward spiral of pornographic dependency*

tension
anxiety
deep loneliness
pain
temptation
flirtation
seduction
yielding
submersion
release
shame
guilt
remorse
resolve to abstain
ignoring the problem
false sense of security
tension
anxiety . . .

In this continuing downward spiral there are ebbs and flows of emotions, some good, some bad. There are periods of relief that give false hopes and there are times so desperate that all caution is thrown to the wind. Looking back over the illustrated downward path you can apply any addictive behavior to the spiraling track – alcoholism, over-eating, drugs, gambling, over-spending, etc.

## Pressure points

A common trigger for addictive behavior is the internalization of real or imagined pressure from one's environment (see Jon's story earlier in this chapter). We often hear about a man having a "mid-life crisis" when the responsibilities of life and family come crashing down, sending him off into bizarre behavioral patterns. This is the stereotypical scenario of a man, married for twenty-five or more years, suddenly leaving his wife and children and taking up with a woman younger than his children.

What has he done? He has felt the increasing pressure of normal family responsibilities without the security of an inner sense of being and affirmation. He has not found a sense of being in his role of husband, in being a father or in his work. He probably never found it as a child with his parents. He just knows that this may be his last chance for happiness and he falsely hopes that he will be able to sustain the rush of emotional affirmation that comes in the first stages of a new relationship. And so he throws aside everything once dear to him and believes he can start over.

It is an illusion. It is only a matter of time before he will realize that the new honey in his life cannot fill the deprivation voids from childhood any more than others have. He needs to be filled with what only God has to give.

Occasionally one hears of a woman doing the same thing, abandoning her husband and children to find a new life for herself so that her needs can be met. She is tired of pouring out herself for others while feeling such an emptiness inside. She makes poor choices. Instead of seeking healing she destroys a family. The sense of being she craves can only come from God.

Most of the men who come to us for prayer about their

addictions to pornography, whether heterosexual or homosexual, will tell us of the cyclic dimensions to their involvement
with porn, depending upon the pressures of their family situations or their businesses. When circumstances are going well,
they may go months or even years without thinking about
previous states of frustration, emptiness and the lure of pornography. But when there are increasingly heavy demands upon
one's life, the old feelings pop up like weeds in a garden.

For one man the pressure point may be a family crisis, such as
an unmarried child expecting a baby; for another it may be an
overwhelming burden of financial responsibility and mounting
debt; for another the illness of a family member that leaves him
feeling helpless; for another, the rejection of losing a job, or a
staggering workload.

Perhaps it has been a long time since he has thought about
pornography, but now, under this intense pressure of his circumstances, he falls right into the cycle. The basic need for attachment and security has always been there but the jolt of facing
something he can't control has set him off. A latent fear of
abandonment may surface, accompanied by the innate need
to be comforted and feel secure. *No one will come for me. I don't
know how to take care of myself, let alone the others who are
depending on me.*

Reluctant to confess his neediness and weakness to anyone,
perhaps even to himself, he is desperate to find a way to cope
with his confusing emotions so that he can function. The lure of
pornography is the most popular coping mechanism the world
has to offer.

## The thrill of pursuit

Once you begin to experiment with pornographic activities the
focus can easily change from the conquest (the orgasmic release)
to the chase. Not every pornographic experience is geared
towards the goal of masturbation or sexual intercourse. There is
a heightened sense of exhilaration and escapism in the pursuit
itself. In the intricate, time-consuming plans and anticipation of
the act there often comes a more thrilling and satisfying high
than the release itself. After the rush of the sexual release the
moment is gone. But in the hours and even days leading up to

the moment there is the sense of an absence of pressure and emptiness. The illusory life takes on such a reality that the unpleasantness of real circumstances pales in comparison. This can even be carried to the extreme situation where literally *nothing* and *no one* matters but the fantasy itself.

One man told us about meticulously planning out a fantasy encounter with a sexual partner for months. The minute details of what he would say, what she would say, what she would look like, how he would feel, where they would meet, what he would give her, etc., kept him so totally occupied that he had no time to worry or deal with the very real problems going on in his family. He began to become absorbed with his fantasy world, aided by Internet porn.

This particular man eventually actually acted out his fantasy. When he finally met with the woman (a stranger he had only "met" on the Internet) for the express purpose of having sexual intercourse, he was disappointed in her immediately. She didn't look like she was supposed to; she didn't sound like his dream woman; she didn't say the right things. However, since he had arranged the whole thing and had been so looking forward to the moment, he went through with it, only to be overwhelmingly disappointed and filled with shame afterwards. Yes, he had the sexual release, but looking back on the whole experience, he would describe the fantasy as being far more exciting than the reality of acting it out.

## Acting out the cycle

### 1. Tension and anxiety

The tension and anxiety produced in your body and mind are like flashing, warning lights and screaming sirens: **There is an internal problem! Get help!** This anxiety may present itself either as an agitated restlessness or as a numbing deadness. Both are warning signs that all is not well.

Suppressed anxieties may be triggered by the pressures of finances, family and/or fatigue. A sense of inadequacy and helplessness begins to pervade every activity. The more you try to accommodate all the demands of your life the more the tension builds:

- Leave me alone!
- You just don't understand!
- Hurry up!
- Shut up!
- Give me some space!

If external circumstances change considerably you may feel better temporarily, but, if ignored, it is just a matter of time before something else triggers the anxieties.

### 2. Deep loneliness and pain

When the initial warning signs are ignored your body may actually experience loneliness and deprivation to the extent that there is physical pain. It may be chest pain, headaches, confusion, stomach cramps or genital tension. It can be manifested in many ways, but all you know is that you have to have relief. You may project your pain out onto others, further alienating those closest to you and bringing even more isolation.

Some of your most piercing accusations of others at this point may really be the long-suppressed cries of the wounded child:

- You don't care what happens to me.
- You're selfish.
- You never really loved me.
- Nobody ever gives me what I need!

### 3. Temptation

In your pain you remember what has alleviated suffering in the past. It may not be a conscious remembering so much as an intuitive sense that this is what you need to get through this one more time. You are tempted by playing with memories in your mind:

- If I could only sneak away for just a little while to do something for myself.
- I need a little time alone to make myself feel better.
- I know what I need better than anyone.
- How can I do this so it will look like I am working?

At this point you can still cry out to God for healing and seek some help for the real problem. This is the time to act on previous healthy choices you have made. Temptation is not a sin; it is what you do about it that matters.

### 4. Flirtation

Temptation, when sustained, leads to flirtation, actually recalling, not just what you can do, but how it will feel. As the anticipation of the act grows more real than the good of reason you are hooked, seduced into a lie of relief and you yield to the pictures, the games, the phone call, the chat room, the magazines, the whatever:

- Yes! I deserve this.
- I need this.
- It will feel great!
- If I work hard this morning I will reward myself this afternoon.

You will begin to bargain with yourself about working now to play later; being considerate to your wife by helping her clean up the kitchen after dinner so that you can later spend some time at the computer.

### 5. Submersion

Once the lie is believed, the decision is made, and the first step is taken, you are submerged. It is like another person has taken over the controls of your life. The pain is forgotten in the excitement of the anticipation, the planning, the total submersion of one's self into the illusion. This stage can last for minutes, hours or even days. For many, it is the most exhilarating stage of the cycle.

It will now have to play to the end until the relief comes. There is a loss of reason and common sense, a departure from reality. You lie to yourself and to others. You are in denial about what you are really doing and your wounded emotions rule.

Elements of danger can even enter in at this point, such as disclosing personal information over the Internet, deciding to meet with strangers to act out fantasies, risking getting caught or even danger for the pleasure of the moment:

- I don't care if I'm caught.
- I don't care who knows.
- I don't care what happens.
- I can't let this end.

This is the point of no return. It is the story of the well-respected city official who is caught in the men's dressing room at the local department store in a homosexual encounter, or the evangelist who is arrested with a prostitute. It is also the husband and father secretly masturbating before the family computer.

### 6. Release
After the release of endorphins into the brain through masturbation or sexual intercourse you feel the release you had anticipated. The tension and anxieties are abated and you have a momentary sense of well-being. The pain may have disappeared but the release is never as satisfying as you thought it would be or as exciting as the anticipation and preparation. There has been no intimate relationship involved in the act to imprint the moment of pleasure into a cumulative memory bank of loving attachment.

### 7. Shame, guilt and remorse
Disdain for what you have done sets in immediately. Right on the coat tails of the illusion of relief comes shame:

- Why did I do that?
- I feel dirty.
- This is disgusting behavior.
- Those are sleazy people, only in it for the money.
- I am a sleazy person, a pervert.
- I am an embarrassment to my family.
- What if they found out?
- What if I'd gotten caught?
- What was I thinking?

Shame is supposed to turn into real guilt. Guilt is a gift from God to show us when we need to confess our sins. *I have sinned.*

*Against my spouse, against my family, and against God. He made me for more than this. I need help.*

In the pornographic cycle however, guilt does not lead to confession of sin as it is supposed to; instead it takes you to a place of feeling sorry for yourself rather than feeling sorry for the action:

- I am so pitiful, just a weak person.
- I should have known better.
- No wonder no one appreciates me.

Genuine remorse is feeling rotten about the fact that you are a sinner and it always leads to confession and forgiveness. Remorse in the pornographic cycle is more concerned about the fact that you either got caught, or might get caught, or are afraid you're getting in over your head, or you are spending too much money entering web sites, or not working hard enough, etc. It's still "all about you."

> *"Godly sorrow brings repentance that leads to salvation, and leaves no regret, but worldly sorrow brings death."*
>
> (2 Corinthians 7:10)

### 8. Resolve to abstain and ignoring the problem

This so-called remorse then leads to a new resolve to abstain:

- I need to try harder.
- I'm not going to do this anymore.
- Next week I'll think about getting an Internet monitor.
- I'm going to burn all those magazines.
- I'm going to be a better spouse and parent.
- I'm going to spend more time doing real work at the office.

This resolve may last a day or a week, perhaps even several months. Because you have made another "new year's resolution" you falsely think the situation is taken care of and so, the problem is ignored – until another set of external circumstances, a word of criticism, a perceived rejection, or a time of loneliness uncovers the old familiar tension and anxiety.

Sometimes a prolonged absence of anxiety for one who has no deep sense of being rooted in his heart, will cause him to feel he doesn't deserve the peace, or that it won't last, and will lead him to sabotage whatever good is happening to him:

- I don't deserve this.
- It never lasts in my life.
- I don't want to be disappointed later.
- It never happens to me.
- Maybe something bad is about to happen.

This dangerous kind of introspection will lead to the destruction of all that is good, thus bringing on the tension and anxiety, once more beginning the cycle.

The cycle is not inevitable, no matter how long or how deeply you have been trapped by it. It is not impossible to come free from the downward and ever-deepening suction of its pull. Coming free demands honesty and perseverance, perhaps the hardest work you have ever done, but if you really want to experience abundant life as God promised and has reserved for you, you can do it. Many others have already done it and will be cheerleaders for you along the way.

Like David, once you decide to totally trust in God and His strength instead of your own, you will have a weapon that can take down the strongest selfish desires, the most deeply imprinted bad habit patterns and the most distorted thought processes. These are giant enemies that seem to call for nuclear weapons, not just determination. Yet God has nuclear power for you to use, if you choose to do it His way.

# Chapter 7

## House Lights Up
### Exposing the problem to the light

*"For God, who said, 'Let light shine out of darkness,' made his light shine in our hearts to give us the light of the knowledge of the glory of God in the face of Christ. But we have this treasure in jars of clay to show that this all-surpassing power is from God and not from us. We are hard pressed on every side, but not crushed; perplexed, but not in despair; persecuted, but not abandoned; struck down, but not destroyed."*
(2 Corinthians 4:6–9)

Admitting to myself I had the problem was the first big step I took. Secondly, I broke the barrier of fear of telling others. Fear can control the mind if it is allowed to do so. This was definitely the hardest step to take. Once it was out in the open and into the light, the burden of fear and secrecy lifted. The fear, I remember, was that of being found out. Once I told my wife, fear no longer had a hold on me. Then I knew I had to talk about it with somebody apart from my wife. I knew a dear couple of Christian friends who also happened to be counselors. They were non-judgmental and were able to keep a confidence. This was extremely important to me when I was feeling so vulnerable.

I am very aware that everyday I need to be careful about what I watch on TV or look at in the bookstore. An even more dangerous element for me is the Internet. This addiction to pornography used to control my life. Now I know I have a choice and I choose God's way.

*Donald*

John Stoltenberg tells about his attendance at a press luncheon given by the Attorney General's Commission on Pornography for magazine editors. A woman member of the Commission asked the question, " 'What's the harm of pornography – a paper cut?' The line got a big laugh."[1]

Once you are committed to answering in truth the question, "So what's the harm with pornography?" then what are you going to do with your answer? Just *knowing* that pornography is a dangerous substitute for true attachment and intimacy, that it brings disastrous, addictive results both to the person involved and those around him, and that it damages the moral fabric of society is not enough. Flailing around in deep water is ludicrous when there are lifelines being thrown to you. You will need to keep your eyes on those lifelines in the midst of the waves and keep swimming steadfastly towards them. They need to become more important to you than the pull of the deep.

## The lifeline of truth

When Jesus told His disciples, *"The truth will set you free,"*[2] He also revealed that He is the truth.[3] Because of that when you are in Him and relying on Him you are empowered to walk in truth, to speak it and cherish it. You soon learn that when you bring all of your life into His truth, you are first stung to the core by the realization that you fall short, and then comforted by the fact that He has a better way. It is His better way that sets you free. This becomes your lifeline.

## Speak truth to yourself

If you have lived in ignorance, denial and with coping mechanisms most of your life, speaking the truth to yourself will be difficult, something you will most likely struggle against for some time. Perhaps your spouse, a friend, or your own conscience has already been telling you that you have a problem with pornography. How have you reacted to these voices? With anger? Denial? Dismissal? Unbelief?

It takes a great deal of courage to take off the defensive armor of the world and stand naked and vulnerable before the mirror, admitting your own weakness and even depravity. Until you are able to do this however, you will have a very difficult time seeing the pain and deprivation of the past that paved the way for your current behavior. Coming out of denial in one area of your life enables you to see reality in many other areas.

One man confided to us,

"I finally had to admit that I am a sex addict. I can't even believe I'm saying that; it sounds so perverted. This was a surprise to me because I never even liked sex all that much; I wasn't obsessed with it the way I thought a sex addict would be. But I realized that everytime I felt inadequate or weak or couldn't face family problems I would revert to a fantasy world and for a period of time, maybe weeks, that's all I wanted to do. I would imagine an idealized woman in my fantasies and believe that she would give me what I lacked. Eventually I would act out the fantasy with someone and that would be the end of it for long periods of time. This behavior, even though it didn't happen very often, kept me from growing into the man I was never allowed to be because of the severe dysfunction in my childhood home. I'm embarrassed to say it but the thing that caused me to finally admit it was getting caught. However, in spite of the pain I caused my wife, we have both grown up and gotten filled up in godly ways. Our marriage is better than ever."

Whether or not this man could be technically classified as a "sex addict" is debatable, but his ability to name his sin, see it in the light of Christ and begin to work on his long-standing neurosis, brought him out of denial and into a glorious healing. As he stated, and as is often the case, he was only willing to do this when "he got caught." A lot of personal and perhaps public embarrassment can be avoided when one is willing to tear off the personae and get real before the Lord.

## Speak truth to God

Speaking the truth to God is called confession. It does not require a priest or minister, although they may be helpful, but it requires a brutal honesty without excuses or rationalization. Look at the entry you made in your journal back in Chapter 4.

Hopefully, that helped you to come out of denial about your involvement with pornography.

One of the sins you may tend to overlook as you make your confession to God (perhaps in the presence of another person) is the sin of adultery. Whether or not you, like Pastor Nors, have never physically touched another person in a sexual way, if you have thought of illusory partners or fantasized about adultery, you have sinned against your marriage partner and against God. To be able to name pornography as the sin of adultery, ask yourself, *Who was I thinking about in the release?* There is your answer.

> *"Is anyone of you in trouble? He should pray . . . If he has sinned, he will be forgiven. Therefore confess your sins to each other and pray for each other so that you may be healed."*
> (James 5:13a–16)

- I have sinned.
- Pornography is a sin against myself, You and others.
- I am guilty of this and many accompanying practices.

## Speak truth to your spouse

If you are married it is vital that you confess your sin to your wife and ask for her forgiveness and her prayer support. Probably she will be more surprised that you value her trust by being honest with her than she will be about your involvement with pornography. You have more serious problems in your marriage than just pornography if your wife has had no clue that you've been distant, avoidant and ambivalent. It will probably come as somewhat of a relief to finally know the facts instead of her worst imaginings.

As we mentioned earlier, women have special antennae for these sorts of things. The following story illustrates this very graphically.

## Carol's story

Carol, a young attractive woman, asked me for prayer about her marriage at a Pastoral Care Ministries conference in the Midwest.

She really praised God for the work He had done in her life and in her husband's over the last few years. About three years before, her relationship with her husband had been dreadful. There had been little communication and intimacy and she soon found out there had been lots of secrets. Eventually, her husband had confessed to her that he had been heavily into pornography on the Internet. It had been consuming so much of his life that he had grown to actually resent her any time she tried to draw him away from it.

Through their dependence on God's strength and some good counsel he had renounced his involvement and had begun to receive a lot of healing for himself and for their relationship. She had been so blessed by the godly marriage they had been building. She had begun to really enjoy the sexual dimension of their relationship and thought everything was going very well.

What she brought to our prayer session was the need to know what was wrong with her. About six months before, she sensed that her husband was pulling away from the intimacy they had established. She had mentioned it to him several times but he would deny it and suggest that it might be her problem, not his.

She had begun to dread sexual intimacy until finally, about a month before we met, she refused to participate at all. She was aware of the hard work her husband had done on their marriage in the past and now wondered what could be wrong with her to sabotage their happiness.

I asked her several questions and we spent some time in prayer. Specifically, I asked God to reveal any hidden reasons for the noticeable differences that began six months before. Basically, I prayed the "paint-the-dragon-red" prayer over her.

Two days later she found me again at the conference to tell me the astounding news. She had called her husband, out on the West Coast, the night before. It was a routine call to tell him about the conference and that she was praying for their marriage. His response was God's answer to our prayers.

Her husband said that he awoke suddenly out of a sound sleep the night before, knowing he had to confess to her what he had been doing. *Six months before*, feeling a great deal of pressure about some work-related problems, he had flirted with Internet pornography once again and had eventually gotten into it deeper than ever. Because of all the hard work they had done before on their marriage, and because of his embarrassment and shame, he had refused to tell her what was going on and had allowed her to take the blame for the current problems they were having. He felt so ashamed and asked her forgiveness and her help.

As Carol related to me what he had said, her emotions were all over the place. She was angry with him for sure, but there was also a genuine relief that she was not crazy and was not imagining things as he had often suggested. Over the last three years she had learned, along with her husband, the true sources of his insecurities. They had both forgiven his parents for emotional neglect in his early years. They had learned to rely on God to fill the deficits he had grown up with. And she had learned that, no matter what she did, she was not equipped to fill the deep voids in his soul. Only God could do that.

She had learned how to pray for him without accusing him, how to affirm him in holy ways, and she had learned how to trust God in what had seemed impossible. Because God had brought healing in the past she knew He could do it again.

It was not OK that her husband had lied to her for months and she would have to choose to forgive him and place her anger at the Cross, but he had assured her on the phone that he was willing to start over with her help and God's. She left for home with hope.

In their case God brought the circumstances to the light in a direct way. If you are confused about your spouse's behavior (or your own), you too may need to ask God to "paint the dragon red" and then trust Him to do so, avoiding accusations and threats that only bring more distrust into the relationship.

## Speak truth to someone you can trust

This is the time to bring all your secrets to the light, vowing not to live in a dark, murky fog anymore. Your wife is probably not the best person to tell all the gory details about your involvement with pornography. This does not mean that you should lie to her or refuse to answer her questions, but any information about specific experiences you have had with pornography that you relate to her voluntarily will most likely be less than helpful.

There's something about the female mind that wants to know all the details about such things her husband has been involved with, even though it is extremely painful. If you give her information that is too explicit then she too, will have the pornographic images to deal with. Most likely she will want to ask you questions that will not help either of you get whole. The best thing to do is, *with her*, prayerfully give to God all the images you have taken into yourself, to be placed upon the Cross. Then, neither of you needs to be burdened by them any longer.

You will need an accountability relationship with another person such as a pastor, friend or counselor. This should be a person who will continue to call you into wholeness, not empathize with you or make light of the struggle you are having. You should make it clear to the person who agrees to meet with you regularly that you want to be accountable. You give this person permission to exhort you, check up on you and challenge you to move forward in your wholeness.

This person should not be your wife. She cannot and should not be the "porn police" for you. This will destroy further the intimacy the two of you are attempting to rebuild.

## Wife talk

This is the time for us to speak to the wives as well as the husbands. You too, need to bring to the light your pain and those hidden feelings of shame and rejection.

Like Carol, the revelation of your husband's secret life of pornography will provoke a myriad of emotions in you, his wife: shock, pain, shame, embarrassment, a sense of rejection, insecurity, anger, disappointment, feelings of inadequacy, betrayal, etc. You may alternately blame yourself:

- If only I were prettier . . . sexier . . . younger . . . thinner . . .

and then blame him:

- How could he do this to me?
- I'll never trust him again . . .
- I won't ever be able to believe anything he tells me . . .

Because of the devastation this kind of invasion brings into a marriage it will be difficult for you to make sound decisions for some time. This is not the time to vehemently announce that you are leaving him, or that he must leave or that you want a divorce. It is also not the time to tell all your friends what has happened, forcing them to take sides, or to turn your children against their father. You need as little pressure as possible from others so that you will be able to hear God clearly.

You will need someone to talk to who will help you hear God. Choose wisely the friend, prayer partner, pastor or counselor who will be there for you but not make biased, rash decisions about your actions. You need godly support at this time, not sentimental sympathy. (Probably, your mother is not your best choice as a support person.)

It will be necessary for you too, to spend time with some of the same steps your husband is taking. You will have to know the appropriate place to put all your negative emotions and choose to forgive him. It will be an act of your will, not your feelings. But out of this choice will come the ability to collaborate with God in the healing process instead of being hindered by your own sin of unforgiveness.

## Forgiveness for the wife

While choosing not to forgive is a sin, choosing to be cautious in the relationship and setting healthy boundaries is good sense. Forgiving does not mean that it was really not that important and didn't matter. It doesn't mean that there are no conse-quences. It doesn't mean that now he's confessed and is sorry, you should just go on as if everything is normal.

Forgiveness is an act of turning over your need to be judge and corrections officer for your husband's crime. You are choosing to put him in God's hands and to trust God to do what is right, just and healing. You are choosing to separate yourself from his sin and not be defined by his problems. This does not mean that you will not care deeply, or be consumed with intense feelings, both good and bad, for a long period of time. While forgiveness is an act of the will at a moment in time, its effects are worked out over a period of time. When Jesus admonished us to forgive seventy times seven,[4] He showed us that there should be no limit on how many times we forgive. Each act of your will to obey God allows more of His healing grace into both you and the one you are forgiving.

The following song was written by our worship leader at a *Journey to Wholeness in Christ* conference while Conlee was teaching on forgiveness.

*"I Choose to Forgive"*

I choose to forgive
I choose to forgive
And release to You those who have wounded me.
I choose to forgive
I choose to forgive
From my heart, by Your grace
I forgive.

Lord, I choose to forgive
I choose to forgive
And accept myself
As You've accepted me
I choose to forgive
I choose to forgive
From my heart, by Your grace
I forgive.[5]

As you indeed release any offender into God's hands you are then free to become the person He intended you to be, no longer defined by another person's transgressions (or even by their successes). Whatever problems your husband has had since birth, whatever ways he has chosen to act out his fears or pain, whatever sins he has committed, do not define who you are. You are not made to carry his shame. You are fearfully and wonderfully made, unique in your relationship with your heavenly Father, who has words of love and affirmation for you.

## A Wife's Shame

I can nearly always recognize the garment of shame when I see it coming towards me. I've seen so many people wearing it that it almost begins to look like one of the faddish styles of our age.

There's the "grunge" look, the "hip-hop" look, the "unisex" look – and the "shame" look. It's sad to see how pervasive it has become, enough to be labeled and easily identified.

The way it often appears to me is like a gray shroud enveloping a body. It hides beauty and hope and enthusiasm. It steals innocence and eternal childlikeness. It masks life. It does its job quite well for it is a grave cloth, containing death.

There is some shame that is the result of godly contrition. This is the sense of guilt over one's own sins that leads to confession, forgiveness and repentance. We might call it a guilty conscience, or being under conviction. God allows this kind of shame in order to provoke one to confess his sins, receive forgiveness and walk in a new direction. This is healing shame; it takes you somewhere.

However, the *shroud of shame* is a garment that should never have been worn by the wearer. It should have been cast aside a long time ago. It belongs to someone else; it even bears the impression of another's shape. And yet, this misbegotten garment is so often worn by the wrong person that it can easily begin to conform to the shape of the wearer as if it belonged.

## Beth's story

Serving on the ministry team at a healing conference, I saw such a shroud-wearer walking toward me at a break. The nametag said "Beth".

Beth had dark circles under her eyes, a sallow complexion, and long, straight hair that has been carelessly unstyled to provide a covering over her lifeless face. As her eyes darted back and forth to make sure no one was close enough to overhear, she pleaded in a whisper, "I really need prayer to make the most important decision of my life."

"Does this affect only you or other people as well?" I asked.

"Other people."

"What other people?"

"My children."

Beth obviously would have preferred a "silver-bullet" prayer without disclosing any details. She wanted to keep her secrets carefully hidden under her shame-shroud. I've prayed with people long enough to know how important it is to open up the shroud and allow some exposure to the light of truth. It's painful yes, but extremely important. So I asked the more than obvious question.

"This is about leaving your husband, isn't it?"

Beth nodded yes, eyes downcast.

I went out on a limb here, "Is he involved in pornography?"

Again she nodded.

"Adultery, too?"

This time she dared to look right at me and she used her voice. This was progress.

"Yes, all of that."

"How long has this been going on?"

"Eighteen years."

"How long have you been married?"

"Eighteen years."

The shame-shroud Beth was wearing had her husband's imprint all over it, but she pulled it tighter around her as if it would make her invisible. "Lord," I prayed, "give me wisdom and minister Your love to Beth!"

A part of Beth's soul had withered several years before. She obviously needed some resurrection power in her life but she had heard all the platitudes and promises. She had quit believing for wholeness; she just wanted to know if God would allow her to take her children and leave her husband. She needed a huge dose of holy hope from God Himself, not from me. This was one of those occasions when the *Lord-give-me-wisdom* prayer was extremely vital. I suddenly felt compelled to ask Beth another personal question: "Is your husband in ministry?"

At this question Beth began to cry.

"He used to be. He was a youth pastor, but after getting involved in pornography he acted out what he saw in magazines with a girl in the youth group at our church and then he was fired and then we had to move and then it was one meaningless job after another."

"Is he willing to get some help?"

"Oh, yes, he's been to pastors, therapists, counselors and even exorcists. Nothing has helped. He says now there must be no hope for him and he is tired of baring his private life to professionals who have no ability to help him change. I tell you the truth, I've given up too. He says he'd like for things to change, but he's such a different person than the man I thought I married, I hardly know what to believe. I don't even know if I want it to work anymore."

I asked Beth if she had read any of the books out on the effects of pornography. She had read *An Affair of the Mind*[6] and *Living with Your Husband's Secret Wars*,[7] both of which I knew to be informative and helpful. For a while she had held some hope that perhaps her husband would join with some other men who also wanted help, but after seeing no movement in that direction she felt terribly desolate, as though she would forever be the wife of a hard-core pornographer, the husband who defied all the help anyone could offer.

My heart went out to Beth. What a weight she carried on her shoulders! I wished I could put an oxygen tube in her nostrils and have her breathe in New Life to rejuvenate the deadness in her countenance. Instead of wishing for very long, I listened to God. He gave me such a strong impression to have Beth speak to Him in her own words.

"Beth, do you remember how to pray?"

"Of course, I know *how* to pray," she replied defensively.

"How do you pray to God?"

She looked down much like a child who is certain she is about to be punished. She waited for the inevitable scolding and braced herself to receive it. Her only response was a long sigh.

"Beth, you have obviously forgotten what it is like to have intimate dialogue with God. Real intimacy has been so distorted for you in your marriage that you have lost the ability to be intimate with God as well. You are missing the most important connection in your life by neglecting those intimate encounters with your heavenly Father and receiving His love. Let's just talk to Him together, okay?"

Beth nodded and I took her hands in mine to pray. Just the touch of my hands on hers opened up a reservoir of tears within her and I could feel resistance begin to well up within her. She was terrified of having her defensive fortress cracked.

I understood her fear. If she broke, who would be strong for her children? Who would be there to protect them? But this was not the time for human compassion; this was an opportunity for God's love to rush in. She needed to hear His voice once again.

I wrapped my arms around her and simply held her, and my

embrace allowed torrents of grief to come forth. Softly, I said to her, "Beth, see Jesus on the Cross, receiving all your grief into Himself. That is the only acceptable place for all this sorrow, anger, grief and shame to go. Allow Him to gather it all up and take it from you."

After a long period of crying and sobbing, Beth relaxed in my arms and I loosed my hold on her and asked, "What did you see Jesus do with all your pain?"

Her eyes were still closed and there was a peace within her as she saw something I could not see.

"Oh, He kept reaching out to me and bringing all the pain up to His chest. It just went inside Him. I thought a few times that He couldn't hold anymore, but then I would see His arms reaching out to me from the Cross and I would feel more pain rise up inside me and I would give it to Him."

She leaned back in a chair, obviously exhausted. I could see how empty she felt. She had been accumulating a lot of grief for eighteen years. It was time to let God fill her with His love.

I anointed her with healing oil by making the sign of the Cross upon her forehead.[8] She continued to lean back in the chair, her face pointed up toward God.

I prayed aloud, "Lord, You have shown Beth Your mighty Cross and she has seen the power of that Cross to take all her shame and pain and grief. I ask You now to allow her to see the Risen Lord who overcame death on the Cross and receive His love and resurrection power into herself. I ask You to embrace Beth in Your love and be her strength and her defense. Please fill her with an overflowing well of Your Holy Spirit . . . and Father, I ask You to speak to her now the words she needs to hear from You."

I waited, knowing that Beth could now hear God's voice in her heart. *Oh, Lord, let Your words bring life to this child who has been dying!*

Her expression told volumes. She began to smile, to brighten up from the inside out and to begin to reflect the beauty of God. It was hard to believe she was the same dark-countenanced woman I had encountered only about twenty minutes before.

Finally I asked her, "What did God say to you?" This was more than just curiosity, although I did want to know what words could bring such a drastic change. I also knew that Beth needed to verbalize the words God gave her, just as she would need to write them in her prayer journal later. Without affirming the words from God in some way it would be easy for them to slip away.

"He said, 'I love you; I have always loved you with an everlasting love.' He said, 'You are beautiful to Me, my precious child.' "

With an encouragement to continue to dialogue with God, to begin a listening prayer journal, and to find a prayer partner, I left Beth, probably never to see her again. Beth's circumstances had not changed. She would have to release a lot more grief, shame, anger and resentment to the Cross. She still had some extremely important decisions to make, responsibilities for her children and a husband deeply involved in sin, but Beth had rediscovered a Divine Connection. She had exchanged her shame-shroud for the gift of hope from her Father. Hope is a beautiful garment.

## A wife's divine transaction

As you choose to exchange your shame, pain, grief, disappointment and anger for God's love you will be relinquishing those things that bind your husband's sin to your soul. In forgiving your husband you can then begin to accept yourself and move on in the healing process of restoring your marriage.

During this process God, in His love, may expose things in your own life that need to be brought to the light. It may be a painful time of personal exploration and discovery for you as well as your husband. Your nerves will already be raw and most likely you will be tempted to short-circuit the process. However, unless you are willing to allow God to do the deep work of restoration in your own life some of the same patterns of behavior will pop up again, triggering the old emotions. This is a time when you will need to remember that living in the freedom of wholeness is well worth the pain of the moment. You are birthing something!

Although you are not *defined* by your husband's problems, the fact is that when he sins, you both have a problem and you both suffer because in marriage you are one flesh. It doesn't mean that there is anything inherently wrong with you because he chooses to sin, but it does mean that because of the covenant of marriage you have entered into, his actions can greatly wound you and cause you deep pain.

## Trust and boundaries for a wife

After the act of forgiving it may be some time before you will be able to whole-heartedly trust your husband again. Both of you need this period of time-out when, without pressure from either side, all your energies can be put into getting whole. This will require a change of mind-set from the normal demands upon one another, especially in the area of sex. There will be times when you will want your husband to desire you and initiate love-making, perhaps to prove that you are still desirable to him and that he is interested in you more than the porn stars.

There will be times when you will feel genuine affection for him and want to express it, wanting to bring healing to him through your love.

There will be other times when you can't stand having him touch you and the thought of sex is disgusting.

These mood swings are not uncommon during the healing process but, when allowed to freely flow, they will only cause confusion and rabbit trails in the restoration period.

It may be advisable for the two of you together, to set some physical boundaries in your relationship with the express purpose of working on the healing process. Perhaps with the help of a counselor, the two of you will decide on a three (more or less) month hiatus from all sexual activity. This will include all pornography, sexual intercourse, and sexual fondling, even not sharing the same bed. In some circumstances it may include living apart for a time. The purpose is not abstinence for its own sake or for division, but abstinence so that all efforts may be made towards healing, with the least amount of pressure upon each other. Genuine affection and affirmation should not be withheld if it is given in non-sexual ways.

During this time your husband will be learning to receive affirmation and deep infilling from God in ways apart from sexual stimulation, and you are learning to trust the reality of his love and sincerity. This takes time and should not be rushed or pressured. At any time during this process, either of you should have the freedom to negotiate lengthening the time of separation.

## Husband alert: a marriage blinded by the light

When one has been in the darkness long enough it is nearly impossible to see clearly when you come out into the light. Things are fuzzy, with halos around them, and you have to squint to keep from being blinded by the brilliance of the sun.

Coming into the light of Christ from long periods of darkness can be just as blinding. All of a sudden the one who has been immersed in pornography sees the world with a new freedom and in a new light. His view may become romanticized, as if now everything is wonderful, beautiful and idealistic. And he may expect his wife to see through the new lens he is now wearing.

Not to put down the miraculous way that Jesus can instantly make all things new,[9] we find it necessary to give a word of caution here. In your new found enthusiasm you can easily be terribly insensitive to others and thereby inhibit their own revelations of the light and subsequent growth in it.

Some of you may understand (or even remember) the phenomenon that took place in the early '70s. It was a time of Holy Spirit renewal sweeping across America. Many people found it intolerable and as a result decided they wanted no part of a personal relationship with Jesus simply because they didn't want to be a part of the "charismania" of the time.

We were a young married couple at that time and the renewal swept over our church and our town with a passion. Most people turned up their noses, scoffing at and shunning what was happening, but some embraced what God was doing with fervor. We were part of the latter group. We encountered a Presence of God far beyond anything we had been taught in church or had even dreamed and desired. Within a twenty-four hour period, our encounter with the living God turned our lives upside-down (or as we like to say, right-side-up!).

Suddenly, everything was different. The grass was greener! The sky bluer! The Bible came alive, eternal truths literally jumping off the page. Our social life changed drastically from cocktail parties and dances at the country club to prayer meetings and revivals. Our interests were radically turned to evangelism and healing. We approached everything spiritual with an intense enthusiasm and a fervor. We were converted! The old had gone; the new had come.

Three decades later I have no doubt of what God did. It has only grown and deepened. What I do regret is that someone didn't lock us up with the Lord for about six months! Even Jesus and Paul went off to secluded places to be taught by the Holy Spirit after huge events of spiritual significance in their lives. In our enthusiasm, zeal and excitement we scared some of our friends and relatives to death. They couldn't believe that such a change in our lives would last; it was too sudden, too intense. Their opinions of our behavior ranged from "flash-in-the-pan" (harmless but nuts) to "bordering on insanity" (seriously deluded and schizoid). Our lack of tact and our insistence that they listen to us left a wake of turned-off people.

There is a similar style of behavior in the husband who has a sudden conversion from pornography to holiness. I'm not saying this sudden "I see the light!" change will happen to everyone who desires it, but it sometimes does happen. The contrast can be frightening to his wife! One day he is argumentative and in denial about his problems and the next he is telling her he is healed and wants to resume a normal sexual relationship. No wonder she puts up a stop sign!

Husbands, when the healing does come in your life, whether in an instant or as a process, respect your wife's emotions. She has been on a roller coaster with you, hoping – denying, believing – distrusting, loving – hating. She needs time to see if what you are espousing is real. She needs time to know that you are not just passing through the "ignoring the problem – false sense of security" stages of the cycle. She deserves all the time it takes. She has defended you in your worst moments; she has made excuses for you to your children so that they wouldn't feel abandoned; she has not left you when there wasn't much reason for her to stay. Give her time to watch and see that what God is doing is real. Time is your gift to her.

Don't let the craziness of your new-found freedom be a stumbling block to the soul-mate God has given you. A little patience and respect will bring lasting benefits that you (and she) won't regret. This will require God's grace and discipline in your life because your past behavior with pornography has been based on a quick-fix, "I want it now" mentality. You have not had the ability to wait for love to come, the patience to know that the comfort you need is just a few moments away. All that will change now and you must lay aside the old habit patterns of your youth and embrace God's eternal way of putting your hope in His eternal love.[10]

## Are you speaking my language?

For some of you I might as well be speaking Greek. You cannot imagine such a complete change coming over you in such a short period of time. To be honest, it may not come that soon at all, but however it comes, it *will* come. Wholeness is God's promise to you. He calls it "Abundant Life."[11] God wants you to have it more than you do. It is the legacy for you from your eternal Father. Without it you are living the life of a pauper.

As you continue reading be prepared for the next chapter. In it you will find some specific steps and prayers for coming free and becoming whole. You will need to enter the next chapter with the following warning:

▶ *According to the Supreme Surgeon General (God Himself) you should not indulge in the following chapter without the risk of spiritual freedom. Obedience to God's Word may impair your ability to continue in sin and may cause a change of heart.*

# Chapter 8

## Final Act

### Coming free from the practice

*"He [God] reached down from on high and took hold of me;*
  *he drew me out of deep waters.*
*He rescued me from my powerful enemy,*
  *from my foes, who were too strong for me.*
*They confronted me in the day of my disaster,*
  *but the LORD was my support.*
*He brought me out into a spacious place;*
  *he rescued me because he delighted in me."*
                              (Psalm 18:16–19)

> If you try to build intimacy with another person before you've
> done the hard work of getting whole on your own, then all your
> relationships will become an attempt to complete yourself.
>                                              *Leslie Parrott*

Up to now you have taken in a lot of information about
pornography and about yourself. By the time you reach this
point I hope you're finally ready to make a life-changing decision
about yourself. *I want to be whole – no matter what it takes!*

This choice must be based on the clear understanding that you
need to renounce the practice of pornography with its accompanying sexual fantasy life and masturbation. To go through the
following steps without a firm decision to put sin behind you
and go for wholeness will be a sham and ineffective.

Although God will be with you in the process all the way, your will is also necessary. He is asking you to collaborate with Him, not just sit passively, waiting for Him to do all the work.

*I told God that if He wanted me to change He could do it.* This is a whiny, passive response that is half-hearted in its intent. Getting whole is hard work; it takes discipline and determination.

The steps that are given are different from a 12-step program. They may include some of the same principles (which are very effective and highly recommended), but there will be an un-diluted emphasis on the person of Jesus Christ, the power of the Holy Spirit and the Father's love to walk with you through this, however long it takes. Instead of meetings with a group, you will be required to meet with Father, Son and Holy Spirit every day. You will need their words and comfort and encouragement which will be like food to your soul. Plan to set apart a time of quiet and privacy each day to learn how to listen to God and share the depths of your heart with Him. Without this you will revert to doing it in your own strength. Your own will power will fail you. God will not.

Keeping a listening prayer journal will be vital as you proceed. You will need to keep a record of all the things God will show you and this will prove to be a wonderful vehicle for pouring out your heart. In seeing the pain you have experienced written out in your own handwriting, you can then nail that pain to the Cross and receive the healing words from the Father that will fill the voids in your life. Opening your prayer journal and your Bible each day will help you focus on the mission of wholeness.

It will take time to go through all these steps. Some will have to be repeated and some continued for the rest of your life. Don't put a time limit on your progress. Decide now that you will go the distance as long as it takes.

If you have already done some of the steps, then simply reaffirm them with God (or others) to keep them alive in your heart.

Father, I pray for your child now who is making a life-changing decision. Allow him/her to take Your truth into the depths of his/her heart. Speak Your healing word over the wounded places of the past. Shine Your light into the darkness and bring forth Your holiness. Enlarge this one's capacity to hear Your Word and receive Your love. I pray for a miracle of restoration for this life in Jesus' name. Amen.

## Step 1: Jesus is Lord

*"Salvation is found in no one else, for there is no other name under heaven given to men by which we must be saved."*
(Acts 4:12)

You may have walked a church aisle decades ago to make a decision to accept Jesus as your Lord and Savior. You may have been in ministry for Him for a long time. You may have assumed He is your Lord because you have heard it all your life. You may have never thought it necessary to say a "sinner's prayer." Wherever you are, whether a seasoned believer or a novice at this Christian commitment, this is the starting place for all of us.

God told us early in our ministry of taking *The Journey to Wholeness in Christ* out to people that it was necessary to begin each seminar with a prayer, giving each person the opportunity to ask Jesus to come more intimately into his/her heart. I was obedient, but at first I was hesitant, thinking surely each person who would come to such an event must have, at the very least, made a commitment of his/her life to Jesus, otherwise why would they be there?

It didn't take long for us to receive letters and testimonies from men and women who had been in church all their lives but had never asked for the intimacy that God promises us through Jesus. They were so grateful for the opportunity, especially husbands and wives who prayed this commitment together, along with the prayer that Jesus would be Lord of their marriage. Our friend, Lee Buck, an enthusiastic evangelist, says, "Never assume anyone is saved!"

Therefore, I am making no assumptions about your salvation, one way or the other. I am simply inviting you to pray an old-fashioned sinner's prayer, the most tried and true way to come into God's kingdom. I encourage you to pray the prayer aloud, following this form and then letting your heart speak directly to God. In your prayer journal, note the date you either committed or re-committed your life to Jesus.

> Lord Jesus Christ, I come to You today, acknowledging that I have sinned.
> These sins have separated me from Your presence because You are a holy God.
> I ask You to forgive me and cleanse me from all my unrighteousness.
> I believe that You died for me to take all my sin, all my anxieties, all my loneliness and all my sickness into Your own body.
> I thank You for Your great love for me, wanting me to be whole.
> I welcome You into my life. Come in, Lord Jesus.
> Come, and be my Savior; come and be my Lord.
> I will serve You with all the strength You give me all the days of my life.
> Amen.

Now, place your hand on your heart and say these words, aloud:

> Jesus lives in me! He dwells in my heart, my mind, my body, my soul, and my spirit. His light has come into my darkness.

Raise one hand to the Father as you keep the other on your heart and say:

> Jesus lives within me! Jesus is in the Father. I am connected to the Father by Jesus in my heart. The Holy Spirit binds us together.

Meditate on these words from John 15:

> *"Remain in me, and I will remain in you."* (verse 4)

> *"If* [you] *remain in me and I in* [you], [you] *will bear much fruit."* (verse 5)

*"If* [you] *do not remain in me,* [you] *are like a branch that is thrown away and withers; such branches are picked up, thrown into the fire and burned."* (verse 6)

*"If you remain in me and my words remain in you, ask whatever you wish, and it will be given you."* (verse 7)

*"As the Father has loved me, so have I loved you. Now, remain in my love."* (verse 9)

## Step 2: Godly sorrow

*"Godly sorrow brings repentance that leads to salvation, and leaves no regret, but worldly sorrow brings death."*
(2 Corinthians 7:10)

Some of you may be participating in this healing process only because you got caught. Without the painful, forced exposure to the light you know you'd still be doing what you used to do to relieve your anxieties. You may be genuinely sorry you got caught and that you caused pain to someone you love. You may be sorry because you are embarrassed and you are feeling deep pain over what you have done. Some of you may have had a scare and are afraid you will get caught so you are seeking help. But getting whole involves *godly sorrow and repentance that makes a difference,* a far different thing than being sorry you got caught.

## Brad's story

*"I got caught!"*

Those three little words tell the story of a family in chaos.

It took Brad a long time to finally get the words out but it was why he came to see us for healing prayer. He was desperate. He didn't really believe that what he had done was all that terrible but he honestly didn't want his wife, Sharon, to be so upset. He couldn't understand why she felt rejected. He kept explaining to us that it had nothing to do with her; he loved his wife and was truly sorry he had hurt her; it was hard for women to understand the way men thought about things; nearly every man he knew did the same things; it didn't really hurt anyone. The bottom line of all his arguments was,

"Everything was OK; if only she hadn't found certain things . . ."

"What really bothers you the most about this whole situation, Brad?" Conlee asked.

Then came the three words . . . *"I got caught."*

It took several prayer appointments for Brad to finally get past his embarrassment of being with us, talking about such personal things. He kept trying to project his own shame and guilt onto his wife, attempting to excuse himself by complaining that if she had been more understanding, more enlightened about what men need, more trusting, not so quick to jump to conclusions, then he wouldn't be in this awkward situation, airing his family's dirty linen before a couple in ministry. In other words, Brad seemed convinced that if he hadn't gotten caught, he would have continued in some illusion of a blissful marriage with no one the wiser about his secret little activities.

Finally, Brad was ready to talk about how he first got started with pornography. When he was twelve years old, while scavenging for some scrap materials for a school project, he had found a couple of his dad's erotic magazines thrown in the trashcan in the alley. After that first encounter, urged on by the new thoughts and emotions the pictures provoked, he began to systematically search the house to see if he could find more. It wasn't long before he discovered his dad's hiding place for "girlie magazines".

Several times a week Brad secretly would check the little niche in the garage behind the workbench where he and his dad often spent time together on woodworking projects. Each time he looked he made sure his mother was either away from home or busily occupied in the other part of the house, and especially he made sure his dad wasn't home. Each time he checked he hoped there would be a new addition to the stash. In spite of all the time he and his dad spent together, the subject of the pictures was never discussed.

From these experiences Brad formed an early impression about the ways in which men and women, husbands and wives, related to one another. First, he learned by example that husbands kept some things secret from their wives. He also became aware that men were attracted to two totally different kinds of women, the kind they married and the kind who took their clothes off and posed in provocative positions. Thus, when Brad married, he never once considered it dishonest that he maintained a secret life apart from that of his wife and children, or that it was unusual to regularly enjoy pornography. To Brad it was simply part of "being a man".

Buying magazines and occasionally going to adult shows satisfied Brad's fascination with pornography until several years before we met. After bringing a computer into their home a whole new level of erotic interest was awakened through the Internet. He was confronted with perverse possibilities he had never thought of. It was available twenty-four hours a day and it was basically free to begin with. His secret could finally be shared with others via chat rooms. He didn't even have to sneak it in the house.

Although he found himself spending more and more time each day apart from his family and deeply involved in the sordid world he encountered, he also became aware of how many other men there who were also involved in Internet sex. It seemed to relieve some of the guilt he sometimes felt about the time he was spending away from his family.

A couple of years before, he used to become extremely upset with Sharon when she would rebuff many of his sexual advances, but the more time he spent in the porno web sites, the more he found that he was losing interest in a physical relationship with his wife. What they had together seemed too tame compared to what he encountered with cybersex. His thoughts were preoccupied more and more with the women he "talked to" on the Internet and the visual images he could call up on the screen. The perverse spin he put on his rationalization of his behavior towards Sharon was that she was probably relieved that he didn't bother her anymore. (Of course, they never discussed it.)

Sharon seldom used the computer in their home office. Her interest only peaked when a parent-teacher meeting informed the parents about how to check up on your children to see what they might be viewing on the Internet. The next day she tried what had been suggested, only to find numerous hits on porn sites. Stunned by what she saw she informed Brad, demanding that he confront their nine-year-old son. At that point Brad 'fessed up and thus began his litany of, "I got caught."

Brad needed to get to the place of having genuine godly sorrow about what he had done to himself and his family so that God could bring healing to the many distorted illusions of intimacy in his life. When you begin to have godly sorrow that leads to repentance you will be well on your way to the salvation of your own soul and your family.

You have already asked Jesus to be the Lord of your life, giving Him permission to make you into His likeness. Now you are giving Him permission to work out this salvation. You will be saved from the hell of self and the detestable practices that your lower self indulges in. You will be saved to become your true self, the one in which the image of God shines forth.

Write out in your prayer journal to God, why you want to give up pornography and all that goes with it.

- Why do you want to be whole, no longer depending on your fantasies to soothe you?

- Do you want help because you nearly got caught or because you really want to change?

If it is difficult for you to know your own heart, ask God to show you the real desires of your heart. Write them out in your journal.

## Step 3: Confession of sin, forgiveness and repentance

### Confession of sin

God already knows all the sin in our hearts before we confess it but when we verbalize our transgressions something happens to us that changes everything. In confession we put ourselves in a humble position, the place we have to be in order to be lifted up. More than merely thinking about our sins and hating ourselves, confessing our sins takes them somewhere outside ourselves – to the Cross.

In making your confession, use honest descriptions of what you have done. Although God loves an honest confession straight from the heart, sometimes using biblical language is best. There is no whitewashing the Bible's descriptions of sin. Adultery is adultery, not having an affair. Theft is not misappropriating funds. Shacking up is fornication, not sowing your wild oats.

When we try to explain to God why and how we did things that displeased Him we get off track. We're not in a courtroom, trying to plea bargain for a lighter sentence. The sentence has already been pronounced. It is death.[1] The only choice left to us is to throw ourselves on His mercy by means of our union with Jesus who has already paid the price of death for us. There are no other choices: either we face eternal death or we are pardoned to enter eternal life through Jesus Christ.

What sins are you confessing? Write them out, specifically and scripturally, before the Lord. If you have been involved in pornography you will need to confess the sin of adultery. Just because you didn't touch another person physically does not excuse you. That is the kind of bargaining you are trying to avoid, remember? You're already on death row because of what you have done, so why lie now?

> *"Jesus said, 'You have heard that it was said, "Do not commit adultery." But I tell you that anyone who looks at a woman lustfully has already committed adultery with her in his heart.'"*
> (Matthew 5:27–28)

Ask yourself, "Who or what am I thinking about in my fantasy life in the moment of release?"

### Forgiveness
The whole transaction of confession does not end with telling God the facts of your sinfulness. The next step is just as vital.

> *"Is anyone of you in trouble? He should pray ... If he has sinned, he will be forgiven. Therefore confess your sins to each other and pray for each other so that you may be healed."*
> (James 5:13a, 15b–16)

When you confess your sins you should expect to be forgiven. It is God's gift to you; this is the divine pardon which means that your sin is no longer on the record.

Without receiving the forgiveness that God has for you, you are literally telling God that you want the death sentence to stay on the books, that it is unimportant to you whether you live or die. If you keep recycling your sinful behavior in your mind, never appropriating God's forgiveness, you will be nurturing the character of the old person within and not the new nature of Jesus in you.

Allow the Lord to give you a symbol or image of what forgiveness looks like. Some people see it as liquid gold being poured from a heavenly urn. Others have seen it as the cleansing waters of the River of Life. We know that forgiveness has cleansing properties because we are told:

> *"If we confess our sins, he is faithful and just and will forgive us our sins and purify us from all unrighteousness."*
>
> (1 John 1:9)

Now that you have confessed your sins before the Lord, on the basis of God's Word, know that He forgives you. Lift your hands and say to Him, *I receive your forgiveness. I allow You to pour it into me, cleansing me from all my unrighteousness.*

Know that your identity throughout the rest of the healing process is that of "Forgiven by Grace". As you receive His forgiveness, allow Him to cleanse all labels that have been placed upon you. Name them before Him, writing them in your journal (dirty, perverted, adulterer, etc.). As you give Him the old labels, receive from Him your true identity. What is the name God speaks over you?

### Repentance

Receiving forgiveness is the fuel for your soul to seek wholeness. Forgiveness empowers you to repent. When we attempt repentance in our own strength it is no more than a short-lived New Year's resolution. *I have really messed up so now I am going to do better.* Now, no longer bound by the sin of the past, you are free to pursue what God has for you. You are like "Christian" in *Pilgrim's Progress.* You may go through some trials and dangerous areas to get to the place you are destined to be, but it is not an impossible journey and each time you make a godly choice the next ones will be easier.

## Nors and Katye re-visited

As promised in Chapter 2, we want to tell you about the important work this Danish couple did in just a few days that produced such spectacular results. Individually, they worked through their complicated issues in the same way. They were willing to be led, in spite of the powerful emotions both of them exhibited, through the steps we just described: confession, forgiveness, and repentance.

We asked the Lord to show both of them their families of origin as He saw them. What both of them had always taken for granted in a permissive society, they saw through God's eyes as perversions of what He created. They both confessed the sins of their parents against them.

Nors confessed the sins of a father who was distant and unaffirming, of a mother wrapped up in self. Katye confessed the sins of parents who were obsessed with sexuality to the extent that they didn't protect their child's innocence.

Seeing their upbringing in reality, they both had much grief they needed to release. We gave them time to see Jesus gently lift this buried grief from their hearts.

With the grief gone, they were both able to forgive their parents, thus releasing them from the intense influence they continued to have in their lives. They both renounced vows they had made about their parents that had put to death the true masculine in Nors and the true feminine in Katye.

*Only after they had dealt with the past* were they ready to tackle their strong feelings towards each other. Nors had to recognize Katye's infuriating responses to his passivity. He painfully saw in himself the same passivity he had seen in his father and was tempted to despise himself even further. What he needed however, was a strengthening of his will to become the man God created him to be. He needed an infusion of God's love to make him a man, not the model of a sick society. Forgiving Katye for her stinging words and rejection of him, he was able to allow God to fill him and call him forth as a man.

One particularly significant transaction he made with God was allowing Him to recall (with all its associated shame) the word Nors always thought described himself. It was a derogatory and belittling word. Nors gave that name to God and received, in exchange, the name God had always had for him. He heard God say it to him and immediately his countenance changed. One word from God can do that to a person. We could have told him the same thing and it would have made little difference. But for a person to hear God speak his real name is a life-changing experience.

We asked God to show both of them significant, symbolic events in their lives that needed healing of memories. Nors was taken back immediately to a situation with classmates in a particularly embarrassing situation in which he reacted foolishly. As we asked Jesus to allow him to see where He was in that situation, the whole impact of the memory was changed. With Jesus he saw it differently and was able to forgive and receive healing.

Katye's significant memory was that of a child in her parents' home. She saw herself confused and frightened, hiding and yet angry with them for shutting her out from their sex games. She also saw Jesus, calling her to Himself to play a game appropriate to her age. This deep demonstration of His love to her greatly assisted her in being able to forgive her parents and accept herself.

After much forgiveness work – forgiving others and receiving God's forgiveness – they were both empowered to become more of what God always intended them to be. Both were ready to be filled anew with His Holy Spirit and be moldable in His hands. Conlee blessed Nors as a man and pronounced a fatherly blessing over him. I held Katye and blessed her in the true feminine, asking God to infuse her with His love, filling every void.

An amazing amount of deep healing was accomplished in their hearts in a very short time. Occasionally, at a particularly anointed conference, God's work is speeded up. In that situation we have come apart from our ordinary lives, have few distractions from the goal of allowing God to have His way, and are surrounded by the many prayers being offered up to God for healing miracles. The work Nors and Katye did usually takes much longer, and indeed they still had much work to do when they returned to their home and the familiarity of their surroundings.

They had a mountaintop experience that then needed to be translated into the plains of life. It would continue to be just as life-transforming at home if they continued the work of listening to God and collaborating with Him.

## Step 4: Disclosure

> *"Have nothing to do with the fruitless deeds of darkness, but rather expose them. For it is shameful even to mention what the disobedient do in secret. But everything exposed by the light becomes visible, for it is light that makes everything visible."*
> (Ephesians 5:11–14)

Trying to be the Lone Ranger in this healing process is not advisable. Your ability to self-deceive has already been proven. It's time to take off your mask and let someone you trust know the score. If you are married, the first person you need to disclose the situation to is your spouse. You have sinned against her and you need to confess that and ask for her forgiveness. Be prepared for her to need time to grant you forgiveness.

Tell her about the plans you have to work on your issues, the reasons you got hooked on pornography as well as giving up the present and any future practice. Ask for her prayers and be willing to set some boundaries in your relationship until you both have sufficient time to absorb God's healing.

If your children have been aware of what you have been doing, confess to them and ask for their forgiveness. This is instilling godly virtue in them and the example of holy response to a holy God.

Tell one other person other than your spouse the truth. Bringing the problem to the light will keep you from lying to yourself and minimizing the situation. Be sure the person you choose to tell can keep a confidence and will not empathize with you, telling you it's not really that bad. The last thing you need is a "friend" who is keeping you from continuing on God's path.

## Jerry's story

When Jerry called Conlee for a prayer appointment he was in a state of despair and great agitation. He felt his world had just crashed in upon him.

Jerry and his wife Betsey, were the parents of two sons, aged thirteen and fifteen. Their home reflected their love for one another and their commitment to God. Yet, unbeknownst to anyone else, Jerry had a porn habit. Since he was a teenager he had been using pornographic magazines to assuage a hunger for intimacy that not even his loving wife could provide.

Jerry's parents had been far too young and immature to know how to nurture their son in proper ways. He had been looking for substitutes when he found the temporary fulfillment of pornography. His need to use it had only grown with time.

Jerry's call to Conlee came on the heels of a recent incident. His thirteen-year-old son had found a stack of pornography in the garage. He shared it with his brother and then with a cousin close to his age. Somehow the cousin's parents found out about what the boys were looking at. Upset, they called Jerry and Betsey. Jerry denied any knowledge of where the magazines came from or how they got in his garage.

Reeling from what he had exposed to his children, Jerry later confessed to Betsey that, not only did the magazines belong to him, but that he had been using them for many years, even before he knew her. He and Betsey needed time to work on their issues, her rejection, anger, disappointment, sense of betrayal, etc. Eventually, with God's help, they did the hard work of reconciliation and their marriage is stronger than ever.

However, the disclosure we want to tell you about is one that had lasting benefits to the future generation. When Jerry arrived at Conlee's office he had his two boys with him. In the presence of his pastor and his sons, Jerry made a full confession of his sin – including his sin against his children and his sin against their mother, his sin of lying and his sin of disobeying God. Never would one see a more broken, contrite man. He was truly a man like David, after Nathan's word to him from God broke the sin in his life.[2]

Jerry asked his sons to forgive him, which they did. In that moment, the hour of Jerry's deepest humiliation, came a powerful godly example to his sons of what a real man is like and what he does. They will never forget that time with their dad. Godly bonds of respect and love were established between the men in that family that had never been there before. We have watched over the last several years as those boys have grown into responsible young men and we have observed the strong bond of love they have for their dad.

Jerry had never had that kind of relationship with his own father. He received it as a gift from God for his own children by his obedience to respond to sin in a biblical way. Whenever you are obedient to God, all kinds of surprisingly wonderful fruit will begin to grow on your family tree.

## Step 5: Accountability

*"Those who know your name will trust in you,*
*for you, L*ORD*, have never forsaken those who seek you."*
(Psalm 9:10)

In addition to your trusted friend, set up an accountability relationship with someone who will not be reluctant to call you into wholeness. This can be a pastor, godly friend or counselor. This is not a person to offer sympathy, but exhortation. It should be someone who can be objective and knows how to hear God.

You may be tempted to keep from telling too many people and choose to have your spouse be your disclosure partner, prayer partner and accountability partner. This is not wise. You and your spouse need to work on your marriage relationship. She does not need to be the porn police for you and that is what will happen. She will feel responsible for every move you make, constantly checking the last viewed sites on the computer, looking through drawers, checking your briefcase, calling you at the office, etc. This does not promote a healing environment for either of you. You may need a parole officer for a while (a clear-headed, godly voice who will keep you from getting off track) but it shouldn't be your wife.

## Power in narrative

It will be helpful for you to write out your story in an objective way, as though giving your testimony. This will enable you to see your situation in reality and assist the person who consents to meet with you on a regular basis.

Your testimony should be a part of your journal. It is important to write it out before the Lord whether or not anyone will ever read it. As you write out your story you, like every other person we know who has done this, will find further insight and healing in your situation. Here is an outline to get you started:

### Guidelines for preparing a testimony

1. **Focus on the goal.**
   - Where are you going in this story?
   - What is the point of your testimony for this particular time? (Obviously, you can't tell your whole life story.)
   - What is God saying through you?

   Title this testimony for self-clarification, for example:
   - *Finding my true self*
   - *The healing of my marriage*
   - *Standing at the cross with my pain*
   - *Exchanging pornography for a sense of being*

2. **Ask God to highlight two or three symbolic events that illustrate your life before His intervention.**
   - Describe these with personal anecdotes.
   - Tell them in such a way that your listener knows who you are.

3. **Define the crisis.**
   - What happened that made you seek help?
   - What did God show you?

4. **Describe the process.**

5. **Describe the root causes that were revealed.**
   - How were they revealed?
   - What were they?

6. **What were the steps to healing?**

7. **How are you now relating to others (and ministering) from your wholeness rather than your brokenness?**
   - How is God glorified in your story?

## Step 6: Seek pastoral and professional help

*"... if the root is holy, so are the branches."* (Romans 11:16b)

Until the root causes are revealed which show you the reasons why you have become so dependent upon pornography and why it is such a struggle for you to quit, you are going to be trying to change your life by the white-knuckle method. Your will power won't work forever. Several falls down the road you will eventually realize the necessity for opening up the locked trunks in your spiritual attic. Why not start now?

Perhaps there have been patterns in your family with difficulties with intimacy. Like Brad, you may never have questioned the behavior of your father or grandfather. Like many others, you may have no memory of neglect or abandonment as a child, but its effects may be directing your life.

Being willing to allow qualified professionals to minister in the areas of deep inner healing takes courage. It is risky in one sense in that you never know what God will reveal. In other ways, you can have great confidence, knowing that what God brings to the light He heals. You should prayerfully choose a pastor, counselor, psychologist or psychiatrist to help you in areas of pastoral counseling or private therapy. It is important that you choose one with a Judeo-Christian belief system, preferably one who operates in the gifts of the Holy Spirit, honoring the Word of God.

It is important that your spiritual counselor helps you to hear God for yourself rather than tells you what they perceive as fact. For instance, many times there may be indications of abuse or neglect in one's childhood that cannot be proven. This is not the kind of proposition to use to encourage a client to confront a parent or make demands. God's way of healing is to make all parties involved as whole as possible.

Choosing a therapist should be done with care and discernment. Not every qualified therapist is a good fit for you. Most people spend more time choosing a lawnmower than a therapist. If a qualified therapist is offended that you want to ask questions about his/her credentials, basic spiritual beliefs, or success rate, then you should look elsewhere. You may need to try several to find one with whom you are compatible.

In addition to private therapy, or instead of it, there are many conferences, seminars and workshops that can be of immense value. Ones that we are personally familiar with are, of course, our own *The Journey to Wholeness in Christ*[3] seminar in which many barriers to wholeness are explored and ministered to. This seminar consists of three to five days of intense sessions with the personal ministry done by a qualified prayer team. It includes teaching, worship and ministry, one on one and in groups.

We also highly recommend *Pastoral Care Ministries*,[4] led by Leanne Payne. Conlee is on the board of this ministry and he and I have served on Leanne's ministry team for more than forty of these five-day seminars and everytime God reveals something to us we had not previously seen in our walk with Him. In such seminars God effectively discloses the root causes for many spiritual problems.

*Living Waters*[5] is a ministry for those with sexual brokenness. Founded by Andy Comiskey of *Desert Streams Ministries*, it is a thirty-week course, designed to help those who struggle with sexual addiction, pornography, and the effects of sexual abuse, frigidity, homosexuality, and lesbianism. I was a women's group leader the first year we began our local program and Conlee is a spiritual advisor for the program that has met in our church for many years.

*Redeemed Lives*,[6] led by Mario Bergner, is also a thirty-week course designed to explore in depth and minister to the deep psychological wounds of one's past. This is a program that has special emphasis on the ministry to those struggling with homosexuality.

There are many more good programs and seminars with which we are familiar, but not intimately knowledgeable. Ask around; find out who has attended programs in your area and ask them questions.

It will be extremely helpful for you to receive healing prayer regularly with the laying-on-of-hands. This impartation of God's healing power to you is like accumulative chemotherapy to the cancer of your soul. You may even need to teach people how to pray for you once you begin to receive God's power through this biblical means of impartation. Conlee and I have done that several times in the past when we were living in areas where people had never learned how to pray effective healing prayer.

Simply by showing them what to do and then receiving God's healing touch through them we were marvelously blessed.

## Step 7: Clean house

*"If your eye causes you to sin, gouge it out and throw it away. It is better for you to enter life with one eye than to have two eyes and be thrown in the fire of hell."* (Matthew 18:9)

This will be a biggie in your progress. How effectively and scrupulously you choose to remove all previous temptations will not only show your intentions for wholeness, it will make the going much easier. You will need to ask God for an objectivity as you go through your house, office and car. Every remnant you find that reminds you of the routine you used to get into in your pornographic pursuits will have to go. This is no time to play "Well, maybe ..." or get sentimental.

Here is a checklist of things to look for:

- erotic magazines
- videos
- photographs
- letters
- music
- erotic art
- erotic toys
- books
- games
- computer software, etc.

It is a good idea to change your e-mail address so that former chat room acquaintances cannot contact you. In fact you may need to either give up your password to the family computer or even put your home computer in storage for a time.

Think about the routine you followed when you sat at the computer: What did you drink? Did you smoke? Did you play music? All of these reminders must go.

Just moving the computer to a different room or location may be a big help to do away with the familiar surroundings.

Consider putting a children's governor on your Internet accessibility and cable channels. You may need to discontinue cable TV entirely or even shut down the TV for a few months. You may go through withdrawal; this is a great symptom to show how great its pull was upon you!

Don't forget to check your desk at work and thoroughly inspect your car or truck. Check your closets, your workshop, your garage, under your bed. Where was your secret hiding place? It's always amazing how many little reminders will be overlooked until a later date when you're feeling particularly weak and vulnerable. Ask the Lord to show you what you are overlooking.

Anything that could be used by someone else for pornographic purposes should be destroyed, not just thrown in the trash. Too many children get hooked by what they find in trash cans.

When our youngest son Ben, who had been throwing his life away in the drug culture for a couple of years, came back to God in a miraculous way that saved his life, he became aware of his need to do a thorough housecleaning. Thankful to God for His deliverance, more than anything he wanted to live a holy life for Him. He looked upon everything from his past that had enhanced his involvement with drugs and alcohol as articles of affection from the devil. He knew that he had served Satan during his drug years and the things he had held in reverence at that time were all reminders of an unholy way of life.

Coming home from college, with a vengeance he stripped his room of posters, boxes of music CDs, T-shirts, letters, jewelry, books, even his long hair was cut very short. Days later I even found him out in the storeroom, throwing away his large collection of G.I. Joe men and equipment he had played with as a little boy. He said he remembered the violent fantasies he had when he had played with them and he knew they shouldn't be around as a reminder.

He then went through his room, his car and his new apartment at college (minus a TV) with prayers of cleansing and blessing, sprinkling holy water in every corner.[7] Finally, he filled his new apartment and his room at home with symbols of Christ's love for him.

Ben's example is a good one. We should not leave one rock unturned when God asks us to clean house. Besides cleansing the temple of the Holy Spirit (our selves), we should make sure that the environment in which we live is scrupulously hallowed as well.

You might consider some kind of a ceremony when you dispose of all the stuff you need to get rid of. Look at it as a sacrifice to God, the doing away with the old man, so that you are ready to put on the new. Perhaps you and your wife can pray together as you dispose of the things that kept you bound to sin, then go through your home with cleansing water and prayers of blessing. After all, this is an event to be remembered!

## Step 8: Avoid temptation

> *"Who may ascend the hill of the LORD?*
> *Who may stand in his holy place?*
> *He who has clean hands and a pure heart,*
> *who does not lift up his soul to an idol*
> *or swear by what is false."* (Psalm 24:3–4)

In addition to a thorough house cleaning you will want to think carefully about those situations and conversations that offered the most powerful temptations for you to turn to porn. Perhaps conversations at coffee breaks at work gave way to sharing provocative web site addresses and information about the latest updates of porn sites. You may need to take your breaks at other times to avoid conversing with people who would keep the pornographic lure alive.

Do telephone calls from certain people always tend to drift to sexual subject matter? You may need to curtail those particular conversations or reveal to those people that you are through with that kind of activity.

Maybe you have to travel alone from time to time and the hotel room with cable TV and pay-per-view access has been your downfall. In ministry we often travel with men on our team who request the hotel to remove the TVs in their rooms before they check in. They know what loneliness can trigger in them and have learned that a good book is better than channel surfing.

When hotels refuse to take out the TV, these men have been known to remove the cable connector and ask us to keep it for them until they check out. While we were traveling in Holland on a ministry trip one friend even moved the TV set into our room until he was ready to leave. He knew that without his wife he could easily fall prey to the cable temptations of Amsterdam.

If browsing in bookstores has been a leisure activity that led you to pornographic magazines, avoid them altogether or only go with a friend who will keep you from straying into no-man's-land.

In addition to cleansing your home, office and car with holy water, consider having a house and/or office blessing[8] This is more than just a meaningful symbol of your new intentions; the prayers of blessing actually invoke a holy presence into the spaces where you spend most of your time. Invoking light where there has been darkness will strengthen you with discernment as you seek to become holy.

## Step 9: Fill the void

> *"Finally, brothers, whatever is true, whatever is noble, whatever is right, whatever is pure, whatever is lovely, whatever is admirable – if anything is excellent or praiseworthy – think about such things."* (Philippians 4:8)

Involvement with pornography can waste an enormous amount of time each day and night. When you decide to renounce it what are you going to do with your new-found time? Hopefully, you will begin to rebuild healthy relationships that have been neglected. But it is vital to begin filling your mind with wholesome godly images to replace the previous distorted ones. Learning to appreciate good books, discussing them with your family, listening to spiritual music, looking at art that celebrates the true beauty of God's creation, developing the art of godly conversation, and especially learning to listen to God, will greatly enhance your desire to rebuild the inner man. In addition you will gain tremendous inner strength and encouragement from realizing you can be satisfied with less titillating subject matter than what you once thought you had to have.

You and your wife might make it a mission to find a symbol of God's redeeming love for your home. You will recognize it when you see it. Our son Ben found a picture of Jesus carrying in his arms a limp young man in jeans, who greatly resembled Ben. The title was simply, "Forgiven." This spoke to Ben's deep heart, continually pointing out to him the love from God that was poured out upon him through Jesus, His Son. Today, in his home with his wife and three children, this picture hangs on the wall of the upstairs hall outside their bedrooms.

## Step 10: Cleanse your imagination

> *"I will sprinkle clean water on you, and you will be clean; I will cleanse you from all your impurities and from all your idols. I will give you a new heart and put a new spirit in you; I will remove from you your heart of stone and give you a heart of flesh."*
> (Ezekiel 36:25–26)

This will be an important step for you to follow for the rest of your life – as it is for all of us. We do not have to spend long hours looking at pornographic pictures to know that our imaginations are polluted. The world around us provides enough impressions and perversions of godly beauty to give us reason to need a spiritual scrubbing on a regular basis.

God has given us imaginations to contain images and symbols of His love. When used in holy ways the imagination will draw us closer to Him, inspire us to accomplish great things to honor Him and maintain a holy awe of His presence. So how do these images and symbols get into our imaginations? They reflect whatever our hearts contain.

Sometimes, called the "thoughts of the heart," the imagination is neither good nor bad. It can reflect good or bad things, depending upon whatever is lodged in the heart. The imagination can be compared to a blank screen that only reveals whatever image is thrown onto it by a projector. For us, our hearts project whatever is in them onto the screens of our imaginations.

If my heart is pure and turned towards God in all ways, my imagination will contain pictures of beauty and goodness. I will look at men and women and see them as creatures made in the image of God. I will be blessed by them and I will give forth blessing. I will see the essence of goodness in all of creation and be inspired to write about it, or preach about it, or paint it, or sing about it, or sculpt it, or bless it. Out of every awesome work of art, great novel, or moving concerto, there was first a seed planted in someone's imagination that came out of a heart that appreciated beauty.

When our hearts become deceived and we allow evil to fill them instead of goodness, vile images become lodged in our imaginations. God saw this in Noah's day,

> *"The LORD saw how great man's wickedness on the earth had become, and that every inclination of the thoughts of his heart was only evil all the time."* (Genesis 6:5)

The Lord was grieved that He had ever made man and would have wiped mankind from the face of the earth if not for the goodness He found in Noah. God looks on the heart and often sees things there we do not see ourselves. As you have turned your heart towards Him, He knows the intentions you have and wants to give you every advantage so that you will continue to grow in His love.

Unfortunately, even though our hearts begin to soften and become ready to be molded by God, there remains a residue of old images on our imaginations. It is as if they were exposed to distortions of truth for so long, some of them have become imprinted upon our screens. In fact, just living in our pagan-infested world we are constantly bombarded with images that lie about God and His creation.

The gross distortions of the images of man and woman are primary examples. Your immersion in pornographic representations of man and woman have left you with perceptions of them that are far from the way God sees them. Woman is not a creature fragmented into body parts designed to stimulate a sexual response. That is a distortion of God's creation: she is a whole person of beauty with a soul and a spirit for whom Jesus died.

Man is not a dominating, sex-oriented creature who is obsessed with hedonistic pleasure. That too is a perversion of the nobility and high calling of a real man.

A prominent man in our church spoke to us once about his concern that he was too wretched to enter into the Holy Communion service. He believed he was under satanic attack. He said that he would have a really good week with God, praying, reading His Bible, obeying what God showed him to do and would be really excited about being in church on Sunday mornings. But then, after he had heard a spiritually moving sermon, confessed his sins, and received God's forgiveness, just as he was quietly preparing to go to the altar to receive Communion, his imagination would be flooded with pornographic images and thoughts, things he never thought about anymore at all, until he was in church. He would feel so filthy that he would just sit in his pew, chastising himself and then go home to begin the process of repenting all over again.

Conlee asked him to remember what he had done just prior to having this happen. He replied, "I had worshiped God, heard the Word read and preached, confessed my sins, received forgiveness and asked God to feed me through the bread and the wine. Then the images popped up. I am just being tormented by Satan."

"What makes you think Satan brought up those thoughts?" asked Conlee. "Did you ever think that after all the holy things you just did, preparing for Communion, that the Holy Spirit was dredging up old junk from the bottom of your heart so that you could be really clean?"

"No, I never thought of that. But what do I do about it?"

Conlee and I led him through a simple little exercise of giving his imagination to the Lord. It is an exercise we all need to practice regularly; we call it "cleansing the imagination." We first learned to do it at *Pastoral Care Ministries* conferences as Leanne Payne would very simply instruct us as a group to give all the ungodly images to Jesus. We began to use it in *The Journey to Wholeness in Christ* seminars, in personal prayer appointments and in our personal lives. It is as effective with children as with adults.

Let's try it:

> Lord, You have given us the gift of imagination and hallowed it by Your presence. Forgive us for not protecting this extraordinary gift and for allowing our imaginations to become filled with things that are vile and full of terror and darkness, perverting the glory of Your creation, and the

creatures You have placed in it. We ask You now to cleanse those parts of us still stained by the sin of the world that we have allowed into our souls. Thank You, Lord.

Now, as those pictures begin to come up – the ungodly thoughts and images of your heart – just pull them right out of your mind and hand them to Jesus. You may need to put a hand to your forehead and lift them right up and out of your imagination. Some of them may seem like a movie reel, they are so prolific. Just keep pulling them all out, giving them to Jesus.

Let every pornographic scene come present and be lifted out – the distortions of man and woman, scenes of violence, horror, pictures of yourself in demeaning roles, domination, humiliation, death, brutality. Take your time and do not be afraid to give all of them to Jesus.

When you seem to be at the end of what comes up, look to see what Jesus does with all the images you have given Him. Where are they now? Write out what you saw in your journal.

Afterwards it is important to ask God to fill your heart and imagination with things that glorify Him. Pray for those things of truth, nobility, righteousness, purity, loveliness, excellence and praise to enter into you. Think on these things as examples of what is given to you by the Holy Spirit. Begin to picture woman as God sees her, man as God sees him. See yourself as God sees you.

## Step 11: Group support

> *"He must hold firmly to the trustworthy message as it has been taught, so that he can encourage others by sound doctrine and refute those who oppose it."*                                    (Titus 1:9)

At some point you will be ready to share your mission with more than just a couple of trusted people. You will begin to have your eyes open to the extent of the epidemic of pornography around you and know you can make a difference. When you have received enough healing that you can discuss your previous addictions without being devastated by the pain or shame, or when you realize that you are no longer defined by what you have done you will be ready to help others. You will speak the language and know exactly what others are struggling with.

At this point, besides meeting with someone one on one, it might be advisable to start a group or join a group already meeting in order to be honest with one another, encourage one another, and pray for one another, being accountable according to God's Word. Not only will this be of great benefit to others who need to know they are not alone, it will also keep you accountable in your continuing walk.

## Step 12: Pray in the Spirit

> *"And pray in the Spirit on all occasions with all kinds of prayers and requests."* (Ephesians 6:18a)

This admonition to pray in the Spirit is the last word in the section in Ephesians 6 about putting on the whole armor of God. After you are encouraged to wear the belt of truth, the breast-plate of righteousness, shoes with the readiness that comes from the gospel of peace, the shield of faith, the helmet of salvation, and the sword of the Spirit, you might think you're ready. Like David fighting Goliath, you are now equipped with spiritual armor, not the armor of the world, to fight your battle. Without realizing you were being outfitted, by the time you reach this twelfth step in getting whole, you are wearing the complete armor. It has been custom made for you, a perfect fit for your particular battle.

But as the infomercials state: "But wait! There's more!" All the spiritual gear you are wearing is going to be effective in deflecting the fiery darts of Satan (the Goliath's) from outside yourself. You will be protected from lies, accusations, deceptions, and perverse teachings when you have put on salvation, truth, righteousness, the gospel of peace, faith and the Word of God.

But what about the depravity that man so easily falls back into as a result of the fall? This needs an internal armor, one not seen, but a governor around the mind, filtering out and purifying the depths of the human heart. Our God does not leave anything to chance. He has given us His Holy Spirit and He teaches us how to pray.

The Spirit is comforter, counselor, truth-bearer, helper, fruit-giver, sanctifier, and power of God. When we allow Him to pray through us we receive the benefit of all His blessings. There are times when we simply do not know how to pray; either we don't understand a situation, or our pain is too great, or we are too weary. We can still pray in the Spirit, allowing the groanings of our deep heart to be brought to the Father by our willingness to let the Holy Spirit pray through us.

Praying in the Spirit is not a spooky or bizarre thing, although some would try to make it so. It is a natural way of prayer for every Christian who has received Jesus into his heart and the infilling of His Holy Spirit. This may or may not be apparent simultaneously with our salvation, although it should be. Jesus brings His Spirit when He comes to take up residence within us. There is nothing else we need from Him. Rather, it is we who need to yield more and more to what He already brings. Many times this "yielding" comes at a later time.

That act of yielding to the power of the Spirit is compared to a baptism. It is receiving the immersion of the Spirit's presence just as we were immersed in water at our baptism. We allow Him to wash over us inside and out, filling us with more and more of God's love.

Out of this collaboration with Him we are given the ability to pray in ways that bypass our understanding. This kind of prayer calls up from deep places within us things we could never put in words, feelings that can not be articulated, desires yet unspoken. It allows us to pray for others in ways that eliminate our selfishness and lack of knowledge.

The purpose of this kind of prayer is always to bring us into the presence of the Father in more intimate ways. Because of this, praying in the Spirit is said to be edifying, building up the Body, able to divide our thoughts from God's thoughts.[9]

Father, send Your Spirit now upon the one who prays for You to come. Let the power of Your Spirit saturate Your child with the warmth of Your Presence. Fill him, O Lord, with all good gifts and give him the tongue of an angel to praise You, both now and through all eternity. Amen.

Praying in the Spirit is a wonderful activity to do when:

- turning on the computer
- channel surfing on TV
- driving your car
- deciding on a movie
- choosing a book
- entering a hotel room
- shopping at the local convenience store
- having nothing else to do.

# Chapter 9

## Dark Theater
*Maintaining purity*

*"Create in me a pure heart, O God,*
*and renew a steadfast spirit within me."*
(Psalm 51:10)

> **Dark theater** is the theatrical term meaning that the theater is closed; there is no show during this particular time.

Our goal has been to help you maintain "dark theater" for the rest of your life. Dark theater means that there will be no further involvement with illusion; all the roles and personae you have known so well have ended and the actor has become a real life person, living in a real family, accomplishing wholesome and worthwhile goals. Your former "theater," whether the Internet porn screen, the videos, the smutty pages, or the illicit encounters, is now dark. The doors are locked and everyone has gone home. There is a real life waiting for you.

You know all too well that there are still "shows" playing all over town. All you have to do is raise the curtain on your own stage and you could be back in performance in a heartbeat. This is the problem with sin. It doesn't go away just because we want it to. Sin doesn't change; *you do!*

Hopefully, at this point, you have made the commitment to keep your theater dark. However, even if you are faithfully working on your spiritual steps, there are more things you need to do that will be vital to staying pure.

## A sense of being

Earlier, in Chapter 3, we discussed at length the incredible plan of attachment and affirmation God has for all his children, and the ways the world thwarts it. You may have made some personal connections to the ways in which many children are denied security in their mother's embrace and safety in their father's strength, both motivated by love.

Perhaps you are aware that you were separated from your mother for considerable periods of time when you were an infant and/or even under the age of three. Although the circumstances may have been justified (illness, death, adoption, etc.) the results from an early deficit of attachment are similar to circumstances borne out of evil or selfishness. Those holes needing mother-love and connection with the feminine do not go away no matter how many years pass. Those who have this deficit will spend a lifetime trying to find ways to fill the void.

Rather than filling the emptiness God's way, we so often find counterfeit ways to attempt to compensate for our inadequacies:

| Counterfeit ways | God's ways |
| --- | --- |
| Coveting | Godly desires |
| Copying | W.W.J.D. |
| Retreating/Hiding | Vulnerability |
| Hardness | Intimacy |
| Promiscuity | Purity of obedience |
| Dependency on others | Dependency on God |
| Blaming | Forgiving |
| Unbelief and anger | New life |

The counterfeit ways destroy relationships and the ability to hear God tell us who we really are and what we really need. They almost always include denial of the real problem. God's ways, while never denying the pain of reality, build relationships and strengthen godly character. There is always healing for the most severely abandoned, wounded and deprived person!

When we minister in this area at *The Journey to Wholeness in Christ* seminars, we help people go through the specific steps towards their healing that you have discovered in this book.

## 1. Define or name your problem

It is important to see your situation through God's eyes, not through the denial of your own heart, or through your own brokenness. Then it is vital to name what you are dealing with. Speak the truth to yourself and to God.

## 2. Dialogue with God

Typically in families where there has been little or no intimacy there is little or no genuine dialogue. Dialogue is the hallmark of intimate relationship. When husbands and wives are close they share the thoughts of their hearts and their desires with each other. When they are not close they seldom really communicate. When they do, it is on a superficial level that reveals nothing about each other.

Families that share in dialogue rather than monologue give each member of the family a right to grow, to mature, to be unique, to be confident, and to be whole. Dialogue implies that your opinion, and not just mine, is important. It is speaking, listening, responding, initiating, waiting, respecting and encouraging. All of this is godly affirmation. A person who grows up in such an environment will be confident in *always becoming*. We will continue to *become* throughout all eternity.

Dialogue with God is the same. We take in His written Word, listen to His voice, cry out our hearts to Him, wait for His response, respect His exhortation, and respond to His encouragement. In participating in such a dance with Him we become the persons He created us to be. This kind of dialogue with God can be learned, but it is far easier for the one who has a secure sense of being and has experienced it in a family environment first, than it is for the one who has never felt the permission to be honest with others for fear of rejection and abandonment.

Learning to appreciate and participate in genuine, meaningful dialogue is essential to overcoming the deep emptiness and anxiety of one's past. But before we are able to even dare to share our hearts with another we need prayer for the deficits to be filled. We will pray for you in that way before this chapter ends.

### 3. Confess your sin

See pages 174–175.

### 4. Receive forgiveness

See pages 175–176.

### 5. Forgive those who have wounded you

We have spoken a lot about receiving forgiveness and about your wife forgiving you for your sins against her, but we need to help you understand how to receive healing from the sins committed against you in your childhood. It is important to seek God's insights as to how your heart became confused, not relying on speculation or suspicion.

When God begins to reveal to you the source of the sins against you it is equally important to honestly and painfully admit before God (and perhaps others in confession) how broken relationships (particularly mother and father) have affected your relationships with same-sex and other-sex relationships. It is very important to acknowledge how these broken relationships have shaped your personality.

Sometimes there is a reluctance to name truthfully the facts about one's childhood. In an effort to honor father and mother, the fifth commandment, it may be difficult to say they sinned against you. To know how to do this in a godly manner, imitate God. How does God honor you when you sin? Does He blame, ridicule, or malign you? No, He calls sin sin and lovingly points it out to you so that you may be aware of it, confess it, and then be forgiven. Can we do any less with our parents?

By refusing to name the sins they commit against us we, in effect, do not honor them, but allow them to continue to sin against us. Naming sin is not pronouncing judgment upon someone – it is bringing sin to the light so that all may be set free, including the sinner! To do it God's way is to do it in love.

Perhaps you are aware that you were left for considerable periods of time as a young child, before your evocative memory of mother's presence could ease your fears. Whether or not your mother's absence was intentional, the sense of loneliness and abandonment you experienced and retained is real. She sinned against you. You may rationalize that she did the best she could, that today you understand, that she didn't know what she was doing, etc., but your heart internalizes resentment and distrust when you are wounded through prolonged emotional neglect.

To cut any bonds that tie us to the pain we experienced as infants we must choose to forgive. Often it is as simple as saying in God's presence, "I forgive you, mama." *Only when God clearly directs*, should one go to a mother with the long sad story, laying our history of sin at her feet as her responsibility. Our sin and our response to hers is still our own responsibility. We make the transaction of forgiveness with God.

If you have blatantly sinned against your mother because of her actions, that is a different situation. You must let God direct you about speaking to her after you spend time in prayer.

Your mother may have been dead for years, or you may never have known her, but still, if unforgiveness towards her is in your heart, now is the time to confess it to God. *I forgive my mother in the Name of Jesus.*

## 6. Let God fill the deficits

With all traces of unforgiveness gone you will be receptive to the infilling of God's presence into the depths of your being, the only way those deficits from childhood can now be filled. It is helpful to know how to pray for yourself and for others for this "sense of being prayer."

Many people with deep mother-love deficits describe the feeling as a big hole in the center of their being. Sometimes they feel as though there is nothing there. They walk around and seemingly function in life, but with a chasm of emptiness at the core of their being. A few people have said they sometimes have to look in a mirror to see if there is really someone there. One man tells of being out of town and being so desolate that he called his secretary, asking her just to talk to him and call him by name to affirm his existence.

These are extreme results of a deep lack of sense of being. More common is an awareness of a lack of a sense of *well-being*. Well-being keeps a person from majoring on self-issues twenty-four hours a day. A person with a sense of well-being is at home with the person God created and thinks very little about his/her own neediness. This person is comfortable within and can focus readily upon God and others. It is the rightful inheritance of one who has been blessed and affirmed in personhood from infancy.

There are varying degrees of one's lack of a sense of being or well-being. However deeply serious or slight the deficit may be in a person, God is calling each of us out of any narcissistic state of being so that we may be free to become the persons He created. Healing prayer is extremely helpful in this process if a person is willing to submit him/herself to God's ways of healing the soul.

We collaborate with Him as we are healed. We cannot sit passively waiting for Him to feel sorry for us and zap us with a sudden change. Rather, He invites us to participate with Him in the healing process.

According to Leanne Payne, "Healing prayer is not the 'instant fix,' nor the bypassing of slow and steady growth. It is that which clears the path and makes such progress possible."[1] The laying-on-of-hands and invocation of the Holy Spirit by another person is extremely helpful in the progressive healing of the deprived soul. At the same time the person receiving prayer will be responsible for ongoing discipline, confession and repentance in order to put to death the old ways of attempting to alleviate emptiness, loneliness and anxiety.

The loving, appropriate touch of a godly man or woman is very helpful in praying such a healing prayer. To place one hand on a person's back and one hand on their upper chest (laying your hand over the person's own prevents any fear of violation or inappropriate touch) is an effective way of symbolizing God's filling and His secure love. If you don't have anyone to pray for you, lay hands on yourself.

> Lord Jesus, I acknowledge the emptiness/anxiety within me. I acknowledge that You want me to know what it is like to be filled with a secure sense of my being, that I belong to You and that I am securely attached to You, the source of my life. I believe that You are the One who can fill all the emptiness within me now with the Father's love. Come, Holy Spirit! Come with Your healing love and fill me.

This is a good time to continue praying in the Spirit. We encourage those who lack a sense of being to pray this often, perhaps daily. The effects of this kind of prayer soak into your soul, accumulating and filling. When being healed a person may need to receive such a prayer regularly.

We often find that when we need such a prayer on a regular basis there is no one who knows how to pray for us in this manner. This is the time simply to teach someone to pray this way by demonstrating what you need. Without explaining your story to another person you can show them by laying hands upon them and praying quietly for that deep filling of God's love into every empty place. Then ask that person to pray for you in the same way. Both of you will be blessed.

We ask people who are beginning this process to ask for prayer in this way at least once a week until they are more aware of God's healing love settling in. Those with a deep deficit of attachment will be like "leaking sieves" for a while. They may be aware of a deep filling of God's presence while receiving prayer and then the next day feel empty again. As we said before, the effects of this kind of prayer accumulate and it is important to continue even though nothing appears to change. You are receiving much more than you realize.

For those of you who have concern over your children, knowing that you as a parent did not know how to affirm them properly and nurture them in their infancy, or if you have adopted children who lack a sense of being, there are suggested prayers at the end of the book.

## 7. Permission to grieve

As you begin to be filled with the love of the Father, a great wave of grief may rise up within you. It may be grief that you never knew was there. If it has been lodged in your heart all your life you need to give yourself permission to release it. This can be frightening if you have had a close rein on your emotions and you suddenly find yourself racked with the sobs of an abandoned child. Releasing grief is healing, however. It is indulging in self-pity that is destructive.

Remember that there is a place for your pain and grief to go – to the Cross. Allow a lifetime of grief and disappointment to be

loosed in God's presence. You may grieve over a lack of affirmation and blessing, fear of abandonment, fear of dying, lack of
nurture and attachment. Stored up grief in your heart will block
the way for further healing.

Sometimes the release of this kind of grief and pain from early
childhood can be so intense that it could be mistaken for a
demonic reaction. When ministering to others be sure to pray for
holy discernment. Ask the person you're praying with, "What is
God showing you? What memory is coming up?"

Twice in my life I have experienced such grief, so intense and
painful I seriously thought I might die. The first time the grief
was over the loss of a real father. It wasn't the loss of my father
whom I grew to love and respect as he found wholeness, the
father who gave his life to Jesus at age sixty-seven and died at age
seventy-two. It was the loss of a father when I was a little girl, the
father who had been so unhealed that he didn't know how to
love and affirm and celebrate my life. This grief (of which I had
never been aware) had accumulated over many years and had
been lodged in my heart, affecting every relationship with others
and myself. I was astonished as God released it and it came forth
in gushes of pain and sorrow.

A couple of years later I experienced another intense grief over
the missed attachment to mother. Although my mother was still
living at the time, the grief that rose up in me was the intense
wailing of an infant who is afraid mama won't return for her. I
had no idea all of that was in me, but when it was gone I was
extremely receptive to new waves of God's love that had never
before found a resting place.

During the time these healings were occurring in me I was in
ministry and was understanding this kind of healing and how to
minister it to others. It made no difference to know it intellectually; I had to experience it for myself in God's time. In fact, at
the time I was being healed of a loss of maternal attachment I
was out of town, alone and isolated from any contact with prayer
partners. In the midst of my pain, I was asking myself, "How
would you minister to someone who came to you with this
problem?" And then whatever God showed me to do, I would do
it to myself! The results were spectacular. They always are when
we cooperate with God!

Having a crucifix as a reminder of the sacrifice Jesus made to take our pain, anger, grief, etc., can be very helpful. The Cross really is the place for all our pain to go! We need symbols of His love for us and reminders of the reality of our transactions.

Most of us can get a bit dramatic in the midst of pain. At the time I was grieving over my relationship with my mother, I had been ministering in a Catholic retreat center in the middle of Kansas. Alone, at the end of the conference, I was totally immersed in my private healing service. Standing on the bed in my little cell-like room, I took down the large crucifix from the wall, placed it on the bed and lay face down on top of it, telling Jesus that I was letting all my pain go into the Cross. You may laugh, but it worked! I knew, as I grieved out my pain in His presence, that there was a place for it to go! No longer did it have to be re-cycled within me, coming up at odd times or affecting my personality.

A few years later I told this story at a conference and one of the men in attendance lived in the vicinity of the Catholic retreat center in Kansas. He went there afterwards, gave the sisters a contribution, and got permission to take the crucifix from the wall of Room 5. He sent it to me, along with "Authentication Papers" for being "A Proper Receptacle for the Pain of a Lack of Sense of Being." I knew it was the same crucifix I had used because Jesus' right hand was loose. I think I must have done that while getting healed. Anyway that crucifix now hangs in our bedroom as a reminder that *there is always a place for my pain to go.*

## 8. Releasing anger

Any long-suppressed anger may be released at the same time. Again, there is only one acceptable place for that anger to go. It is not to be projected out onto others or turned in on self; it is to go to the Cross. This is the place of sacrifice.

Getting rid of suppressed anger can bring about drastic changes in a person's personality. It allows trust and intimacy to be established with God and with others.

## 9. Facing physical pain in healing

It is possible for long-suppressed abandonment, rejection, loneliness, grief, anxiety and anger to lodge in one's body as physical pain. When one begins to be emotionally healed, allowing God to reveal the sources of the problem and letting the suppressed emotions come up and out, very real physical pain can accompany the emerging emotions. This may be very confusing to the person being healed. We have ministered to several people who have experienced this phenomenon.

When the strong physical pain begins to be apparent, such as stomach cramps, chest pain, or headaches, the temptation is to back off from the source of the pain, shut down the healing process and medicate. For most people continuing in this disruptive cycle means they never go as far as the root causes and they continue to deal with symptoms, never getting whole.

One particular man we ministered to off and on for quite a while never would move ahead with the healing God wanted to bring to him. His cycles of depression, loneliness, neediness and sense of rejection, would lead him to seek help. When he would come just to the brink of being willing to start dealing with his lack of sense of being and his ambivalence towards women he would experience intense stomach pain.

Instead of standing and hurting at the Cross until the help he needed came to him, he would run for medication. His medication followed a pattern that could be charted very easily after several months. First he would become the whining little boy, crying and complaining that he was not getting what he wanted. In his case it was all the undivided attention of his wife and children to the extent that the whole world should revolve around him. But enough was never enough. After a week or so of demanding his family's attention, he would find that their attention didn't ease his pain. Then he would spew hot, molten, anger all over his family, doing bizarre, destructive things that left lasting, painful impressions on everyone around him.

Eventually his eruptions soothed his pain and he would act as though everything was normal while his family would reel for weeks in the aftermath of another volcano. When he finally refused to seek further help and made it impossible for anyone to talk to him, he moved away to "find himself," leaving his wife to care for their children.

This man's medication wasn't pornography, but it could have been. Whatever eases the pain is the easy way out. Jesus invites us to bring our pain to the Cross and stand there with Him as He ministers to the deep heart. It may not be the "easiest way out" but it will be the most satisfying, complete, rewarding, hard work you will ever do. What is more important is that this kind of redemptive suffering brings wholeness.

## 10. Renounce Baal

In ancient Israel and throughout the Middle East, the most well-known pagan god was Baal, the god of sexual orgy, along with his consort, Ashteroth. The Old Testament is full of admonishments from God to His people to "Tear down your altars to Baal and the detestable Asherah poles!"[2]

Although you won't find the word "pornography" in the Scriptures, it will apply when describing the accouterments of Baal worship. Everything that is the antithesis of God's standards of holy sexuality in marriage was encouraged in the pagan ceremonies to honor Baal and Ashteroth. The end result of all such worship was then and still is, death. The coveted sacrifice was oneself or one's child, with no substitutionary animal as in the Temple, or Messiah Himself, as on Calvary.

To this day Baal worship attracts demons who celebrate at his altar. His modern altar for the neo-pagans and even Christians who have gone astray is the altar of sexual indulgence with no restraints. Our society is embracing it and as a result we are losing our respect and desire for holy living.

Paul gave a clear and firm reprimand to Christian Corinthians who were indulging in the practices of the pagans in their society at the same time as they were professing to follow Jesus, the Messiah:

*"Therefore, my dear friends, flee from idolatry."*
(1 Corinthians 10:14)

*"Do not those who eat the sacrifices participate in the altar?"*
(1 Corinthians 10:18)

*"The sacrifices of pagans are offered to demons, not to God, and I do not want you to be participants with demons. You cannot drink the cup of the Lord and the cup of demons too; you cannot have a part in both the Lord's table and the table of demons."*
(1 Corinthians 10:20–21)

Paul was admonishing these Christians that if they participate in the practices of pagans and indulge in what they do as they worship their gods, they might as well be worshiping Baal too. Baal accepts the worship of his devotees and takes seriously their activities and sacrifices. As he accepts the sacrifices, the pagan god then considers the practitioner as one who belongs to him. We are clearly told that we cannot worship two gods or serve two masters.[3] You must choose whom you will serve![4]

God opened my eyes only once to see the phallic demons who celebrate at Baal's altar. I hope I never see them again. They are hideous little things, disgusting and vile, too despicable to describe in detail. When He allowed me to see them I knew that a particular ministry situation we were dealing with was Baal worship and it had to be confessed to God and renounced. As Conlee and I and two prayer partners obeyed God, the results were not spectacular, but the obedient action was effective. Within a couple of weeks healing began in remarkable ways.

Your involvement with Baal worship through pornography, sexual fantasy and masturbation has infected your home because your actions have erected an altar to Baal and because of that he has claimed you as his own. Let God's words ring in your ears, *"Tear down your altar to Baal!"*

The way we tear down strongholds is to confess our sins, receive God's forgiveness and then renounce the idols in Jesus' name. Then we are empowered to build a new altar to a holy God.

> I renounce you, Baal, in the name of Jesus Christ. I renounce you, Ashteroth, in the name of Jesus Christ. I renounce all accompanying demons who have flocked around your altar. In the power of the Holy Spirit I tear it down and cleanse my home by the Blood of Jesus Christ.

You may want to use holy water in this cleansing prayer as a symbol of what Jesus is doing and of His water of Life which renews and heals. (Read Ezekiel 36:24–29a.) Then erect a proper altar by praising Jesus and the work He has accomplished for you. Praise and worship builds a holy altar because it is a sacrifice of your heart.

## 11. Healing of memories

Memories, both remembered and beyond our remembrance, can be healed in two ways:

1.  As we invite Jesus to be present in the memory, knowing that He is present in all times, eternal past, present and eternal future, we use our sanctified imaginations to see Him and hear His healing words for us.

2.  We choose to forgive those who have wounded us in the past. Unforgiveness binds pain and sin to the soul, so that when we choose to forgive, we release the sins of others to God and are free to become whole without the weight of another's problems.

I have been present with a few people who came present to their own births, some even while in the womb. The pain they endured as God brought them present to past fears, rejections, or sense of abandonment was unimaginable, but the healing they received was spectacular.

A twenty-three year old woman came to me seeking healing prayer for intense fears and anxiety. She couldn't remember a time when she hadn't felt this way. We asked God to reveal the memory of that fear first entering in. She immediately had a violent reaction to an unseen threat, writhing and screaming, fearful of dying in a most graphic way. She kept screaming, "Don't kill me! I want to live!"

She had been taken by the Holy Spirit to be present to her time in the womb, where she first experienced the fears that had continued into adulthood. In spite of the trauma she encountered she was comforted by the presence of Jesus who affirmed her with His love and gave her His life. A peace came upon her before she left. She intuitively knew that her mother had attempted an abortion. I encouraged her to ask her mother about the circumstances of her conception and pregnancy, without placing any blame or making accusations.

She approached her mother in a few days, telling her she was receiving some spiritual counseling and wanted to know something about her time *in utero*. Her mother burst into tears, confessing the attempted abortion, her fears of pregnancy, her guilt and her inability to ever love her daughter. God's revelation to this young woman opened up a most amazing healing for a whole family because it was done in a holy, redemptive way. Even the mother was freed to become whole as her fears and guilt were brought to the light of Christ and she could receive His forgiveness.

At *Pastoral Care Ministries* conferences there is the opportunity for the whole group of participants to receive healing of memories prayers, covering every aspect of their lives, from conception to the present. It takes about an hour and remarkable deep healings occur in very quiet ways during this prayer.

At *The Journey to Wholeness in Christ* we incorporate a prayer for the healing of very early memories, with ministry for a sense of being. We pray for everyone from the time of conception through birth. The prayer has been adapted from the one Leanne Payne prays, because she taught us how to pray in this way. This prayer seems to cement the sense of being affirmation in very gentle and complete ways.

We would like to pray it over you now. Some parts of the prayer may not be pertinent to your situation, but every time you enter into this prayer God will show you something new and bring a deeper healing. It is not a prayer to receive lightly or quickly. There are places in the prayer where you should pause for as long as it takes to hear what God is saying to your heart, or see pictures of your early life that He is showing you.

Set aside a special time to experience this prayer. You should be in a quiet place without fear of interruption. Take the phone off the hook. Devote yourself to God's presence and allow Him to hold you as you pray.

Listening to God as you receive the prayer is vital. There are obvious places within the prayer that are marked to remind you to stop and listen to the words coming to you from God. It is His voice, not the words of the prayer that bring you healing. Don't rush. This kind of prayer takes time, relaxation and concentration. It might be necessary for you to quiet your mind before beginning. Listening to a quiet praise song, reading a comforting scripture, or using your holy imagination to see God and crawl up on His lap might be helpful.

Probably you will want to let God lead you through this prayer several times over the next several months. If you are married you may want to go through it with your marriage partner sometime. You may want to ask someone to pray it for you so that you can close your eyes and tune into what God is saying. I have known one man who recorded the prayer so that he could listen to it attentively, stopping the tape when God began to speak to him.

Perhaps you have never prayed this way before. If you find yourself analyzing the prayer and dissecting what God is doing, it is helpful to recognize that tendency and confess it to God, asking Him to give you the strength to choose to focus on Him. Then begin again.

Remember, God is your Healer and the Restorer of your soul!

## Healing of memories prayer for a sense of being

> Heavenly Father, dearest Abba, I welcome Your presence.
> I embrace Your love as a blanket of protection around me as I let all my weight down upon You.
> You are the One who calls each person into being.
> You are the One who is present as each child is being formed in mother's womb.
> You are the One who welcomes and affirms each child into the world.
> You are the One who is there to receive those who are abandoned, frightened, or unfulfilled.
> You are the One who sees any traces of wounds still residing in my heart from childhood.
> I acknowledge that You alone can fill the deficits that I am just beginning to understand – and even those I will never understand.
> I come to You and say, Father, You are the healer. Father, have mercy upon me!

> Father, I confess the sins of this fallen world that have distorted Your perfect plans for Your children. Your plans have been so grossly distorted that many infants are born without any sense of being related to mother and without a sense of peace in her love.

Father, forgive me for any ways I have encouraged or
   spread this widespread sin of neglect and
   abandonment...
   - through the love of Mammon above my love for
     You, that has encouraged mothers to leave their
     infants for the workplace,
   - through the promotion of self above sacrifice,
   - through seeking what is right in my own eyes rather
     than looking to You, my Creator,
   - through the neglect of Your Word that guides us as
     parents and grandparents.

I confess to You, Father, the sins of my parents.
I especially pray for my relationship with my mother and
   any ways she sinned against me, disrupting our
   relationship.
I name her sin to You, Lord, as I understand it.

I choose now to forgive her for sinning against me.
I forgive her for not being able to relate to me in healthy
   ways.
I forgive you, mother, for not being there for me when I
   felt abandoned.

I confess to You, Father, all the other circumstances that
   have happened because of living in this fallen world,
   other than her sin against me, that contributed to a
   lack of connectedness between my mother and me.
I forgive her for dying.
I forgive her for being sick.
I forgive her for putting me up for adoption.
I forgive her for having to go to work.
I forgive her for having too many responsibilities to care
   for me.

I lift my mother up into Your hands, Lord, and I bless the
real person in her, the one You created her to be.
I ask You to give me a picture of her as a whole woman.
Thank you, mother, for giving birth to me ... for
collaborating with God, whether you knew Him or
not, in giving me life.

Lord, I confess to You, that for whatever reason, I never
made a secure attachment to my mother, or either I
lost it at some point in my development.
I have felt as if there is no place for me to fit in;
as though I never stand on solid ground,
as though I am never accepted,
as though I am related to no one,
as though I am desperately alone in every situation.
Enter into each empty place, Lord, with Your everlasting
love.
Give me a true sense of being.
Fill me with the Love I need in order to be related to
others.

I confess, Lord, that I have tried to alleviate my emptiness,
pain, loneliness, anxiety, and tension through
undesirable behavior, and by ungodly activities.
Forgive me, Lord, for losing hope in You...
- for draining other people instead of turning to You,
- for turning to pornography rather than You for
comfort,
- for the substitute of fantasy, masturbation and sex
for the reality of Your love,
- for looking to substances – overeating, alcohol,
drugs, cigarettes to alleviate my anxiety.
Forgive me for abusing my body in so many ways to drive
away the emptiness.

Forgive me for perpetuating the sins that have been
committed against me by sinning in the same ways
against my children.

---

Lord, as You forgive this one who makes these confessions to You
and who has extended forgiveness to others, fill him/her with a
new, godly, holy peace within. Gather up all the loneliness and
tension and emptiness and fear and gnawing anxiety and take it
from his heart and his body.

Enter into those places now with the power of Your love. Let
Your peace enter into his physical body where any tension has
lodged, especially the genital area where that tension has
become eroticized. Transform his lonely heart into a garden of
solitude where You are found.

---

Lord, I ask that You let the memories of my conception
come present to me.
At the very moment I was conceived You were there.
You know all the circumstances of my conception, O Lord,
where there was
illegitimacy,
unlove between my parents,
generational sins within my family lines, such as
- idolatry
- cruelty
- incest
- adultery
- murder
- bestiality
- negativity
- fears
I choose to forgive those family members of my past, even
my generational ancestors. I forgive my...
- parents,
- brothers and sisters,
- grandparents of many generations,
- aunts,

- uncles,
- cousins.

Lord, I choose to be free from their sins.

By forgiving them and being loosed from their sins, I now also loose the effects of any curses that have been made on my family line.

I loose the curses of...

- racial prejudice,
- the occult,
- any alliances with darkness.

*"A curse without a cause shall not alight."*

(Proverbs 26:2 NKJV)

Upon my confession and extension of forgiveness all causes for curses to alight on me are removed. Thank You, Lord, for lifting any curses from me and showering me with Your blessings. I celebrate my freedom in You as You cleanse me with Your Blood, removing all generational sin and bondage.

As I was being formed in my mother's womb, You were there, Lord.

I ask You to free me from...

- any rejections I experienced in her womb,
- any fears or anxieties I experienced through the circumstances of my parents' lives,
- any attempted abortion or miscarriage, or invasions of the womb, such as:
  - amniocentesis,
  - any fear of death that was transferred to my heart,
  - any sense that I should not have been born,
  - any way I did not feel safe as I was being formed,
  - any sense that my family would not be a safe place for me to be born into.

I extend forgiveness to my parents.

Thank You, Lord.

At the moment of my birth, Lord, You were there to
welcome me.
I give You the fears of any trauma at that time...
- pain of labor,
- breech birth,
- panic of emergency C-section,
- premature labor,
- birthing techniques,
- forced delay of birth,
- forceps,
- fetal monitors,
- any violence,
- loud noises,
- blinding lights,
- words spoken over me,
- physical deformities.

I ask You to reveal to me any trauma that occurred during
time I spent away from my mother immediately
following my birth, because of...
- isolation of an incubator,
- illness,
- pain associated with treatment,
- circumcision,
- loss of a twin,
- sense of abandonment,
- fears,
- grief,
- sorrow,
- rejection.

I choose to forgive doctors, nurses, hospital staff,
- their attitudes and policies...

Lord, I ask You to hold me tightly and pour Your Love into
all the deprived and frightened places within my
heart.

Lord, I ask You to bring up any early memory of feeling
abandoned and neglected,
I ask You to allow me to see You in that memory...

- where You are,
- what You are doing,
- what You are saying to me.

Lord, let Your love now give me the sense of attachment I missed getting at the appropriate time. I receive Your embrace and Your affirmation.

I receive the name You have for me.

Lord, I confess that I repress my need for attachment to others in healthy ways. Loving relationships with others are so difficult for me. As You have shown me the root causes of this problem, I ask for Your healing by the power of Your love.
Thank You, Lord.

Lord, I confess that I need healthy relationships with women.
Out of fear and distrust I often have avoided women.
Out of my unfulfilled needs for attachment I have clung to women in unhealthy ways.
I have been ambivalent with women,
  loving and disrespecting them,
  wanting them and avoiding them.
Forgive me, Lord, as I remember all the women in my life that I have wounded by my actions and words.

I ask You, Lord, to free me from this behavior and fill all the deficits of mother-love within me.

Lord, I confess that I was bonded to my mother in such an
unhealthy way that I never came free from her in
appropriate ways. I had no godly, masculine voice in
my life, calling me away from her at the appropriate
time, into my own identity. I know I need to separate
my identity from that of my mother.

I choose to forgive both my mother and my father in Jesus'
Name.

I ask You to show me if there is still any diseased umbilical
cord attaching me to my mother.

I allow You, Lord, to cut these cords and properly attach
me to Yourself for my true identity.

In Jesus' name, I renounce any vows I made to never be
like my mother.

I ask You to free me from any ungodly effects of those
vows so that I may relate aright to the good in my
mother and in all women.

Lord, I choose to lift my father up to You now, seeing him
in Your presence. I pray for my relationship with my
father and especially, any ways he sinned against me.

I confess the sins of my father before You, that he may be
healed.

I choose to forgive him, Lord, for sinning against me. I
forgive him for not being able to call me forth into my
true self, for not giving me the security and
encouragement to relate to all creation as a whole
person.

I forgive him for not sending his love to me even as I was
growing in the womb.

I forgive him for not loving my mother.

I forgive him for not providing a safe home of protection
for me as a child.
I forgive him for not affirming me as a man (woman).
I forgive him for being so wounded himself that he could
not love in meaningful ways.
I forgive him for being abusive in words and/or in actions.
I forgive him for abandoning our family.
I forgive him for bringing pornography into our family and
polluting our home.

I ask to see You, my heavenly Father, present as I was born.
Please let me hear Your masculine voice, calling me
forth, into the person You created me to be. I receive
Your blessing of love as I wait in Your presence.

In Your presence, I give you any internalized fears of the
masculine presence...
- any fears of my father,
- fears of the false masculine,
- fears of criticism from men,
- fears of abandonment,
- fears of abuse,
- fears of death.
I ask you to resymbolize for me what it means to be a man
in the image of God.

In Jesus' name, I renounce any vows I made to never be
like my father.
I ask You to release me from any ungodly effects of those
vows so that I may see men in a holy way and relate to
the good in my father and in all men.

Lord, I ask You to bless both my mother and my father, in Jesus' name. I thank You that, through them, You have given me life. May each of them grow into the full potential You have always had for them.

I pray all this in Jesus' Name.

Now, Lord, I ask for a new heart and a new spirit to be birthed in Your child who has prayed these prayers. May You strengthen the will to always choose what You would choose. And may Your deep peace fill to overflowing with all your Love and sense of being that You long for all Your children to possess. Amen.

# Chapter 10

## Reviews
*The testimonies of strugglers and overcomers*

*"They overcame him* [the Accuser] *by the blood of the Lamb
and by the word of their testimony;
they did not love their loves so much as to shrink from death."*
(Revelation 12:11)

I am very recently recovering from my struggle [with sexual addiction], and one of the biggest things that has helped me has been to see other men struggling with the same issue. The church needs to step up to the plate because good men are being lost in this spiritual battle!

*Jason*[1]

When you can begin to tell your story in honesty, without embellishment or over-spirituality, and without having your pain define who you are, you are well on your way to becoming whole.

When you can see objectively through the wounds of your past and the wounds you have inflicted upon others, you will begin to believe (and experience) that God forgives and trans-forms your life.

The three-fold way of achieving the life of an overcomer is beautifully outlined for us in Revelations 12:11:

1.  The blood of the Lamb
2.  The word of testimony
3.  Death to self

Your testimony is the story of your dying to self, and allowing the power of the blood of the Lamb transform you into resurrection life. You are writing your testimony today as you struggle in your desire to become whole. You are choosing to give up what the world and your unhealed soul says you deserve.

You will have "friends" who will not understand your choices. You will have to turn your back on what they say if their values do not line up with God's. You may have to set strong boundaries in some old relationships. You will be sacrificing your old desires for the sake of those you love. There is resurrection power in all these choices.

You have the power to overcome the strong temptations of the world when you are willing to die to self and allow Jesus to live in you. You will want to shrink from this kind of death because it will be painful. Dying is hard work; it hurts. No one else can do it for you. But, because you are choosing to be an overcomer, you won't shrink from it. You will face your pain, standing in the Cross. And you will not stand alone; Jesus will stand with You. He has been there before. He stood alone so you won't have to, and He endured.

## The desires of your heart

At this moment, what are the desires of your heart? Write them in your prayer journal.

Are you willing to put them on the Cross, giving them to Jesus? What does He do with your desires?

Some of our desires are our Ishmaels. We have decided what is right in our own eyes and we have grasped it, believing it would bring us happiness. Instead those desires have brought misery to us and to others. Abraham loved Ishmael. It was hard for him to give him up, but he obeyed God for the sake of the promise.

Some of our desires are our Isaacs. They are promises from God and we have waited a long time for them. But still, we may be called to lay them on the altar. Our good desires may be too grandiose, needing to be refined by the hand of God. Or they may be too small, needing God's love to enlarge them for us.

Whatever we are not willing to sacrifice we will fail to see resurrection power flowing through. We often don't see immediate results of our sacrifices. But be assured, the principle of resurrection power is always flowing!

## The power of your testimony

We can have power in our testimonies only by looking back through the Cross, seeing the sacrifice Jesus made for us, and being aware of the sacrifices we are willing to make for Him. Your testimony can help others become free; it is an encouragement, a helping hand on the journey to wholeness.

Besides helping others, your testimony (and you do have one!) enables you to become aware of the enormous sacrifice Jesus has made for you and the vast amounts of resurrection power that are already in your life, even though there is still much work to be done.

The following stories of other strugglers and overcomers are offered as their sacrifices and thanksgivings to the Lord who is completing them. Each one of them is at a different stage of the journey. Not all are healed yet as much as is possible, but each one is trusting in the Lord, willing to collaborate with Him to get the job done.

### Mike's story[2]

It's amazing the terrifying thoughts that run through your mind when you're holding a gun to your head. In my case, I was the most unlikely person in the world to be sitting there in the darkness of my car with a .357 caliber Magnum trembling in my hand and aimed squarely at my head.

After all, I was the pastor of a successful, growing, central Florida church. I had a wonderful family – a beautiful wife and two lovely children. Four years earlier, my wife and I had arrived in the city with great expectations for building a church. It was a Saturday morning when I was first confronted with a growing trash heap that was accumulating outside our home. I was out on the front lawn picking up when I noticed a paperback book by the roadside. Out of curiosity I picked it up and started leafing through the pages. It didn't take long to realize it was pornographic – no dirty pictures, but a collection of pornographic stories that immediately carved crystal clear sexual images in my mind.

I tossed out the book, not realizing the mental replicas couldn't be forgotten quite so easily. After a week or two those images began coming back to my mind with a vengeance. Soon I began waking up in the middle of the night thinking about them. As the months passed, they became the first things I thought about when I awoke in the morning and the last things I pictured before I went to sleep at night.

It wasn't long before I ventured into the world of pornographic magazines and videos. During my lunch hour, any private moment I could get, I spent looking at them. After each time, I became overwhelmed with feelings of shame. I would promise myself and God that I would never do it again, yet after the emotion of guilt would fade, I would find myself visiting the places I'd swore I'd never go to again.

The fascination progressed until I had to experience more than a simple magazine or video could provide. That's when I first visited a massage parlor.

During this time I still kept up my pastoral duties. Absolutely no one had any idea of my double life. My escapades seemed to take place in three-month cycles. For three months I would experience relief and life free as a pastor, family man and friend. But then, triggered by a TV program, a magazine ad, or a comment on the radio, I would find myself once again inside an adult bookstore, in a massage parlor, or calling an escort service.

While sitting there in the darkened car, images of the past flooded through my mind. The hiding, the disguises, the shame, the disappointment came rushing forward like a raging army of darkness. Somehow, by the grace of God, I was so afraid of dying that I didn't have the courage to pull the trigger.

That night I confessed everything to my wife. Holding nothing back, I told her my nightmarish history. Of course, she was devastated. I fully expected her to leave, but I hadn't counted on the depth of her commitment to God and His unlimited grace in the face of a horrific circumstance.

I did know that the healing and recovery might take years. I started sleeping on the couch knowing that, although there was forgiveness at the cross, the consequences of my sin would take great time and even greater effort to repair.

Although it was the most difficult time of my life, over the next few years God would begin to work a miracle in my life and in the life of my family. Along with my wife's determination not to give up, God graciously helped us break the bondage of that horrible stronghold and begin a new life together.

Insecurity is the doorway of deception. A revelation of God's love is the only way to shut the door of insecurity. Finding our security in His love establishes our heart and releases His ability in the face of temptation.

I no longer succumb to the temptation of pornography. I don't need to fill a void of rejection by trying to be empowered by sex. I am loved! I am accepted by God. The power of God's love gives us the strength to believe, the desire to press on, the freedom to love, the courage to laugh in the face of adversity, and the faith to live holy.

### Susan's story

I first learned of my husband's addiction to pornography over five years ago. We are divorced today. I wish I could say that there was a happy ending between the two of us, however, I can say that God has restored me to wholeness, and I faithfully and with a tender heart, am able to pray for Josh, my ex-husband, each and every day.

Recently, in the past two months, I have felt God asking me to be willing to reconcile with him. My response to God was, that would be the biggest miracle I can only begin to imagine in part, as there is so much wreckage, not only to myself, but the church body in which we served, my children, and our friends. God didn't give me a time frame, so I have simply said I am willing, laying it at the foot of the cross, and moving forward in my own walk, ministry and journey to wholeness.

Both my husband and I were leaders in our church. I was the women's counselor on staff as well as a worship leader, and developed and facilitated a group for battered women. My husband too, was on the worship team, and was a counselor in a secular treatment center, plus did a men's anger management group.

I believe we were seen as a couple with tremendous potential, anointing and respect among church members and the pastoral staff. Josh and I had only been married for about one year, when I noticed his behavior as that of what I will call "relapse." We both are in recovery for alcohol addiction (14 years for me, 10 years for him).

I went to our best friend and made the comment, "I think Josh is in relapse and is going to drink." Our friend said the word "Pornography". In that moment I knew he was right, yet my scope of understanding about this addiction was very narrow and totally limited. The biggest picture I had was *Playboy* (mere child's play in the real world of porn). So I went home and asked Josh if he had looked at pornography. He said, "Yes, last week."

I left it at that, with a mind that was spinning. The next morning the Holy Spirit prompted me to ask how long had he been looking at pornography. His answer changed my life forever. He said since he was fourteen. It was on that day that my life changed. I could never have imagined the things I was to learn and the truths I was to face over the next two to three years.

From that moment on, for the next several years, I spent every waking moment searching, seeking, praying, learning, confronting, crying, being counseled, etc., etc., etc. I clung to the Scriptures, and cried out constantly to God for the truth, so I would be set free and so my husband would be set free.

I learned how steeped Josh was in every imaginable piece of porn – prostitutes, private strippers, voyeurism, movies, Internet, dumpster hopping, magazines, lying, stealing, minimizing, blaming, entitlement, compartmentalization, justification, rationalization. You name it, I believe every base was covered.

In spite of all this, I can only praise God for His faithfulness. He protected me at every turn from disease, from financial ruin, and from not getting sucked into the cycle of addiction with my husband. I was being blamed for everything – bad sex, not loving enough, not being a good enough wife.

Fortunately, we were with a counselor who would say, "You know, Josh, if you were not practicing your addiction, and you were saying these things about Susan, then we would take a serious look. But you are not acting from a place that is clear or whole, so for today what you say holds no water."

What a blessing that was to me to have someone see the truth. I know many women who have been sent home to pray harder, be a better lover, quit exaggerating, on and on. It can make you crazy! I did have my moments of outburst, and acting badly. I certainly didn't do it all right...

I sought God like crazy, and put myself in places of accountability at all times, even when I was not such a pretty sight to see. At times I felt like my entire life was on the big screen, and trust me, with such subject matter like this, people have very strong views. Others need to minimize everything because they are so uncomfortable with the subject.

I was always honest because I knew everything in my life depended on my walk with the Lord. I was not willing to relinquish nor compromise that. It was awful, painful, lonely, scary, overwhelming, humiliating, embarrassing, and at times, very confusing. Yet I clung to Jesus for life itself.

Three years ago Josh and I went to a Christian healing conference out of town and he proclaimed that he had a real healing with Jesus. However, during the week of the conference, he would daily leave and go into the city to act out. I returned home alone, leaving him a letter, begging him to stay to get help through the ministry there. He refused, stating I had abandoned him, and that he was filing for divorce. I said no divorce, but he would not listen.

While at that conference I bought your book, *The Journey to Wholeness in Christ*. Because I do better with a task-oriented book, it was very helpful to me. My journey from that conference lasted forty more days, with revelation after revelation, healing after healing. Not only did I use the book, but now it is part of the curriculum at a small Christian college as a result of what it did in my life and the testimony I have been able to share.

What I believe happened to Josh, that so many face, is this: God did give him a way out which did not exclude walking through the healing process which was to come after his initial face to face encounter with Jesus. God asked him then to journey with Him into what I call "the pool of pain." It is here that we get to walk through all that has been placed upon us by family, abusers, and the consequences of our own choices.

It is in that pool of pain that we get set free, however we have to be willing to go into that place of unfamiliarity, with complete abandonment and trust in God. Eventually the pain will subside and complete and absolute healing will take place. What I believe often happens is that the pain or the fear of pain is so great that people stick a toe in the pool and then run back to that with which they are so familiar and which Satan makes appear so enticing and acceptable.

For the past three and a half years I have been on the fast track to healing. Initially the first year that Josh left, which was two years into the discovery of his addiction, I had many defining moments. One was on New Year's Day, as I drove around for hours looking for a place to go. As a single woman who had mostly married friends, there is definitely a season of not belonging anywhere. It was on that desperate day that I came to a crossroad.

Either I was going to plummet into the sea of depression, or I was going to fight to keep my head above water. I cried out to God and said, "Help! I refuse to go down." He gently said, "Your purpose is to invest in the lives of people."

Lots has happened since that day, more than I can or will share, yet I am free, and I am in love with Jesus. He recently asked me if I would pick up my cross to follow Him, leaving all behind. My answer was, "Yes, Lord!"

I am so excited to be able to pursue God violently, as it says in the Scripture, in complete abandonment, knowing there is no safer place. He has promised me no limits, so I am holding Him to His promise. I want to be part of the end time revival, and to see the mighty works of our Creator. I know that I am on the right path.

This past year God walked me through a complete forgiveness for Josh. There was a time that the nicest name I could call him was "bastard," but today I do have sweet memories of good times and I truly bless the gifts he does carry. I can't yet imagine him free from this horrific addiction, yet God is in the business of miracles. This would have to rank #1 on my list of miracles if it does happen!

In love and hope for those still afflicted and tangled in this awful web of sexual addiction, I cry out and pray for the truth to set the captives free.

### Jake's story

In my ministry as a lay Christian counselor I have met hundreds of men who have greatly suffered and who have paid a very high cost for being addicted to pornography. The suffering has been shame, guilt, brokenness and distance from God and from loved ones. The cost has been broken marriages, inordinate amounts of time spent planning, finding and using pornography, less time and less intimacy with family, cross-addictions, loss of jobs, physical impairments, including sexually transmitted diseases, and ultimately, loss of life.

I consider this to be both (1) an illness (addiction/obsession), not unlike alcoholism or drug addiction, and (2) a spiritual battle involving Satan's attempt to destroy and corrupt God's creation, His beloved children.

I firmly believe that through the wonderful grace and mercy of God, the compassion (He too was broken and experienced pain and suffering) and healing powers of our Savior Jesus Christ (the addict is dying and desperately needs to be saved), and the conviction and direction from the Holy Spirit, that a person lost to pornography can find new life/recover/restoration by being thoroughly "transformed." I approach such transformation from a holistic approach, i.e. "allow the Lord to change you from the inside-out, heart, mind, body and soul."

I strongly believe that for men there is a direct connection between addiction to pornography and relational problems with fathers. I feel this connection is also true with male homosexuals. The common denominator appears to be this: a father who was or is unable to show demonstrable love and affection to his son. My heart breaks when I hear a man say, "If only my father could tell me just one time that he loves me it would mean the world to me. I would have given anything to have received just one hug or one kiss from my father."

That love that God intended us to receive from our fathers, to fill our souls with a sense of belonging, to feel fully accepted and valued as being precious and worthy is missing and has a tremendous impact on the very soul of the child. The pornography addict seeks to fill up this tremendous hole/gap in his soul by using (acting out) counterfeit intimacy and self love. We are trying to numb the pain of loneliness and unworthiness (message: "My father didn't love me so I must not be serving of love. I'm unlovable. I'm not worthy!"), and the fear and the lack of intimacy in our lives. Love and intimacy were not modeled to us by our fathers.

The story of the Cross is in fact the story of transformation for those who come to Jesus with contrite and broken hearts, who with bended knees cry out for help and for redemption. It is there and then when Jesus Christ answers our cries and begins His awesome work of transformation and healing. Praise God!

Last but not least, I encourage each person I counsel to surround themselves with prayer. Asking a wife to pray, asking prayer teams at church to pray, seeking soaking prayers and intercessory prayers are all crucial ingredients for healing, transformation, and restoration. I explain to the people I counsel that without God's intervention the battle will be lost. With God there is great hope; without God life becomes hopeless.

I am passionate about this because this is my story. My father kept pornographic magazines in our house and I discovered them when I was twelve. My father was a prominent physician who spent most of his life practicing medicine, gambling, drinking and taking drugs. I was terrified of his alcohol-induced rages and I can never remember him ever hugging me or kissing me or demonstrably expressing love and affection for me. What especially broke my heart was the time and love he openly showed to his horses.

In graduate school we were asked one day to share who showed you the most unconditional love when you were a child. I answered honestly, "My dog." I was one of three students with this response – how sad!

I prayed each day from the age of 12 to 14 that my father would die so that my mother would no longer have to suffer and that I would never again have to be shamed and humiliated by him. One day the headmaster of my school pulled me out of class and told me that my father had died. I later found out that he had committed suicide.

In high school I occasionally used pornography. While attending college and for the next 20 years I looked at pornographic movies and magazines and was a full-blown addict by the time I got married. I used to show pornographic movies in my home to my friends and I ultimately got a wake-up call from one of those friends. While attending a wedding, this friend introduced me to his fiancée as "I'd like you to meet Mr. Pornography." I felt terribly shamed and guilt-laden.

For the first ten years of my married life I would share pornographic magazines with my best friend. I needed more and more pornography to satiate my needs and was starting to go down the spiral. In my mind I felt that I now had to possibly get my wife involved by entertaining sex with other couples. She was disgusted by the idea.

I would spend inordinate amounts of time and money procuring pornography and during one period of time I would sneak out of the house at 2 or 3 am to purchase magazines.

In my late 30s I gave my life to Christ and fortunately came under the guidance of men belonging to a ministry called The Pittsburgh Experiment. These men gently encouraged me to allow God to show me areas in my life and character that needed to be changed. Much to my surprise and great shame, my little girl found a stash of pornography I had hidden in our house. I cannot tell you how broken and literally destroyed I felt. I fell to my knees on the floor like a piece of putty and implored God to forgive me, to help me, and to remove this incident from my child's mind.

This began a process of great delivery, healing and restoration. I was convicted to share with my wife that I was addicted to pornography and that I needed help. I was encouraged to share my heart with those men who loved and always supported me in The Pittsburgh Experiment.

One of my most poignant memories is the time I was a patient in a hospital. Resting in my bed in my hospital gown, I suddenly had an insatiable desire and need for pornography. I hurriedly put on an overcoat and walked out of the hospital in search of the closest convenience store. Finding one nearby, I practically ran to the magazine section and began to reach out to grab a pornographic magazine. As my hand neared the magazine it began to shake and tremor uncontrollably as if it had been stopped by an invisible force. I stood there trembling for many minutes and then I suddenly realized what was taking place.

A battle for my life (my mind, body and soul) was being acted out, and I needed to make a choice immediately. That day I was victorious because I chose God and through His mercy and grace I was able to put my hands down, walk back to the hospital, and focus on His great desire to save me and protect me.

My best business friend died as a result of the spiraling effects of a pornography addiction. He called me up one day and said, "Jake, I need to meet with you immediately. I have something to share with you." We met at a restaurant where he disclosed that he had been living a secret life from his wife, family and friends. Many years before he had become addicted to pornography and had slipped down the spiral in his need for more and more satiation. He finally got to the point that he tried homosexuality and fully entered into a bisexual lifestyle. He stated that he had never told anyone but now he was scared that he might have contracted AIDS and that maybe his wife was infected.

I told him I would walk with him and be supportive of getting his life right with God, but that he had to (1) get tested, and (2) tell his wife. Approximately one week later, immediately after he received the test results, we met and he shared with me the sad news that he in fact did have AIDS. As he cried and I cried with him, he shared with me that he probably would be dead within the next year. His funeral six months later was one of the saddest I have ever attended.

His wife and three young children were there and all I could think of is "this, but for the mercy and grace of God, could have been me. Thank You God, for saving my life!"

The last time my friend was able to talk to me he shared something that still moves me. He said, "Jake, all I ever wanted in life was to have experienced the love of my father and he never was able to show me that love. Sex with the men had little to do with sex – it had everything to do with feeling a sense of being loved, of belonging, something I so much wanted to receive from my father."

### Simon's story

My relationship with my mother was not all that bad, though I never felt close to her. She was not domineering, nor was she naive. She supported me in the activities I was interested in and encouraged me to participate in church activities. But I never felt the bond with her that I did with my father. I didn't feel unloved by her, just not close.

I always related much more to my father, enjoying his male companionship. To me, my dad was someone who could fix everything, play every kind of sport and be good at all of them. He was a youth minister and I was always proud to see him up in front of everyone. He seemed larger than life to me.

I first discovered pornography when I was seven. I found some pages that had been torn out of a magazine and hidden in some bushes by a couple of my friends. The feeling I got when I saw those pictures felt like a rush of adrenaline through my body. It felt great.

I first realized pornography was a problem for me after I got married. I knew it was going to cause a big gap in my relationship with my wife. During the height of my porn indulgence I probably looked at it every day for two to three months and then got rid of it for six months to a year. Then I would start again.

My relationship to the Lord was not very close. I thought it was at the time, but looking back it was very minimal. I would pray, only after the guilt preyed on me, and then I would ask God to take it away from me.

Before my wife knew what I was up to, she thought I was not very interested in sex. The duration of time we would go without sex was more than she cared to go. When my wife found out about my pornography usage, it was a massive blow to our relationship. All trust vanished and a sense of betrayal set in. She was angry, heart-broken, and felt rejected.

The day she found out was a heart-wrenching experience, and yet full of release. It was as if the wall I had put up came crashing down to provide a way out. We talked about how long I had the problem with porn, and she helped me through it.

When I asked God how this got hold of me He showed me a picture I used to look at when I was about four years old. It was a picture in a child's book of an Indian woman with her back turned and not wearing a shirt. Though the picture was not revealing at all, it was a starting point of my interest.

My healing process has taken a long time and is getting better from day to day. Without the support of my wonderful wife, falling back into pornography would be easy. She is constantly keeping me accountable. On a scale of 1–10 with 10 being the hardest thing I have ever done, getting porn out of my life has been a 9.

I have to give the Lord credit for opening my eyes to the poisonous effects of pornography. But I give my wife credit for standing by me and working with me through it. It took her about four months to begin to trust me again. My relationship with her is better now that it has ever been. Our frequency of having sex has increased and the Lord has made it much more fulfilling. I feel much more open to talk with her about sensitive topics and my attitude toward her is more peaceful.

The Internet is what I have struggled with most. I still have strong temptations to go back to pornography on it. The smallest thought can creep into my head and make me want to look for porn on the Internet. Keeping it out of our home and not having easy access to it helps with the healing process. This is the reason I don't use the Internet very often. Also, getting involved with a men's Bible study has helped.

My relationship with the Lord has changed a lot. I am able to trust Him with this area of my life and am grateful that He gave me a way out. I know He always provides a way out of any bad situation; our job is to find it. Accepting myself is a daily struggle and I have come to realize two things: God can accept me and love me in spite of my imperfections, and my wife has vowed to stay with me and love me. Those two things allow me to accept myself more.

I know now that the mildest form of pornography (if there is such a thing) will always result in hurt lives. The ones you love the most will feel betrayed. When I feel the temptation the most I go to 1 Peter 1:13–16:

> *"Therefore, prepare your minds for action; be self-controlled; set your hope fully on the grace to be given you when Jesus Christ is revealed. As obedient children, do not conform to the evil desires you had when you lived in ignorance. But just as he who called you is holy, so be holy in all you do; for it is written: 'Be holy, because I am holy.'*

### Marie's story

Signa, I attended your workshop on pornography last week and it was excellent. I have been a youth and children's minister for several years in Canada. I'm writing because I just finished a lengthy conversation with a father whose teenage sons are starting to access pornography on the Internet. I've had several parents approach me on the subject throughout the past several months and I am needing resources that I might be able to recommend to parents in this regard. I am surprised with how many parents don't want to talk with their kids directly – they'd rather discontinue their Internet services or move the computer to a more public location in the home than actually talk to their kids about why they are doing these things.

I also want to let you know that your workshop was a great help to me personally. I've struggled with an addiction to pornography for 19 of my 30 years and have felt a tremendous amount of shame about it because it is so often described as a "male problem." I was hooked by it so young under abusive circumstances, and I'm in ministry. I pretty much thought of myself as a sick freak all these years. I don't have a "road to Damascus" healing to report, but I can tell you that last week was the first time in eight conferences that I was able to see Jesus on the Cross and give all of those filthy images to Him. Until this year I was never able to look up and see Christ crucified. I was also made painfully aware that while my addictions fill a void in my soul, albeit in unhealthy ways, they are also destroying my creativity and imagination while fueling both my propensity to dissociate, my sexual neurosis and the black depression I've suffered for years. All of this truth seems to have penetrated the depth of my self-deception and I have had the freedom to choose not to indulge in pornography for more than a week now. This is pretty incredible to me as it was a daily struggle for me. Thank you so much for telling it like it really is.

# Appendix

## Praying for Children for a Sense of Being

When parents begin to understand the long-lasting deficits that a lack of sense of being can cause in their children, they will begin to grieve over ways in which they have contributed to their child's deficits. When they become convicted of their own sins and/or ignorance of parenthood they will be filled with a heavy sorrow and self-condemnation.

However, godly conviction of sin leads to a guilt and sorrow unto repentance rather than a grief unto self-hatred and self-condemnation. It is important to take your grief and sorrow to the Cross, giving it to Jesus, and asking Him how to pray effectively for your child.

We suggest the following prayer for you who have contributed to a lack of sense of being in your children, whether they are still infants or grandparents. It is never too late for God to work His miracles in anyone's life.

Lord, I ask You to give me divine insight into my
relationship with my child. Help me to see our
situation in truth, neither exaggerated nor diminished.
Show me the relationship as You see it.
Where there was sin or ignorance on my part that led to
the neglect of my child, reveal that to me in truth.
Show me, Lord, the physical, emotional, and spiritual
voids in my child due to my negligence.
Lord, I confess this to You as sin. I ask You to forgive me
and cleanse me. Wash my sorrow from me and release

my child from my sin and the sins of society. Lord,
You make up the deficit in my child as only You can.
Fill the empty places in my child's heart and heal any
division between us.
In Jesus name, Amen.

There are some instances when it might be helpful for a parent to confess his/her sins of neglect directly to the child. Be sure to *know God is leading you to do this* before you strike out with a confession which your child may be totally unprepared to handle. If you are feeling led to do this, please pray first:

Lord, please prepare my child to receive my confession in
an appropriate time and way, and empower my child
to extend forgiveness to me.

You may need to be willing to turn loose of your child if you have used him/her to fill your own emptiness. If you prayed the prayers in Chapter 9 you will be more equipped to release your children so that they can be free to become all God created them to be.

You may need to pray for their broken wills to be mended.

You may need to pray for their repressed wills to be set free.

## Ministering a sense of being to little children

If you have small children you can greatly assist in their whole-ness by:

1.   Prayer

2.   Play

3.   Pretend

### *1. Prayer*

Unless they are very wounded, little children are extremely receptive to prayer. They love the laying-on-of-hands and have an acute awareness of God's presence.

If however, there is resistance to prayer, there is still a way to impart God's healing power into their lives in a very personal way. While they are asleep, place your hands on them and pray or sing over them. Praying in the Spirit is extremely effective at this time. The Holy Spirit knows what your child needs more than you do.

Children who have been troubled even as they sleep, as evidenced by their knotted and tangled sheets during the night, begin to rest in peace within a few weeks of this kind of prayer over them.

Pray for them to have an awareness of God's love and peace. Pray that He will fill their hearts with all they need. Pray that any deficits will be filled by Him. Pray for an enlarged capacity for them to receive and give love. Pray as God leads you for the specific needs of your child.

### 2. Play

No other activity allows you to give your child your undivided attention as much as "play." Just by setting aside time on a frequent, regular basis to do what your child wants to do at his/ her level, is saying to your child, "You are more important to me than anything else at this moment. I'm giving you my undivided attention."

Tell your child that within a certain time limit (thirty minutes, an hour, the afternoon, when the little hand gets to a certain number on the clock, etc.) he may choose whatever he wants to do with you alone. And then do it!

In the activity of play, like no other, you are living in the present moment. The person you share that with, uninterrupted, is receiving an abundance of affirmation. He is worth it! Over time this activity, when done with boundaries and love, will begin to fill voids still unfulfilled.

### 3. Pretend

Tell your child the story of his/her birth. Tell him how much he was wanted; how much not only you as his parents wanted him, but how much God wanted him to be born. Describe what it was like while you waited and prepared for his arrival, going to the hospital, seeing him for the first time, etc.

Allow him to "play like" he is being born, thus re-enacting his glorious arrival. Holding him closely, tell him how securely he was protected within the womb. Put a blanket over him and

then, throwing it off, say, "And then you were born!" Dancing
with him, kissing him, or holding him, relate your joy in having
him be your child.

If the circumstances of his birth are less that what were just
described, relate to Him in truth of the joy Jesus had at his birth
and demonstrate the love Jesus felt as He welcomed him into the
world with His open arms. Ask him if he remembers seeing Jesus
at the moment he was born. You may be surprised at his answer!

If your child is adopted you can still play this game. Tell your
child that a mother who loved him very much allowed him to
grow within her until it was time to be born, going through the
same motions. Describe how God heard your prayers for a baby.
Then describe to him in great detail your joy at seeing him for
the first time and what he looked like, what he did, etc. Even the
smallest detail will bring an infilling of belonging to your child.

# Notes

## Chapter 1

1. The American Family Association revealed that 80% of all sex depicted on prime-time TV is outside marriage.

2. MUD (Multiple User Dimension, Multiple User Dungeon, or Multiple User Dialogue) is a computer program which users can log into and explore. Each user takes control of a computerized persona/avatar/incarnation/character. They can walk around, chat with other characters, explore dangerous monster-infested areas, solve puzzles, engage in sexual activities, and create every item of their own environment. The player invents his own world and his own persona. The relationships are all illusory. All morality, law and order is up to the player. To keep from getting killed off a player must be extremely committed to his role, which adds to the spiritual danger of the illusionary activity.

3. Genoa City and Port Charles are the ficticious locales for the network soap operas, *The Young and the Restless* (CBS) and *General Hospital* (ABC), respectively.

4. These are two popular heroines for romance novel readers. The Skye O'Malley series is authored by Bertrice Small (Kensington Books, NY); the Claire Randall series of romantic time travel is authored by Diana Gabaldon (Dell Books). Both series contain some sexually explicit material.

5. Larry's baby-sitter might have been an older boy and the results would have been similar.

6. Conlee was ordained to full-time ministry in 1987, with a Masters of Divinity degree. He is senior pastor of a large

241

downtown church which emphasizes the healing ministry along with bringing people into salvation, truth and the intimacy of worship. Together we have been praying for people for wholeness since 1972, as well as serving on the ministry team of *Pastoral Care Ministries*, led by Leanne Payne. In 1992, we began *The Journey to Wholeness in Christ* seminars which have been held several times a year in many U.S. cities, Canada, Europe and Israel. A major objective of this ministry is to equip local faith communities to effectively minister healing prayer as part of the normal rhythms of their life in Christ.

7. Write for newsletter to *Pastoral Care Ministries*, P.O. Box 1313, Wheaton, IL 30189, or check web site at www.leannepayne.org

8. John 8:32.

9. *Restoring the Christian Soul*, Leanne Payne, Baker Books, 1991, p. 188.

## Chapter 2

1. *New Webster's Dictionary of the English Language*, Lexicon Publications, Danbury, CT, 1993.

2. According to Naomi Wolf, "For the first time in history, children are growing up whose earliest sexual imprinting derives not from a living human being, or fantasies of their own ... [but from] mass-produced, deliberately dehumanizing and inhuman [images]" (quoting from *The Beauty Myth*, p. 162, in *The Price We Pay*, Laura Lederer and Richard Delgado, Hill and Wang, N.Y., 1995, p. 122).

3. *Sexual anorexia* is a term used by some psychologists for explaining the total disinterest in sex that frequently occurs in a marriage when one's partner is sexually addicted to pornography and/or adultery. It is the shutting down of one's sexuality, walling one's self off from the pain and shame associated with the proximity of sexual impropriety. This may even occur when a person is unaware of the spouse's addiction, but there is a sensing of a separation between them from an unknown source. (The term may also be applied to the person caught up in a sexual addiction who, in advanced stages, may completely turn off his sexuality towards flesh and blood relationships, preferring the fantasy world and fantasy sex with themselves and their illusory partners.)

4. Paul Harvey gives an even more graphic illustration of the same principle: When Eskimos traditionally hunt wolves they repeatedly dip the blade of a sharp hunting knife in animal blood, allow it to freeze, dip it again and allow it to freeze, until a thick layer of frozen blood is covering the knife. The knife is then placed, blade end up, in the snow with the blood exposed. As a wolf begins to lick the blood away he becomes so frenetically absorbed in the act that he never realizes he eventually is eating his own blood. The wolf bleeds to death and his predator is victorious with very little effort.

5. Quoting Michelle J. Anderson, "Silencing Women's Speech," *The Price We Pay*, Laura Lederer and Richard Delgado, Hill and Wang, NY, 1995, p. 123.

6. U.S. News and World Report, 2-20-98.

7. "Enough is Enough" brochure (1997) and Adult Video News (1997).

8. "The Promise Keeper" newsletter, July/August 1998.

9. *An Affair of the Mind*, Laurie Hall, Tyndale House, 1996.

10. Ibid.

11. "The Promise Keeper" newsletter, July/August 1998.

12. Romance Writers of America, database, 2000.

13. *USA Today*, 9-5-97 and *UPI News*, 11-19-97.

14. "U.S. News & World Report" (2-10-97) cited in *When Good Men are Tempted*, Bill Perkins, Zondervan, Grand Rapids, 1997.

15. WorldNetDaily (8-11-00), "Porn-Gate," MSNBC, Lisa Napoli (8-10-00).

16. Koss and Dinero (1998), Shere Hite (1981), Donnerstein and Linz (1984), Cowan (1993).

17. Zillman and Bryant (1982).

18. Malamuth and Check (1985), Briere, Corne, Runtz and Malamuth (1984).

19. Interview with Ted Bundy and Dr. James Dobson of Focus on the Family (1-24-88). Quote from Ted Bundy: "In the beginning pornography fuels this kind of thought process . . . Like an addiction, you keep craving something that is harder, harder, something that gives you a greater sense of excitement until you reach a point where the pornography only goes so far, you

reach that jumping off point where you begin to wonder if maybe actually doing it would give you that which is beyond just reading or looking at it."

20. Quote from Arthur Gary Bishop: "Pornography was not the only negative influence in my life, but its effect on me was devastating. I am a homosexual pedophile convicted of murder and pornography was a determining factor in my downfall."

21. "A Plan for Personal Success," MyComputer.com's EZpolls.

22. MSNBC, February, 2001.

23. American Family Association.

24. *The Road Ahead*, Bill Gates, Penquin USA (1996).

25. Computer Industry Almanac, Inc., 2000.

26. *Caught in the Net*, Dr. Kimberly S. Young, John Wiley & Sons, 1998, p. 23.

27. CBS.

28. Ibid.

29. Today's "Ties the Knot" series, *Today Show*, NBC, summer 2000, 2001, 2002, 2003.

30. Today's "Build a House for Auction" series, *Today Show*, NBC, spring 2001.

31. *Caught in the Net*, Dr. Kimberly S. Young, John Wiley & Sons, 1998.

32. As Conlee and I talked about this newest trend, he imagined the following scenario: As a husband and wife become unhappy and distant from each other, they lose themselves in their chat rooms on the Net. Unbeknownst to each other, they both pour out their loneliness and look for cyberlovers. They eventually find their electronic soulmates and chat for months, developing more and more online intimacy. They eventually arrange an in-person meeting. Of course, they meet each other. (When someone eventually writes the book or screenplay we want royalties!)

33. *Caught in the Net*, Dr. Kimberly S. Young, John Wiley & Sons, 1998, p. 46.

34. *Life on the Screen: Identity in the Age of the Internet*, Sherry Tuttle, quoted in *Caught in the Net*, Dr. Kimberly S. Young, John Wiley & Sons (1998), p. 106.

35. *Homosexuality and the Politics of Truth*, Jeffrey Satinover, Baker Books, 1996.

36. *Caught in the Net*, Dr. Kimberly S. Young, John Wiley & Sons, NY, 1998.

37. *Washington Times*, Jim Dyar, "Cyberporn Held Responsible for Increase in Sex Addiction," January 26, 2000, quoted in "Dangers and Disappointments," Ryan Hosley and Steve Watters, "Focus on the Family Online."

## Chapter 3

1. Genesis 2:18. God prepared in Adam a longing and desire for woman before Adam was ever aware of her existence. This is a major factor in the principle that *together* they will form the image of God. There will be a unity, a complementarity between them. Adam does not have all the fullness of God's nature without woman. He alone cannot fulfill God's commandment to him. He does not contain all it takes to be fruitful and multiply or to rule the earth. He needs a complementary companion. Without her he cannot create life; without her he cannot have dominion over the rest of creation in a wholly God-like manner. It takes both man and woman, side by side, to show the whole nature of God, His gentle, nurturing, responsive love and also His objective initiatives of setting boundaries, pressing through difficulties and protecting those He loves. By naming the animals, Adam saw how very alone he was. *"But for Adam no suitable helper was found"* (Genesis 2:20b). God said, *"I will make a helper suitable for him"* (Genesis 2:18b). *With the woman* the man was able to fulfill God's commissions: "Be fruitful and multiply," "tame the earth," and "rule over the creatures of God." A "helper" is defined as someone who provides what the person cannot be or do for himself, far more than just an assistant. The same word [help] is also used for God as *"an ever-present help in trouble"* (Psalm 46:1b). This shows how man and woman move toward becoming one flesh. They provide for one another something neither can become alone. This is a process. It is not the automatic result of having sexual intercourse. The man and woman continue to remain two distinct persons, but joined together by God in marriage, now have a unique unity. This

unity functions as God's image on the earth. This is God's ideal beginning. See *Creation and Blessing*, Allen P. Ross, Baker Books, 1996, Chapter 6.

2. Genesis 1:28: *"Be fruitful and increase in number ... "*

3. I have chosen to use masculine pronouns to describe the infant, to distinguish more easily between mother and child.

4. This example is taught very graphically and beautifully by Mario Bergner who leads Redeemed Lives training sessions to illustrate the importance of secure attachment to mother until evocative memory is established.

5. This presents a basic disagreement we have with popular child care books such as *On Becoming Baby Wise* by Gary Ezzo and Robert Bucknam (Multnomah, Sisters, Oregon, 1998), which advocate training a baby to sleep through the night before the age of eight weeks by allowing the baby to cry. The authors never take into consideration that any prolonged absence of mother's presence *before* evocative memory is established can cause genuine deficits to the infant's soul. What a small price a few month's constant attention to the needs of a new baby is to insure the lasting effects of security and stability in a human life! For further information regarding the dangers of this kind of parenting request via email a packet of material concerning *Baby Wise* Parenting from Dr. Matt Aney at ANEYBODY@aol.com.

6. Ephesians 3:17b–19.

7. Frank Lake, *Clinical Theology*, Crossroad, New York, 1987, pp. 58, 63.

8. See John 8:12.

9. Dr. Robert Lewis, "Men's Fraternity," tape series of *Manhood Curriculum*, Cross Reference, Little Rock.

10. Ibid.

11. It is interesting to note that studies of new mothers from many cultures show conclusively the same thing: If the mother is given the encouragement and opportunity to have unlimited amounts of time immediately after giving birth to bond with her newborn child something amazing happens. Not only does the child become at peace and feel secure in her arms, but the *new mother actually undergoes a change as well.* Her reactions are the same world-wide. First she will pick up her infant and stroke

his face with her fingertips. At this the baby will become quiet
and turn towards her touch. Soon she begins to touch his head
and body with the palm of her hand. Within a few minutes she
puts him to her breast. The baby responds immediately. The
mother becomes at peace and all her focus is on her newborn.
And this is immediately after undergoing the most difficult
work she will ever accomplish! During the next few days she
will want to spend many hours just being alone with her baby,
looking at him, cuddling him, and getting to know him. She
should be allowed to do this and not expected to return too
soon to the routine chores of caring for a family. If help is to be
provided for the mother it should be in the form of housework
and cooking, not the care of the newborn. Being with her infant
should be her sole responsibility for the first few days. During
this period of intimate contact she comes to the amazing
realization in an inexplicable way that this child is really hers
and she is totally responsible for him. Something internal has
happened to her that does not happen to the mother who has
little or no contact with her newborn. The mother who has
rightly bonded with her child learns his rhythms and adapts her
own to his. They respond to one another. It is like a dance to
watch them together. She modifies her voice to his movements.
The child relates to her eyes. He focuses on her face and its
expressions. There is an interweaving of responses and this
creates a dialogue that is vital to both of them. Through this
natural observation we can see that something happens to the
mother as well as to the baby. How this contrasts from the
once-typical hospital procedures of whisking the newborn out
of the mother's body and into a sterile nursery for testing,
treatment and isolation, often not being reunited with mother
for several hours! Many of these mothers have a difficult time
with the most basic maternal responses when they are reunited
with their infants. See *A Secure Base, Parent-Child Attachment
and Healthy Human Development*, John Bowlby, Basic Books,
1988.

12.  *Parenthood By Proxy: Don't Have Them If You Won't Raise Them*,
     Dr. Laura Schlessinger, Cliff Street Books, 2000, p. 10.

13.  Ibid. Quote from Lloyd Olivia Davis, *Topeka Capital-Journal*
     (2-2-95).

14. We have been present with many adult men and women who, while getting in touch with the root causes of their fears and anxieties, have been taken by God to the earliest moments of their sense of abandonment. It is quite something to hear the wails of the abandoned infant coming out of their deeply buried pain. There is no other sound like it and it is easily recognizable. These wails come from the deepest recesses of their hearts and only God can reveal it, release it and heal its wounds.

15. *A Secure Base, Parent-Child Attachment and Healthy Human Development*, John Bowlby, Basic Books, 1988.

16. See *The Journey to Wholeness in Christ*, Signa Bodishbaugh, Journey Press, 2002, pp. 227–231.

17. Prolonged separation from mother due to illness at an even later age can be extremely traumatic for an older child, often interpreted in the child's mind as rejection, abandonment and/ or distrust of the feminine.

18. *Clinical Theology*, Frank Lake, Crossroad, 1987.

19. Ibid, p. 39.

20. Ibid.

21. Genesis 6:5, KJV.

22. Dr. Robert Lewis, "Men's Fraternity," tape series of *Manhood Curriculum*, Cross Reference, Little Rock.

23. A fetish is an object (e.g. women's undergarments, shoes, hair, etc.) that constellates high emotional response, such as a sexual response or an imagined sense of well being when in contact with the object. It can be a part of a fantasy or a remembered and perhaps suppressed reality. It masquerades as genuine relationship.

24. Lori Rentzel, *Emotional Dependency* (InterVarsity Press, Downers Grove, IL, 1990).

25. Ibid.

26. *The Healing Presence*, Leanne Payne, Baker Books, 1989, pp. 72–75.

## Chapter 4

1. *The Price We Pay*, Laura Lederer and Richard Delgado, Hill and Wang, NY, 1995, p. 5 (bracketed inserts mine).

2. This pattern of seeking secretive ways to alleviate loneliness in my childhood is the same pattern followed today by others who lack a God-given sense of being. The huge difference is what today's seekers are finding!

3. *"For where your treasure is, there your heart will be also"* (Matthew 6:21).

4. Philippians 4:8.

5. These statistics were compiled by Tim and Beverly LaHaye, marriage and family counselors and authors. They were accurate before the proliferation of Internet time by family members in recent years. The ungodly information and images absorbed by family members today must be much worse.

6. J. Bryant, testimony to the Attorney General's Commission on Pornography Hearings, Houston, TX; 1985, transcript. 128–57.

7. "Net Sites Co-Opted by Pornographers," Stephen Labaton, *The New York Times* (9-23-99).

8. Ibid.

9. "Porn Site Owners Charged with Billing for Free Services," Cecily Barnes, *The New York Times* (8-23-2000).

10. *Men's Health*, Greg Gutfeld, "The Sex Drive," October, 1999, p. 121.

11. Ibid.

12. *Washington Post*, "A Case of 'Let the Surfer Beware,'" Don Oldenburg, April 12, 2000, p. C4, quoted in "Dangers and Disappointments," Ryan Hosley and Steve Watters, on "Focus on the Family Online."

13. Ibid.

14. Strategic Telemedia.

15. The North County Coalition Against Pornography.

16. There are ways to decode network addresses to determine the senders as well as several anti-spam resources you can investigate by asking your Internet Service Provider.

17. *Newsweek*, Jennifer Tanaka, April 10, 2000.

18. "Kids Will Find It," Lisa Napoli, MSNBC, August 9, 2000.

19. Ibid.

20. In our ministry we have actually seen a few cases where God sovereignly reversed the hard effects of pornography and years

of sexual promiscuity. In one case a woman who had been a prostitute for many years in New York City was so filled and cleansed with God's Spirit that she experienced the joy of having her innocence restored. Another woman who had been unable to enjoy healthy sexual relations with her husband because of the promiscuity of her past was marvelously forgiven by God, cleansed and had her virginity restored physically in a most miraculous way. Her marriage was healed by the grace of God.

21. "The Positives and Perils of the Internet", Donna Rice Hughes (12-1-99).

22. *Christianity Today*, Editorial, "We've Got Porn," June 12, 2000.

23. Ibid.

24. 1 Samuel 17:45.

## Chapter 5

1. "Christianity Today, Inc.", editorial, June 12, 2000.

2. Ibid.

3. Ibid.

4. "Sultans of Smut," Mike Brunker, MSNBC, August 2000.

5. Financial statement information by New Frontier Media, Inc., July, 2001.

6. Ibid.

7. Ibid.

8. Ibid.

9. "Porn Industry Thriving," *L.A. Times*, 9/1/99.

10. "Sultans of Smut," Mike Brunker, MSNBC, Las Vegas, 8/9/00.

11. Ibid.

12. Ibid.

13. "The Business of Pornography," Eric Schlosser, U.S. News Online, 2/10/97.

14. Philipians 4:8.

15. "Preserving the Presence of the Past," J. L. McGaugh, *American Psychologist*, February 1983.

16. "Cybersex Gives Birth to a Psychological Disorder," Jane Brody, *New York Times*, May 16, 2000.

17. "What's Good About Sex?" J. Budziszewski, *Citizen*, November, 1999.

18. *The Christian Family*, Larry Christenson, Bethany Fellowship, 1970.

19. Ibid, p. 20.

20. "What's Good About Sex?" J. Budziszewski, *Citizen*, November, 1999.

21. "Pornography's Effect on Adults and Children," Dr. Victor B. Cline, *Morality in Media*, New York.

22. Ibid.

23. "Porn Again?", Steve Watters, quoting Maggie Gallagher, *New Man*, May/June, 2001, p. 25.

24. I will continue to use the masculine personal pronoun in order to simplify the narrative. In no way does this imply that women are not tempted in similar ways.

### Chapter 7

1. John Stoltenberg, "The Triangular Politics of Pornography," *The Price We Pay*, Lederer and Delgado, Hill and Wang, NY, 1995, pp. 177–178.

2. John 8:32b.

3. John 14:6.

4. Matthew 18:22.

5. "I Choose to Forgive," Kirk Dearman, Expressions of Praise, 1993.

6. *An Affair of the Mind*, Laurie Hall, Tyndale House, 1996.

7. *Living with Your Husband's Secret Wars*, Marsha Means, Fleming H. Revell, 2000.

8. Although this may seem like a very Catholic action for some of our readers, let us assure you that there is great power in the symbol of the mighty Cross. Oil of healing, combined with human touch (which God often uses) and the symbol of the Cross (the only receptacle for our pain) being imprinted upon one's forehead enable a person in a mysterious way to be open to whatever God is imparting. We, the ministers, become mere agents for His healing power. Many times we are totally

unaware of the deep healing taking place. It is our job to point the person to Him and stay out of the way.

9.  *"Therefore, if anyone is in Christ, he is a new creation; the old has gone, the new has come!"* (1 Corinthians 5:17).

10. Psalm 147:11b.

11. John 10:10.

## Chapter 8

1.  *"For the wages of sin is death, but the gift of God is eternal life in Christ Jesus our Lord"* (Romans 6:23).

2.  See Psalm 51.

3.  *The Journey to Wholeness in Christ*, P.O. Box 50635, Mobile, AL 36605, Phone: 251-643-7755, Fax: 251-643-7626, e-mail: bodishba@aol.com. Newsletter available by request.

4.  *P.C.M.*, P.O. Box 1313, Wheaton IL 60189, Phone: 630-510-0487, Fax: 630-510-0617, email: WheatonPCM@aol.com, website: www.LeannePayne.org. Newsletter available by request.

5.  *Living Waters* and *Desert Streams Ministries*, P.O. Box 17635, Anaheim, CA 92817, Phone: 714-779-6899, Fax: 714-7-1-1880, e-mail: info@desertstream.org. Newsletter available by request.

6.  *Redeemed Lives*, P.O. Box 1211, Wheaton, IL 60189, Phone: 630-668-0661, Fax: 630-668-0730, e-mail: RLivesOffice@aol.com. Newsletter available by request.

7.  An explanation and prayers for the proper use of holy water, as well as prayers for the cleansing and blessing of a home, can be found in the appendix of *The Journey to Wholeness in Christ*, Signa Bodishbaugh, Journey Press, 2002.

8.  Ibid. You can find prayers for a house blessing in the Appendix.

9.  Hebrews 4:12.

## Chapter 9

1.  *The Healing Presence*, Leanne Payne, Crossway Books, p. 55.

2.  Judges 2:2; 6:25; 1 Samuel 7:3.

3.  Matthew 6:24.

4.  Joshua 24:15.

## Chapter 10

1. "Is the Church Doing Enough to Help Sex Addicts?", *New Man*, May/June, 2001.

2. Excerpted from "How do You Overcome Sex Addiction?", Mike Fehlauer, *New Man*, May/June, 2001, pp. 40–41.

If you have enjoyed this book and would like to help us to
send a copy of it and many other titles to needy pastors in the
**Third World**, please write for further information
or send your gift to:

**Sovereign World Trust**
**PO Box 777, Tonbridge**
**Kent TN11 0ZS**
**United Kingdom**

or to the **'Sovereign World'** distributor in your country.

Visit our website at **www.sovereign-world.org**
for a full range of Sovereign World books.